T0323808

Value Management in Healthcare

How to Establish a Value Management Office to Support Value-Based Outcomes in Healthcare

Endorsements

"Value-based healthcare is one of the most important concepts in health reform to emerge in the past 100 years of modern medicine. The concept, developed by Harvard Business School Professor Michael Porter, asks that the industry reshapes how it is organized and what it measures to improve outcomes and control costs. It is a concept that is embraced by patients, clinicians, administrators, and payers. While sometimes thought to be strictly conceptual, Nathan Tierney has assembled a book that takes health care organizations through a step-by-step process of how to create and run a value management office. He covers not only the basics of the value-based healthcare framework but addresses key issues like change and project management. This well written and concise guide will be essential for any organization embarking on a value-based health care journey."

- Dr. Thomas Feeley, MD Anderson and Senior Fellow Harvard Business School

"Value. Value based care. Value optimization. Policy makers and providers alike are pressing on all fronts to drive healthcare to a better place based on "value." The risk is that value becomes a hollow, overused term with little or no quantifiable meaning. Nathan Tierney has compiled an excellent resource to help us avoid such a fate. Building upon the concept of a Value Management Office, Mr. Tierney provides us with a blueprint on how and why to create such an office, how to quantify value, and how to achieve a shared understanding and vision of what success looks like. This detailed roadmap is a must read for all in healthcare as a guide to understanding how to build value into our health delivery systems and to deliver measurable value-oriented outcomes."

**- H. Stephen Lieber,
President & CEO HIMSS**

"As healthcare organizations transition from traditional fee-for-service to value-based models of reimbursement, they're re-engineering the way they do business. They need processes and solutions that help them define and achieve outcomes-based success. The Value Realization Framework describes the underlying principles organizations need to mark their progress. It's another tool that can help organizations meet the operational, regulatory and quality demands of health care today and in the future."

- Paul M. Black, CEO Allscripts

"Beautiful writing!"

**- Dr. Regina Herzlinger, Harvard Business School and
Author of *Who Killed Healthcare?***

"For hospital executives, healthcare professionals, policymakers, patient rights advocates, and anyone interested in understanding how and why outcomes must drive strategy, Nathan's book has it all. With most comprehensive coverage and detailed examples of outcomes based value creation, it is a handbook to design and implement transformational programs. A thorough guide to truly understand what healthcare is all about—a must-read for leaders who sincerely want to make a change."

**- Al Naqvi, President of American Institute of
Artificial Intelligence, Professor, Formerly CFO of
Illinois Health and Science healthcare system**

"Whenever thinking of innovation in healthcare—whether you are in public or private hospital, whether you consider radical or gradual change, whether you work for pharmaceutical company or digital healthcare startup, and whatever healthcare policy your nation has—you may find yourself facing the fact that 'value-based healthcare' is the key to solve your problem. If you need a comprehensive guide to tackle your own issue, this book is the one you are finding. Nathan made outstanding efforts on this book to provide practical tips and insights based on his learning and experiences as a healthcare innovator."

- Charles (Dong Cheol) Kim,
Chief of Future Insights and Strategy,
Samsung Life Public Welfare Foundation •
Samsung Medical Center

"We humans usually struggle wrapping our heads around the abstract concept of "value," regardless the domain. Measuring it, oftentimes seems some sort of a subjective exercise. When we talk health, it's even more difficult to measure it, though we all know very well, we feel it in our pockets and hearts, when we or our loved ones are receiving a valuable treatment. That's precisely why it is so important for patients and healthcare professionals alike to measure it and create a culture around it.

The value based health care delivery paradigm has been around for a while, but it is through rigorous and experience-based books like the one in your hands that organizations of all kinds are actually able to make a successful transition into this new world.

Nathan Tierney's work, product of his non-paralleled experience in an organization that sets the pace for the rest of us and his contagious passion for the subject, is at the same time a pragmatic and very useful toolset and a roadmap to successfully lead your organization to embracing value."

- Rafael Garrido Rivas,
Managing Partner everis USA, an NTT Data Company

"Nathan Tierney has developed a much needed, comprehensive, and multi-dimensional framework for healthcare professionals who are interested in improving the value of their outcomes ... The complexity of connecting operational performance measures (CSF, KPI and KRIs) of initiatives with strategic business objectives is exchanged with clarity ... Read this book—and learn from one of the best."

- Dr. Ajay Asthana, President, Pretium Analytics

"Nathan's book is a beautiful dance of countermeasures, root cause, and the required processes to ensure optimal outcomes for all involved. Critical Success Factors (CSF) will always remind me of those good ole days when I used to hold my breath while performing a difficult spinal tap in the ER at 3am. Transforming complex healthcare industry can now begin with this must read where true value based healthcare can drive better outcomes for the patients efficiently."

- Sonya Kim, MD, MBA, CEO & Founder, One Caring Team.

"As a public health physician practicing in one of the African countries, I can dispassionately say that Nathan Tierney in this book has instilled a new vitality into healthcare management by translating this day to day discussion into a compelling intriguing read, applicable to both the realities of today and the future of implementing value management in health care. His descriptions which I tag *call to action* brings forth the needed creation, management and measurement of values in health services, with incomparable concepts that improve services and create fervent customers."

- Bola I. Gobir MD. MSc. Interim Country Director (Nigeria), Assistant Professor Center for International Health, Education, and Biosecurity (CIHEB);

Maryland Global Initiatives Corporation (MGIC), Institute of Human Virology University of Maryland Baltimore School of Medicine

"Healthcare is experiencing transformation across the world, from the developed markets to emerging markets. The core concept is how to deliver value, better clinical results, more cost effectiveness and shareholders' value through industry innovation. Nathan Tierney's book just provides the health care industry a valuable guide on value-based analysis from a health care provider's point of view, not just concept but real practice. The knowledge within the book will be indispensable for the health care industry to innovate and help more patients."

- George Wang, MBA, General Manager of Cardiovascular and Specialty Solutions Group, Johnson and Johnson Medical China

"Nathan Tierney addresses perhaps the most pressing issue in American healthcare today—the universal need to align management techniques with health outcomes. In what should be required reading for experts and those just beginning the journey that is value-based healthcare, he presents a step-by-step guide to implementing the change needed to succeed, in a reference that can be returned to again and again. From outlining the fundamental shift required for organizations to compete in today's healthcare environment, to presenting key measurements of progression and success, Tierney has produced an accessible guide to how a value management office can be set up for success."

- Niall Wallace, CEO Infonaut Inc.

"Nathan has drawn on his diverse and sometimes intense life experiences to successfully develop a resource for all health organisations to use when implementing a value driven approach to health care. Whether a commissioner or a provider of health care, the value based healthcare approach enables organisations to frame their strategic, tactical and operational response to better deliver outcomes that really matter to patients and the population served.

Nathan describes, in a very practical and "real" way, the journey from theory through to practice for organisations wishing to embrace a value and outcomes based system of healthcare. Change management is the key, influencing and convincing the most important professionals in any healthcare system is critical to successfully changing an organisations culture and mind set. Who can argue with improving value and outcomes for the people we treat?

From a financial perspective better outcomes and leaner patient pathways equal higher efficiency and less wastage— music to my ears!

I foresee this being a key reference document to support the Harvard approach to healthcare improvement, certainly a publication I will be recommending to colleagues in Wales and the UK."

- Rob Holcombe, MSc, FCCA, Assistant Finance Director, Aneurin Bevan University Health Board, Wales, UK

"This book presents an evidence-, value based decision making philosophy sorely lacking in today's antiquated medical system. This book should be required reading for all legislators, presidents, hospital CEOs and administrators. Timely and relevant to today's healthcare dilemmas."

**- Fernando Burstein MD, FACS, FAAP,
Clinical Professor Plastic and Reconstructive
Surgery, Emory University,
Director of Craniofacial Surgery
Children's Healthcare of Atlanta**

"A Veteran, Nathan Tierney has combined his passion for this country and the system that cares for her Veterans, drawing from an unmatched fund of knowledge, skills, and experience in information technology, analytics, and business acumen to create a portrait of value that is founded upon the dignity of the individual. With our rising healthcare costs, nearing 20% of the Gross Domestic Product, organizations must come to terms with the economic implications of not immediately reigning in wasteful spending that inversely affects the triple aim, creating a triple threat: worse economic health, poor population and personal health, and reckless care. Tierney's Value Management in Healthcare eradicates this triple threat through a clear and precise approach that any health care organization can adopt. Built on the seminal treatise by Porter and Teisberg that refocused the trajectory U.S. healthcare system from supply centric transactional outcomes to consumer-driven and value-based patient-centered outcomes that matter, Tierney synthesizes the best tools in competitive strategy and operations management, such as the balanced scorecard, developed by Robert Kaplan, into an executable framework for all health care organizations to measure and deliver value that respects and reconciles the limited resources that are required to achieve the best outcomes for patients, in a replicable and scalable framework that not only thrives within the digital age driven by big data, but also fosters a Learning Health System built on a virtuous cycle of continuous improvement sustained on a platform of better health and better care, while balanced upon stewardship of resources. Not only is it imperative that health care organizations implement an executable value management framework to enhance operational efficiency and alignment with patient outcomes, but our nation and children depend upon it. *Value Management in Healthcare* will provide the blueprint and charter for health care organizations as they navigate the era of value-based care."

- David Massaro, MD, Deputy Chief Medical Officer VISN 9, U.S. Department of Veterans Affairs

"There is no industry or business in the world that measures its services by something other than their added value. Yet, value-based healthcare delivery is a relatively new concept in the healthcare industry.

Although we have witnessed a global trend moving towards the development of value-based healthcare services, the United States is lagging behind many developed countries in this regard. The current fee-for-service model that incentivizes doctors and hospitals to increase volume and, possibly, demand for services, is perhaps one of the main causes of rising healthcare costs and the U.S. Strategies to prioritize value over volume are still in their infancy, due to many confounding factors.

In this book, Nathan Tierney has eloquently described the fundamental problem in the healthcare industry and has elegantly presented evidence-based practical algorithms and solutions to establish a value-based healthcare management plan/initiative. Any change in healthcare delivery is going to be slow, fraught with challenges. But such progress will not even begin unless all the main players, including the public, healthcare providers and legislators understand and acknowledge the need for change. *Value Management in Healthcare* is a concise, well-written book for all parties to learn about the current problem, the urgent need for change, and the potential solutions."

**- Shahin Tabatabaei, MD, Director,
MGH Prostate Health Program,
Department of Urology,
Massachusetts General Hospital**

"*Value Management in Healthcare* by Nathan W. Tierney, outlines how Healthcare Delivery Organizations (HDOs) apply Value Management methodologies in order to revive their processes. Currently, the health care structure is failing all patients, providers, and payers due to the zero-sum competition design. Everis has been a leader and champion for Value Management within healthcare systems and is very proud to be a contributor to this awesome book. The efforts promoted through the book have already been nationally recognized. On November 30, 2016, Nathan and the everis team won an award at the Predictive Analytics Summit in Chicago for 'Best Use of Data for a Public Good'. This award was presented to the group who has 'used data to help government and services solve society's biggest problems'.

Everis focuses on the patient, and more specifically the patient's Value, as the center of the HDO's establishment. Stemming from their expertise with Value Management, everis has recently ventured into Digital Transformation for hospitals. Digital Transformation within healthcare involves the creation of new solutions which can easily be adopted, and therefore information and data is turned into shared knowledge. Overall, a higher patient's Value, equal to Outcomes over Costs, is achieved through everis' continued patient-centric mission. Both Value Management and Digital Transformation can be utilized to best fulfill better outcomes and lower costs for any hospital."

- Mario Chao, ehCOS CEO

"Every CEO and senior executive whose successful tenure depends on achieving digital transformation of their business units should read this book and know how to stand up a value management office to achieve outcomes-oriented results and delivering measurable value from information technology efforts. Every CIO and IT executive whose success and longevity as a leader depends on enhancing their strategic role and engaging with business line sponsors should follow the value management approach outlined in this book. Every healthcare leader who is accountable for outcomes and results for their organization's clinical and IT performance and whose standing depends on happy, engaged clinicians and patients should understand the importance of the value management in asking the right questions and demanding good performance from their information technology partners and suppliers.

Nathan Tierney has incorporated practical, scalable management tools based on lessons learned leading the value management office at the Veterans Health Administration and for the Department of Veteran's Affairs. Included are excellent use cases and evidence-based results from real-world projects on local, regional, and national levels of implementation, as well as projects that span the focus from clinical transformation to information technology implementation. The tools and methods are easy to follow and practical to implement but incorporate very insightful and impactful ideas on how digital, data, and information technologies can transform business outcomes for an enterprise in a predictable way. For IT teams, using the value management office approach can help bridge the expectations gap between promise and performance to achieve lasting strategic impact and directly beneficial outcomes for customers, vendors, and end-user alike."

- Aneel Advani, MD, Assoc Prof (Adj), Johns Hopkins and former CMIO Indian Health Service, Associate Director for Technology, CDC

Value Management in Healthcare

How to Establish a Value Management Office to Support Value-Based Outcomes in Healthcare

By

Nathan William Tierney

CRC Press
Taylor & Francis Group
Boca Raton London New York

CRC Press is an imprint of the
Taylor & Francis Group, an **informa** business
A PRODUCTIVITY PRESS BOOK

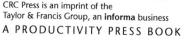

CRC Press
Taylor & Francis Group
6000 Broken Sound Parkway NW, Suite 300
Boca Raton, FL 33487-2742

First issued in paperback 2020

ISBN 13: 978-0-367-73566-1 (pbk)
ISBN 13: 978-1-138-10442-6 (hbk)

Library of Congress Cataloging-in-Publication Data

Names: Tierney, Nathan William, author.
Title: Value management in healthcare : how to establish a value management office to support value-based outcomes in healthcare / Nathan William Tierney.
Description: Boca Raton : Taylor & Francis, 2018. | Includes bibliographical references and index.
Identifiers: LCCN 2017019857| ISBN 9781138104426 (hardback : alk. paper) | ISBN 9781315102245 (eBook)
Subjects: | MESH: Quality of Health Care--organization & administration | Patient Satisfaction | Efficiency, Organizational
Classification: LCC RA399.A1 | NLM W 84.41 | DDC 362.1068--dc23
LC record available at https://lccn.loc.gov/2017019857

For Leeza, Joshua, Sebastian, and Indra, your
love makes my world go round.

Contents

Foreword

As a means of communication, stories convey understanding. Storytelling is the most powerful communication tool we have, and through these stories, we can lead and define future moments. Within the healthcare community, a place is needed where organizations can share their own value stories.

There are four factors that determine why storytelling is so powerful, and why it is possible to make implementing a Value Management Office a successful story:

- *History*: Since the beginning of our existence, humans have shared stories of their experiences, whether through cave paintings, drama, or literature. Alexander Fleming's 1928 discovery of penicillin led to the treatment of infections, which has had a distinct impact on health outcomes.
- *Cultures*: At their root, cultures are just a collected group of stories and experiences. We as Americans are completely different from the Spanish in how we became a nation, our view of the world, our language, and in many other ways by how we have grouped our own unique stories. As an example, while others have embraced universal healthcare, we in the United States have not, but we conduct more than double the number of MRI and CT tests compared to other OECD countries.

- *Remembrance*: Stories have helped us remember and correlate items of similar and differing interest in a way that is expandable in our own personal learning experience ($2+2=4$ and later we learn $4 \times 6 = 24$). An invasive surgery can have a lasting impact on a health outcome, but at its procedural root, education and remembrance shape the quality of the surgery and its outcome.
- *Identity*: Identity is shaped by the unique stories people tell and those other people share. For most of us, these stories are the ones we want to share and are comfortable sharing, not those about the unpleasant things in life. As a healthcare provider, what is your selfless identity shaped by?

Struck by my own experiences at Walter Reed Medical Hospital, stories from our returning warriors, and work at the Department of Veterans Affairs, I have wondered, "How do we harness the power of storytelling and place it into a narrative that resonates with people?" The resounding answer is full transparency and telling our story of how we are incrementally improving the delivery of healthcare value outcomes. As Dr. Pamela Rutledge, author of *The Psychological Power of Storytelling*, said, "When organizations, causes, brands or individuals identify and develop a core story, they create and display authentic meaning and purpose that others can believe, participate with, and share. This is the basis for cultural and social change."

Putting Healthcare Value into Perspective: A Father's Point of View

On March 14, 2004, while deployed overseas, my life took a dramatic turn for the worst—my three-year-old son died. His accident was rare and at the time only occurred 358 times a year in the United States, but that was one too many—a parent should never outlive their child. Following my third tour to the Middle East, I was again deployed and was not there on that fateful day. The experience left an indelible mark on my life, shattered my view of emergency care, and created an almost debilitating anxiety about future fatherhood. Despite serving in special operations for my military career, in my heart, I knew I was not strong enough to get back up should I lose someone as precious as Joshua again. So, what does a father or a parent do when it comes to a life-changing health event for their child? Don't we all want the best outcomes for our children's health? How do we measure a value so that as parents we can make the right decision about medical care for our children ... and ourselves?

I am not overly religious, but God or some sort of Irish luck befell me on September 7, 2013—the day our son Sebastian entered this world. Both my wife and I had gone through the ups and downs of the adoption process, and at times thought we'd never be matched or that the day would never come when we'd be able to adopt; yet there we were in a Florida hospital room, blessed by a young selfless birth mother who gave us the amazing parental responsibility to love, care for, and protect Sebastian. From day one, Sebastian asserted himself as a strong-willed baby who despite life's challenges will always get back up. His spirit and "intestinal fortitude" was proven repeatedly as he found himself in physical therapy from the age of five months old to twenty-two months old, and as he and top-notch physical therapists worked to overcome his torticollis and plagiocephaly. Despite the physical therapy, Botox injections, vision therapy, and two cranial-facial helmets, our son was in the rare 0.5% of children that required surgery.

As parents faced with the decision to allow surgery on our baby, we did what anyone would do—we researched the procedure, read countless articles and blogs, consulted multiple surgeons, had heated arguments about the pros and cons, and tried in vain to find some way to control the outcome for our son. We, like many of you reading, sought peace of mind about the quality and safety of the operation, and a successful health outcome that improved functionality and reduced pain. Yet nowhere in our research did we find some clear and measurable outcomes for the provider or the hospital. In fact, we even encountered a surgeon's refusal to discuss his outcomes or even disclose how many times he had performed the surgery before! Ultimately, much of our decision came down to where the provider had gone to school and our comfort in dealing with him in the past. We wrongly associated that a surgeon who studied at a widely recognized school, Johns Hopkins, must be better than one who studied at the University of California Los Angeles (UCLA). However, just because you studied at a leading institution, or work at a reputable hospital, does not mean you will deliver a better outcome.

My wife Leeza is my rock. In truth, she led our research efforts and utilized social media relentlessly to reach out to other parents. It is her hard work that ultimately changed our minds on what surgeon and path to take. We landed in Florida on a Thursday morning in August. On Saturday, Sebastian was scheduled for surgery at the local hospital with Dr. A. After landing, my wife turned on her cell phone and seconds later the text alert dinged. It was a lady who my wife had become acquainted with via social media (Facebook) and whose son previously had the surgery. The message was simple, "Call me when you get this. Do not get your surgery with Dr. A." Alarmed, my wife immediately called the lady in the terminal. Over the 35-minute discussion, we learned that the woman previously scheduled her son (same age as Sebastian) for the surgery with Dr. A, but cancelled because of poorer health outcomes. Instead, she chose a doctor in Atlanta who had pioneered an endoscopic procedure. Dr. A's procedure was more invasive, had a higher chance of complications, required additional Botox injections following surgery (which required anesthesia and hospitalization), and had a greater chance of a repeat procedure being needed. Sebastian would also have a visible x-shaped scar on his neck because of the needed incision to miss the carotid artery. Dr. Burstein's procedure was less invasive, required 12 weeks of physical therapy post-operation but no additional Botox injections or hospitalization, had a predictable restoration of full range of motion, and left a minimal scar behind the left ear. It seemed like a no-brainer, but we had yet to meet Dr. Burstein or "Google" him to learn more, and already had a surgery scheduled in 2 days. However, with just one phone call, he sent reading material and agreed to Skype the next day to discuss.

On Friday, we Skyped with Dr. Burstein, and not only did he field our relentless questions, but he also had the data to show that his procedure would yield a better outcome. The peace of mind he provided when discussing what to expect was invaluable; we made the decision to go with Dr. Burstein.

Not only did we cancel the planned surgery the following day with Dr. A, but we also flew to Atlanta on Sunday. We met with Dr. Burstein in person on Monday and the following day he conducted the surgery.

It was tough, really tough, watching our son be wheeled away for surgery and not being with him during the operation. I prayed that I would see my son again. Self-doubt about whether we had made the right decision, and whether our son would be okay, did creep into our minds while we waited. Yet we took comfort in that we had made an informed decision based on value-based outcomes for what mattered most—our son.

For those of you with children, or even those of you without, I hope my story resonates with you as does this question, "How do you today choose your doctor?" Through word of mouth, a Yelp review, or based on where the provider went to school or which hospital he or she works at? The truth is that most of us make the decision without understanding value—a now three-year-old boy enjoys a full-throttle toddler life because a provider was transparent with his outcomes. Wouldn't it be great if everyone else did the same?

Acknowledgments

An untapped repository of knowledge lays dormant—awaiting the call to awake. Through a standards-based Value Management approach for healthcare organizations, a collaboration of government, academia, and organizations can provide leadership to improve health outcomes and ultimately deliver value. The measurement of health outcomes and cost facilitates consumer-driven healthcare, academic rigor, corporate innovation, and egalitarianism. However, without selfless servants and leadership, we cannot achieve social change or deliver value. Fortunately for me, I've been blessed throughout my life to have mentors and lasting friendships with people who are willing to answer the call. Each of their personal journeys is different, but their experiences, thoughtfulness, and commitment to improving global healthcare delivery by focusing on value is inspiring. It is because of each of them that this book was written and I am in debt to their kindness and "tough love." Special thanks to everis for providing me with incalculable data and support, especially Thomas Day, Rick Miranda, Gregory Viggiano, Paige Hagstrom, Daniela Bazoberry, and Lilia Fernandez. To my Spanish friend Francisco Fernandez Galeano, I feel like you have become a brother and somewhat of a Dr. Phil counselor for listening to me ramble. Our 2 a.m. discussion about propensity modeling in Boston over a few old fashioneds is a memory I will never forget. None of this within the Department of Veterans Affairs or elsewhere could have been possible without you.

Countless doctors have been gracious enough to impart their wisdom and expertise in developing a value-based approach toward improving health outcomes. In my opinion, these individuals are at the forefront of healthcare delivery and are the true heroes in transforming our broken healthcare system: MD Anderson's Dr. Thomas Feeley, Harvard Business School's Dr. Michael Porter, Dr. Robert Kaplan. My friend Dr. Mahek Shah of Harvard Business School has provided an invaluable wealth of information and help in executing this approach within the Department of Veterans Affairs. Thank you Mahek for always asking the perfect question, "Did you think about this?" and discussing how to accomplish this mission. You are a thought leader in this field and have taught me so much.

Thank you to my colleagues, and early champions, within the Department of Veterans Affairs, Dr. Jonathan Nebeker, David Waltman, Fred Mingo, and Dr. David Massaro. David is a true champion of value management. Without his help, none of our work within the Department of Veterans Affairs would have been possible. Listening to David speak on the topic of value-based care and his ability to quickly coordinate clinicians for a pilot study in mental health was inspirational. Together we always found "small victories" in implementing the Value Realization Framework.

For those who have served in the military, we can all remember that non-commissioned officer (NCO) or senior leader taking the personal time to mentor us and show us what "right looks like." Through this combination of leadership and mentorship, we can also grow, rise up the ranks, and have productive military careers. However, where is that leadership or mentorship when a man or woman on active duty transitions to veteran status? Often it is disjointed because of an overall lack of mentorship. Thankfully, in crossing the chasm from military to the private sector, I was blessed to have met Alan Silverman. He is a successful entrepreneur and businessperson who has selflessly given more of himself to the causes he believes in than anyone else I have met. His work on behalf of fallen special operators has helped countless families. Thank you, Alan, for taking me under your wing and teaching me how to translate and hone my previously learned skills for accomplishing this mission. You have influenced and shaped my post-military life more than anyone in the world and I am beyond grateful for having you in my life.

Lastly, but most importantly, to my wife Leeza. You inspire me, honey, to rise to the occasion of any challenge and see the color in this world. Your nonprofit work abroad, empathy, and how you care for our children is a testament to what living a selfless, purpose-driven life is all about. Thank you, Beautiful, for all your support and help in uniting people with passion around a common purpose—value.

List of Figures

List of Tables

Chapter 1

Executive Summary

Introduction

In healthcare, the overarching goal for providers, as well as other stakeholders, must be to improve value for patients. Here, value is defined as the health outcomes achieved that matter most to patients relative to the cost of achieving those outcomes. Improving value requires either improving one or more outcomes without raising costs, or lowering costs without compromising outcomes, or both.[1] Outcomes empower patients, clinicians, and payers and will influence the future healthcare delivery landscape in three distinct ways:

1. Patients shall choose the providers for their care based on outcome value scores.
2. Providers shall be data-informed to make targeted improvements and learn.
3. Payers shall measure return on investment and direct patients to high-value providers.*

---

* Adapted from the International Consortium for Health Outcomes Measurement (2012). Available at: http://www.ichom.org/.

In the absence of a value-based approach toward achieving desired outcomes, patients, clinicians, and payers suffer the consequences of inefficient and poor quality care, dissatisfaction, and increased medical costs that rob each of self-actualization.[2] This evidence-based book seeks to provide Healthcare Delivery Organizations with a Value Realization Framework and methodology for the establishment of Value Management Offices in order to support quality of care and the safe delivery of value-based outcomes that matter most to patients, clinicians, and payers.

> The universal development and reporting of outcomes at the medical condition level is the single highest priority to improve the performance of the health care system.
>
> **Michael E. Porter and Elizabeth O. Teisberg[3]**

Problems Facing Healthcare Delivery Organizations

Globally, countries are investigating new healthcare delivery strategies to prioritize value-based outcomes over volume. National governments are introducing policies, implementing new reimbursement methods, and collaborating with health organizations to enact change. The new laser-beam focus on achieving the best health outcomes for patients at the lowest cost will transform the healthcare industry.

Companies are also interested in value-based outcomes. These companies pay high prices for employee health data in order to predict risks and health needs. The implications for this situation are significant for employees, employers, and insurers. As an example, if a company thought you were at risk for diabetes, it may offer an incentive to join a weight-loss program or send personalized reminders to visit a doctor for a checkup.[4] Employers do have a vested interest in healthy and productive employees as well as a fiduciary interest in what they pay for employee healthcare insurance, but does the use of health-related data constitute the improper use of the employer and employee relationship?

> Provider organizations understand that, without a change in their model of doing business, they can only hope to be the last iceberg to melt. Facing lower payment rates and potential loss of market share, they have no choice but to improve value and be able to "prove it."
>
> **Michael Porter and Tom Lee**[5]

Recommendations for Healthcare Delivery Organizations

It is recommended that organizations create a Value Management Office to serve as a center of excellence for determining evidence-based outcome measurements. This facilitates the creation of value-based care and payment models. Value-based care and payment models support information technology (IT) governance by evaluating business case investments and projected benefits to link people, processes, and technology. Patients and providers should work together to define and drive the industry toward value (Figure 1.1).*

The implementation of a collaborative Value Management Office enables organizations to evaluate projected and realized strategic, operational, and financial benefits from major

---

* Adapted from the International Consortium for Health Outcomes Measurement Intro Presentation (2015). Available at: www.salute.gov.it/portale/temi/documenti/dispositiviMedici/conferenza/54.pdf.

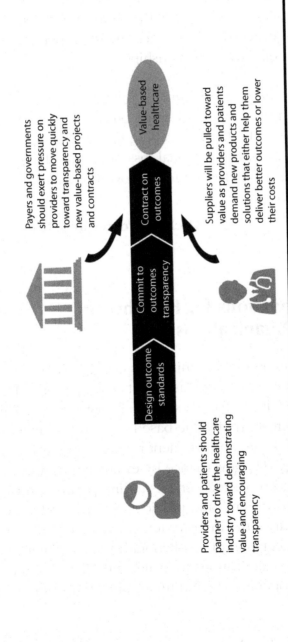

Payers and governments should exert pressure on providers to move quickly toward transparency and new value-based projects and contracts

Value-based healthcare

Contract on outcomes

Commit to outcomes transparency

Design outcome standards

Suppliers will be pulled toward value as providers and patients demand new products and solutions that either help them deliver better outcomes or lower their costs

Providers and patients should partner to drive the healthcare industry toward demonstrating value and encouraging transparency

Figure 1.1   Value through coordination.

business process changes and enterprise initiatives, and establishes critical value-based care models. The shared vision is for Healthcare Delivery Organizations to apply value management as a way of doing business to ensure the efficient deployment of capital, improved clinical outcomes, and the achievement of strategic, operational, and financial objectives.

Healthcare organizations are examining innovative ways to deliver improved patient outcomes at a lower cost. This has involved traditional process improvement methodologies, which have been effective in reducing traditional defects and improving efficiency. However, these efforts have failed to utilize new technologies, analytics, and value frameworks that provide both horizontal and vertical alignment for value-based healthcare.

The Value Realization Framework provides the methodology for aligning mission, vision, and values with concrete Critical Success Factors (agency goals), measurable Key Results Indicators (outcomes), and objective and measurable Key Performance Indicators (actions). The methodology seeks to ensure quality of care and patient safety, and the implementation of Health Information Technology Programs that improve service delivery, product delivery, information security, fiscal management, clinical outcomes, and operational metrics (Figure 1.2).

This standards-based process also ensures that present IT systems continuously perform as required, contribute to overall business goals, and deliver expected outcome-oriented results.

Conclusion

The Hippocratic Oath *Primum non nocere* (First do no harm) calls on the healthcare community to ethically uphold the highest standards of providing safe and quality care to those in need. This calling goes beyond minimizing mortality rates

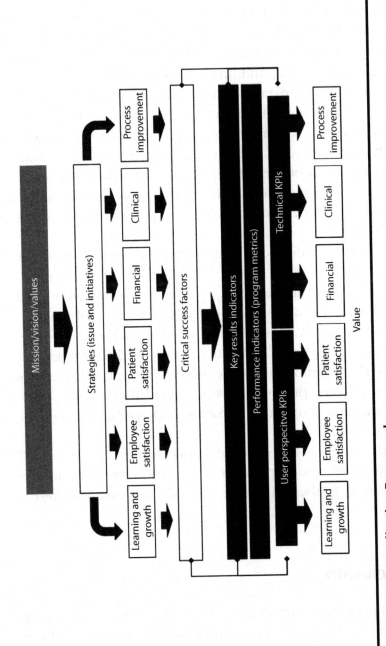

Figure 1.2   Value Realization Framework.

and instead requires standards with which to achieve a predicted outcome. A standard is something quantifiable and is used as a measure or model in a comparative evaluation to determine the value of an outcome. Without standards, there can be no improvement, which is why establishing a center of excellence to determine outcome measurements is so critical. Only through the establishment of a Value Management Office and a standards-based Value Realization Framework will Healthcare Delivery Organizations truly shift from reactive to proactive in the provision of value-based care. This shift is the catalyst for change within our healthcare system that empowers patients, clinicians, and payers by delivering the desired clinical, financial, patient satisfaction, employee satisfaction, process improvement, and learning and growth outcomes from the perspective of the individual—not the institution. *If*

$$\text{Value} = \text{Outcomes}\,(\text{Benefits})\,/\,\text{Costs}\,(\text{Inputs}),$$

then the value story is providing any patient regardless of sex, age, race, or location, a safe and quality health outcome relative to the cost of achieving those outcomes. A Value Management Office can help be the conduit for telling your organization's value story.

Book Purpose

This book emphasizes the importance of establishing a Value Management Office within healthcare organizations to enhance business decision making and maximize value across all of an organization's strategic dimensions. The purpose is not to create another layer of bureaucracy, but rather to ensure that a process to define success and achieve desired outcomes is realized. The Value Realization Framework is explained in detail, highlighting how healthcare organizations can use an effective value outcome-based approach to provide an accurate and current picture of its progress toward achieving its strategic initiatives. This book is designed to build on the principles of learning to provide the reader with four main capabilities:

- *Foundation*: Key concepts of value management, its definitions, and its importance.
- *Application*: Building on a foundational understanding, a use case is provided related to Consultation Management and a step-by-step application of the Value Realization Framework.
- *Understanding*: Integrate three critical dimensions (clinical, program, and technology) for achieving value-based outcomes and present a Common Operating Picture (COP).
- *Correlation*: Discussion of the application of Business Intelligence, propensity modeling, and techniques for making data-driven decisions without sacrificing the human element.

Included in this book are the basic principles of Value Management, practical examples, a few tools for your proverbial "toolkit," and steps toward creating an organization's own Value Management Office.

Book Structure

In 1972, Bernice McCarthy developed the 4MAT System, an eight-step cycle of instruction designed to help instructors organize their teaching based on the different ways that people learn. It is a process for delivering instruction in a way that appeals to all types of learners. The system engages, informs, and allows for learned material application. According to McCarthy, "Inherent in the 4MAT System are two major premises: (1) People have major learning styles and hemispheric (right-mode/left-mode) processing preferences; and (2) Designing and using multiple instructional strategies in a systematic framework to teach to these preferences can improve teaching and learning."[6] An essential component of this method is for instructors to understand and present their material conceptually, and explain the relevance of material to be learned. The 4MAT System focuses on four areas:

- Concepts
- Essential questions
- Content and standards
- Outcomes

The basis for 4MAT is rooted in the two major differences in how people learn: (1) how people perceive; and (2) how people process.[6] No one uses one response to the total exclusion of the other. The resulting structure defines the qualities of the four major learning styles:

- *Type I (Imaginative learners)*: These individuals seek personal associations and meaning, and perceive information concretely and process it reflectively. Generally, these individuals integrate experience with the self and are interested in people and culture to understand all sides. These individuals want to make connections and ask, "Why is this important?"
- *Type II (Analytic learners)*: These individuals seek facts, perceive information abstractly, and process it reflectively. Typically, these individuals are avid readers, need details, and have high verbal skills. These individuals need to formulate ideas and ask, "What is this thing and what does it do?"
- *Type III (Common sense learners)*: These individuals think and do, think pragmatically, perceive information abstractly, and process information actively. Generally, these individuals are skills-oriented people who like to

experiment and solve problems, and resent being told the answers. These individuals seek to apply ideas and ask, "How does this really work?"

■ *Type IV (Dynamic learners)*: These individuals perceive information concretely but process it actively, and they learn by trial and error and self-discovery. Usually, these individuals are risk-takers, adaptable, and seek to influence others and frequently reach correct conclusions despite the lack of logical justification. These individuals seek to create original conclusions and often ask, "What if I did this?"

According to McCarthy, "Learning style issues lead directly to instructional issues, which lead directly to curriculum issues, and their attendant ambiguities about the nature of evaluation."[7] It is essential to educate the reader on Healthcare Value Management regardless of an individual's learning style, and I have arranged this book to accomplish that goal.

At the beginning of each chapter, learning objectives are presented by asking the questions *why, what, how, and what if.* Each chapter closes with a summary of the key points to remember. Hopefully, this approach can begin a greater discussion on how healthcare can cross the current value chasm.

References

1. Porter, M. E. and Lee, T. H., MD. 2013. The strategy that will fix health care. Available at: https://hbr.org/2013/10/the-strategy-that-will-fix-health-care. Accessed October 12, 2016.
2. Maslow, A. H. 1943. Psychological review: A theory of human motivation. *Psychol. Rev.* 50(4): 370–396.
3. Porter, M. E. and Teisberg, E. O. 2006. *Redefining Health Care: Creating Value-Based Competition on Results.* Harvard Business Press.

4. Wired Magazine. 2015. Security this week: Employers are paying data firms to predict your health risks. Available at: http://www.wired.com/2016/02/security-this-week-employers-are-paying-data-firms-to-predict-your-health-risks/. Accessed February 20, 2016.
5. Porter and Lee (2013).
6. McCarthy, B. (1972). Using the 4MAT system to bring learning styles to schools (p. 31). Source: http://www.4mat.eu/4mat-who-developed-it.aspx.
7. McCarthy, B. (1972). Using the 4MAT system to bring learning styles to schools (p. 37.) Source: http://www.4mat.eu/4mat-who-developed-it.aspx.

Chapter 2

Healthcare Landscape

Learning Objectives

After reading this chapter, the reader will be able to answer the following questions:

- Why is it important to understand the rapidly changing healthcare landscape?
- What are other countries actively doing to achieve value-based healthcare standards?
- How will implementing a value-based approach improve outcomes while also reducing costs?
- What if organizations created a Value Management Office?

Global Trends

The global healthcare landscape is radically changing and experiencing a notable increase in the demand of healthcare services from in-country providers. Health experts attribute the increase to

- An aging population
- Growing affluence
- A surge in the treatment of chronic illnesses
- A more knowledgeable patient population*

National governments and healthcare providers have struggled to respond to this dynamic landscape, causing the quality of care administered by healthcare networks to plummet, costs to rise, and patients to become increasingly unsatisfied with their healthcare options.[1] Leading the change to resolve the systemic issues plaguing the patient population are countries from the developing world that are attempting to understand and tackle their respective challenges head-on.

Health expenditures are significant and keep growing in the industrialized world without a clear correlation between levels of healthcare spending and quality/outcomes. By completing a comprehensive evaluation of their respective healthcare environments, countries are identifying the leading causes fueling the misalignment between healthcare supply and demand.

It is critical that governments and Healthcare Delivery Organizations (HDOs) remember that "…the Organization for Economic Co-operation and Development (OECD) still predicts that public spending on health in its member states will raise from an average of 6% of GDP across its member states in 2006–10 to around 9.5% of GDP in 2060. With no cost containment, that proportion would reach 14%" (Figure 2.1).

The causes for the trailing response from healthcare networks stem from people, processes, and technology. Currently, the stakeholders comprising national healthcare networks, which include providers (e.g., hospitals), suppliers (e.g., pharmaceuticals), buyers (e.g., patients), and payers (e.g., health insurance companies), do not have sufficient incentives to

---

* *Economist Intelligence Unit*. November 2015. Value-based healthcare: An update.

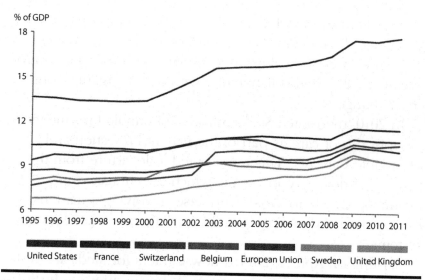

Figure 2.1   Healthcare expenditure percentage of GDP. (From World Development Indicators, World Bank, 2012.)

deliver the best quality care relative to costs. In many countries, including the United States, the prevailing provider model is fee-for-service, which encourages providers (doctors and hospitals) to maximize patient volume (e.g., visits and treatments) and possibly contribute to the surge in demand for services.

At the same time, healthcare operations have not scaled proportionally to the demand for healthcare services. For the healthcare network serving the United States Department of Veteran Affairs, this has translated to long wait times for routine services. Older technology systems are beginning to be updated, but have yet to catch up with patient expectations. The introduction of electronic medical record (EMR) solutions has provided some improvements, but many technology platforms still need upgrades.*

Around the world, countries are examining a new healthcare delivery strategy that prioritizes value over volume. This

---

* Ibid.

strategy focuses on achieving the best health outcomes for patients at the lowest cost.[1] In an effort to shift to a value-based approach to healthcare, national governments are introducing policies and collaborating with health organizations to enact change.

In 2010, the United States introduced bundled payments for episodes of care as part of the Patient Protection and Affordable Care Act. This represented a departure from the practice of defensive medicine, which encourages over-treatment, largely to avoid court cases involving omissions. Instead, bundled payments build on diagnosis-related group systems.*

Starting on April 1, 2015, a new Centers for Medicare and Medicaid Services (CMS) requirement began affecting healthcare organizations and physicians. A 5.75% upfront withholding of bundled payment reimbursement is now contingent on readmission rates, value-based purchasing, and hospital-acquired infections. Data analytics is now a critical component in this new environment. Organizations that control their data can negotiate better payments from insurance payers and CMS. If organizations can prove that they are providing better outcomes, they can negotiate better payments (Table 2.1).

> We know [very little] about whether, where, and how health services achieve the outcomes that patients are looking for. We want health ministers today and in the future to do something about this.
>
> **Boston Consulting Group**
> *Strengthening International Comparison of Health System Performance Issues Paper May 2015 https:// es.slideshare.net/leongi1/bcs. Slide 15. From OECD report at https://www.oecd.org/about/47747755.pdf.*

---

* *Economist* (2015).

Table 2.1   Global Value-Based Healthcare Developments

France	France introduced a new cost-effectiveness focus into its Health Technology Assessment (HTA) system in January 2014. Medicines are now assessed by cost efficiency as well as by clinical evaluation and both assessments form the framework for price negotiations with pharmaceutical companies.
UK	In 2014, the United Kingdom proposed introducing a broader "value-based assessment" that takes into account direct and indirect costs of treatment.
Germany	Germany's Institute of Quality and Efficiency in Healthcare (IQWiG) has focused on greater transparency in its decision making with new guidelines issued in April 2015.
Japan	Japan is considering the introduction of economic evaluations for pharmaceuticals with the next drug price review in 2015 (2015 is seen as a likely date for implementation). This approach could increase the price differentials between generic and patented drugs, and also exclude some drugs from Japan's National Health Institute (NHI) list.
China	China abolished price controls for the majority of drugs, laying the groundwork for the introduction of a health technology assessment. The Chinese government has been working with several international organizations, including the international arm of the United Kingdom's National Institute for Health and Care Excellence (NICE), to develop evidence-based care pathways that will help control costs as health spending increases.
Thailand	Thailand teamed up with NICE International, the U.S.-based Center for Global Development, and major UK universities to launch the international Decision Support Initiative (iDSI). Its aim is to raise awareness about evidence-based healthcare in developing markets.

Value-Based Trends

Healthcare organizations are examining innovative ways to deliver improved patient outcomes at a lower cost. This approach has involved traditional process improvement methodologies, effectively reducing traditional defects and increasing efficiency. However, these efforts have not involved using new technologies, analytics, and value frameworks to provide both horizontal and vertical alignment. Additionally, the lack of a standards-based Value Realization Framework impacts healthcare organizations processing new bundled payments, directly linking the value of financial and patient outcomes (Table 2.2).

Building a technology platform that provides improved outcomes alignment and measurement is critical to value-based management methods. These new technology platforms will integrate older siloed healthcare systems used by different departments, locations, types of service, and types of data.* Because systems integration is key to successful operations, healthcare organizations deciding to adopt a value-based management approach usually transform their technology platforms early in the process. To ensure that these transformations are successful, organizations create "value management offices" to centralize expertise, manage enterprise activities, and champion sustainable operational change (Table 2.3).

In 2013, Michael E. Porter and Thomas H. Lee proposed the Value Agenda in the Harvard Business Review as the strategic agenda for moving to a high-value healthcare delivery system. As stated by Porter and Lee in their article "The strategy that will fix health care," "Embracing the goal of value at the senior management and board levels is essential, because the value agenda requires a fundamental departure from the past." This strategic agenda for moving to a high-value healthcare delivery system has six components. They are interdependent and mutually reinforcing.

---

* Porter and Lee (2013).

Table 2.2   Changes Required for Value-Based Health Management

	Traditional Health Systems	*Value-Based Health Systems*
Reimbursement	By volume of healthcare activity or product	By patient outcome compared with alternatives
Regulatory approval requirements and process	Demonstrate high-quality manufacturing standards, clinical safety, and clinical effectiveness, but only against a placebo	Formal systems in the United States and the European Union now require clinical effectiveness to be proven against comparative therapies for best outcome over cost
Pricing of supplies	By volume purchased	Relative pricing correlated with health benefit delivered per unit of input
Data and records	Lack of measurement of health outcomes, leading to an inability to purchase or manage performance against this metric	Transparency of input (activity and product volume) and outcomes
Health system planning	Lack of planning against present and future needs	Integrated and collaborative care, budgeted and planned for in accordance with population health needs, access, and universal coverage of essential services

Note: Economist Intelligence Unit.

Table 2.3 Examples of Value Management Offices in Healthcare

Healthcare Organization	Value Management Office
University of Texas MD Anderson Cancer Center	• Established Value Management Office in 2008 • Provides expertise (analytics, project management, etc.) • Measures outcomes that are most important to patients, significant for clinicians, and suitable for value-based reimbursement contracts • Led the pilot, and the eventual full implementation, to institute Time-Driven Activity-Based Costing • Integrated outcome measurement and reporting into EMR system
Hospital for Special Survey (HSS)	• Established Value Management Office in 2014 • Institutionalizes continuous value improvement • Provides greater coordination and resource focus for the value agenda • Improves the collection of outcome measures • Integrates quality data into care delivery • Expands from process excellence to population management

■ *Organize into Integrated Practice Units (IPUs)*: The first principle in structuring the healthcare organization is to organize around the patient and their needs, which requires a shift from siloed organization by specialty department and discrete service to organizing around the patient's medical conditions.

■ *Measure outcomes and costs for every patient*: Rapid improvement in any field requires continuously measuring results and performance. Any organization improves by tracking progress over time and comparing their performance within and outside their organization.

■ *Move to bundled payments for care cycles*: The payment approach that is best aligned with value is the bundled payment. Well-designed bundled payments directly encourage teamwork and high-value care. Payment is tied to overall care for a patient.

■ *Integrate care delivery systems*: To achieve true system integration, organizations must focus on the following initiatives: defining the scope of services, concentrating volume in fewer locations, choosing the right location for each service line, and integrating care for patients across locations.

■ *Expand geographic reach*: If value is going to increase, the superior providers for particular medical conditions need to serve more patients through the strategic expansion of excellent IPUs. Geographic expansion should focus on improving value, not just increasing volume.

■ *Build an enabling information technology platform*: The preceding five components of the value agenda are enabled by a supporting information technology (IT) platform. For example, the IT system can help the parts of an IPU work with one another, enable measurement and new reimbursement approaches, and tie the parts of a well-structured delivery system together.

As illustrated in Table 2.3, leaders are beginning to establish Value Management Offices. The Value Management Office is designed to create value initiatives and accelerate the dissemination and adoption of the organizational value agenda.

> Implementing the value agenda is not a one-shot effort; it is an open-ended commitment. It is a journey that providers embark on, starting with the adoption of the goal of value, a culture of patients first, and the expectation of constant, measurable improvement.

> **Michael Porter and Tom Lee***

In another example from the Mayo Clinic involving a Value-Improvement Program, Derek A. Haas and Richard A. Helmers

---

* Porter and Lee (2013).

cite that "others can learn from Mayo's disciplined approach for value realization projects." In the Mayo Clinic, each value-improvement project is being required to fulfill the following conditions.[2]

■ Gain senior leadership support, including an approved charter
■ Select a project team with the right skill sets
■ Engage local physicians for each medical condition studied
■ Measure both costs and outcomes for comparative analyses of care variation
■ Test process improvement suggestions
■ Record and share end-of-project learnings

Summary of Key Points to Remember:

■ Why is it important to understand the rapidly changing healthcare landscape?
HDOs have wrestled with balancing quality, service, and cost for years. The importance and urgency around measuring and communicating real metrics has grown in the last decade. However, even today, most hospital leaders cannot articulate or demonstrate the "value" they provide to patients and payers. Instead of developing a strategic direction that is based around a core value proposition, they focus their strategic efforts on tactical decisions such as physician recruitment, facility expansion, and physician alignment. In the healthcare paradigm of the next decade, the alignment of various tactical initiatives will require a more coherent understanding of the hospital's core value positioning. For most hospitals, quality (i.e., clinical outcomes and patient safety) will become the most visible indicator of value. The introduction of a Value Realization Framework will help healthcare providers increase their value positioning based on the quality they provide.

■ What are other countries actively doing to achieve value-based healthcare standards?
Many countries are exploring new healthcare delivery strategies to prioritize value-based outcomes over volume. Governments are implementing new reimbursement methods, such as bundled payments versus fee-for-service payments in the United States. These new policies and payment methods tied to individual patient outcomes will have a profound impact on the healthcare industry.

■ How will implementing a value-based approach improve outcomes while also reducing costs?
A value-based approach toward improving outcomes replaces an old mind-set that simple process improvement changes or staff/service cutbacks will somehow deliver value. Using the Value Realization Framework for total organizational alignment with a focus on patient conditions brings accurate cost and value measurement into healthcare delivery.

■ What if organizations created a Value Management Office?
The results of the MD Cancer Center in Houston, Hospital for Special Survey are obvious—these organizations have delivered quality outcomes for patients at reduced costs. The main objective for these organizations was to deliver desired patient outcomes at a reasonable cost that includes the entire cycle of care for the patient's condition.

References

1. Porter, M. E. and Lee, T. H., MD. 2013. The strategy that will fix health care. *Harvard Business Review.* Available at: https://hbr.org/2013/10/the-strategy-that-will-fix-health-care. Accessed October 12, 2016.
2. Haas, D. A., Helmers, R. A. et al. 2015. The Mayo Clinic model for running a value-improvement program. Available at: https://hbr.org/2015/10/the-mayo-clinic-model-for-running-a-value-improvement-program. Accessed October 12, 2016.

Chapter 3

How to Measure Value

Learning Objectives

After reading this chapter, the reader will be able to answer the following questions:

- Why are the healthcare perspectives and outcomes on a Balanced Scorecard important?
- What is value as an equation?
- How does an organization link value as a program in a health outcomes setting?
- What if each program or health information technology (IT) project had value defined from the start?

Key Terms to Remember

The ability to differentiate between inputs, outputs, and outcomes is essential to Value Management, as is determining the linkage between program deliverables and intended outcomes. Input, output, and outcome measures must be precisely defined and aligned in a cause and effect relationship in order to deliver value to the stakeholder. Key concepts used throughout this book that constitute the core of Value Management include the following terms:

- *Outcomes*: A measure of results and benefits from strategic initiatives across six perspectives in healthcare, such as patient and employee satisfaction, clinical and financial outcomes, process improvement, and learning and growth.
- *Critical Success Factors (CSFs)*: "The key areas where an organization must perform well on a consistent basis to achieve its mission."[*]
- *Key Results Indicators (KRIs)*: A "measure of the results from your business actions which are critical in tracking progress and defining success."[1]
- *Performance Indicators (PIs)*: A "particular characteristic or dimension used to measure intended changes defined by an organizational unit's results framework. Performance indicators are used to observe progress and to measure actual results compared to expected results. They serve to answer 'how' or 'whether' a unit is progressing toward its objectives, rather than 'why' or 'why not' such progress is being made. Performance indicators are usually expressed in quantifiable terms, and should be objective and measurable (e.g., numeric values, percentages, scores, and indices)."[2]
- *Key Performance Indicators (KPIs)*: A "measure of the actions and events that lead to a result and are considered to be critical to the success of your business as their data is crucial in creating strategies and aligning goals."[2]

---

[*] Carnegie Mellon definition of Critical Success Factors. From Caralli, R. A. 2015. The critical success factor method: Establishing a foundation for enterprise security management.

- User perspective KPIs: System performance that impacts usability and customer satisfaction based on availability, efficiency, and the accuracy of the systems.
- Technical KPIs: System performance that impacts managing the collective enterprise architecture and the network functionality of systems.
- Value elements: A quantifiable, calculated benefit that is worth the investment.

It is critical that effectiveness is defined first, that is, the desired outcomes prior to planning for efficiency, otherwise, there is the risk of doing the wrong things well.

Value Myths

As healthcare organizations grapple with increasing costs and demand for quality outcomes, there has circulated many myths related to implementing Value Management as a way of doing business. As eloquently noted by Kaplan and Porter, the first three myths apply to healthcare costs and reluctance to change.[3] Myths 4 and 5 have stymied progress in applying a standards-based approach toward horizontally and vertically measuring value within Healthcare Delivery Organizations. Only through education and standards based on facts can such myths be dispelled.

- *Myth 1*: Charges are a good surrogate for provider costs.
- *Myth 2*: Hospital overhead costs are too complex to allocate accurately.
- *Myth 3*: Most healthcare costs are fixed.
- *Myth 4*: KRIs are the same thing as KPIs.
- *Myth 5*: The assumption that spending money on a new IT capability or service will result in a desired outcome.

A Healthcare Value-Based Balanced Scorecard

In 1995, Robert S. Kaplan and David P. Norton proposed the Balanced Scorecard theory and management approach in Harvard Business Review. Subsequently, in 1996, they published their book, *The Balanced Scorecard*, and refined the approach in their second book, *The Strategy-Focused Organization* (2000).[4] As defined by Kaplan and Norton (1996), "The Balanced Scorecard translates an organization's mission and strategy into a comprehensive set of performance measures that provides the framework for a strategic measurement and management system."[5] This strategic management system measures organizational performance in four "balanced" perspectives:

- *Financial*: Summarizes "the readily measurable economic consequences of actions already taken"
- *Customer*: Contains measures that "identify the customer and market segments in which the business unit will compete and the measures of the business unit's performance in these targeted segments"
- *Internal business process*: Measures the "critical internal processes in which the organization must excel"
- *Learning and growth*: Measures the "infrastructure that the organization must build to create long-term growth and improvement"

In this book, these perspectives to Healthcare Value Management are adapted. The result is a combination of process and stakeholder perspectives of a business that are encapsulated in the Value Scorecard, which is now comprised of six perspectives:

- *Financial*: Increase revenue by leveraging data to quickly negotiate with payers (i.e., private insurance/Medicare)

- *Clinical*: Improve clinical data-driven decision making to deliver high-quality and safe patient-centered care
- *Process improvement*: Decrease clinical, administrative, and other resource costs (e.g., elimination of paper/material costs) and improve efficiencies
- *Learning and growth*: Increase expertise and adaptability by capturing lessons learned and improving best practices
- *Patient satisfaction*: Measure value of patient satisfaction and experience
- *Employee satisfaction*: Measure value and patient experience, which leads to improved recruiting, retraining, and retaining of employees

To create a Balanced Scorecard, an organization's leadership must translate the mission, vision, and strategy (or issue or initiative) into a scorecard. The measures are traditionally arranged into four perspectives (now six for healthcare); however, scorecards can be tailored to meet organizational needs. The scorecard should contain both KRIs (outcome measures) that indicate performance, along with the KPIs (performance-drivers) that track organizational performance. This "balanced" framework enables an organization's leadership to execute the following four strategic management processes:

- Clarify and translate vision and strategy
- Communicate and link strategic objectives and measures
- Plan, set targets, and align strategic initiatives
- Enhance strategic feedback and learning

These four strategic management processes are the keys to the Balanced Scorecard theory.

In 2001, Kaplan and Norton found that the implementation of strategy is as important as the development of strategy. They proposed the following five strategic management principles:

- Translate the strategy into operational terms
- Align the organization to the strategy
- Make strategy everyone's everyday job
- Make strategy a continual process
- Mobilize change through executive leadership

Within these five principles, there are several new elements added to the Balanced Scorecard approach:

- *Strategy Maps*: Strategy aligned with the *value* proposition.
- *Personal scorecards*: Strategy aligned with personal objectives.
- *Balanced paychecks*: Incentive compensation aligned with team-based goals (scorecard).
- *Strategic and operational budgeting*: Strategy funded.
- *Open reporting*: All employees attend information and management meetings to discuss performance.
- *Change management*: The Balanced Scorecard is a change management program, enabled by the scorecard.

The Balanced Scorecard Strategy Map illustrates an organization's strategy and the measures of success for the strategy. In short, the map provides a visual aid for achieving value through action.

This book introduces a Balanced Scorecard Strategy Map for healthcare applications, based on the approach created by Kaplan and Norton. The strategy for improving healthcare value focuses on two main strategies: quality of care and productivity. In healthcare, the balance between the quality of service provided to the patient and the cost of service is key. The combination of both strategies results in the patient value proposition (Figure 3.1).

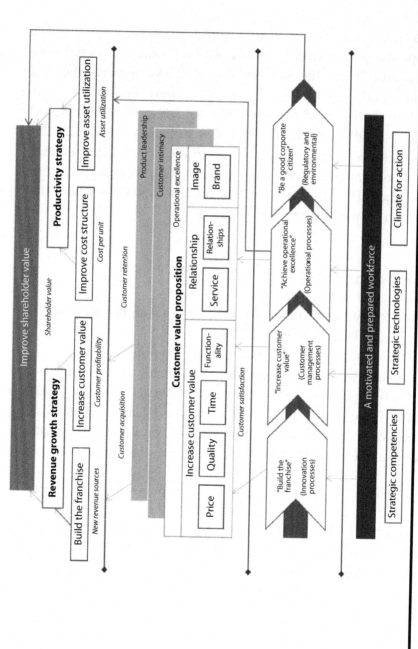

Figure 3.1   Balanced Scorecard Strategy Map.

Value Calculation Trends

To calculate and communicate value, a common method is to apply a cash flow analysis, comparing the costs and benefits over time. The analysis is used to measure the value of a proposed project over a period of time, usually to determine the useful life of the solution. The analysis compares the cost savings and hospital benefits of a proposed solution versus the total investment and costs in order to determine if the project makes sense financially. Typically, organizations compare the "business as usual" financials, where the organization continues to operate as it intends to without the proposed solution (as-is model), with a predictive model of financials where the solution is implemented (to-be model).

Value Equation

In the following sections, the proposed Value Equation for Healthcare is described.

The Value Equation is the optimum combination of whole-life costs and benefits needed to meet the customer/patient's requirements. It is the balance between outputs and inputs. Benefits are stakeholder outcomes (Value Realization Framework outcomes, not only financial) and costs are inputs that must be expended in order to achieve the desired outcome.

$$\text{Efficiency} = \text{outcomes}/\text{output}. \quad \text{Effectiveness} = \text{inputs}/\text{outputs}$$

In order to realize value, both effectiveness and efficiency must be taken into consideration. When combined with the relationship between efficiency and effectiveness, the following equations are presented.*

---

* Davies R. N.; Davies A. J. (2011). *Value Management Translating Aspirations into Performance*. Burlington, VT: Goward Publishing Company.

$$\text{Value Equation} = \frac{\text{Outcome}}{\text{Outputs}} \times \frac{\text{Outputs}}{\text{Inputs}}$$

that is

$$\text{Value Equation} = \text{Effectiveness} \times \text{Efficiency}$$

Example: For access to care for mental health (MH) appointments, the Value Equation can be expressed as

$$\text{Value Equation} = \text{Timely} \frac{\text{Appointments}}{\text{Total}} \text{Appointments}$$

$$\times \text{Total Appointments/Cost}$$

that is

$$\text{Value Equation} = \text{Timely MH Appointments} \times \text{Cost}$$

Value as a Process

Standardized processes provide the means by which success can be repeated. Business processes deliver value when the processes are standardized and continuously followed. There can be no improvement without standards, nor can there be repeatable value for our stakeholders. A standardized process is comprised of one or more activities that transform inputs into outputs and is enabled by resources under the influence of controls.

The value of a process is the degree to which stakeholder outcomes exceed the cost of inputs and resources (Figure 3.2).*

$$\text{Value} = \text{Outcomes} - \text{Resources}$$

Value as a Business (Healthcare Organization)

The core process inherent to any business is the value chain, which defines the critical activities and the products

---

* Integration Definition for Function Modeling (IDEF0). Federal Information Processing Standards Publication 183 (FIPS 183). http://www.idef.com/idefo-function_modeling_method/. Accessed October 20, 2016.

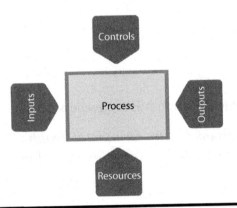

Figure 3.2   Process value definition.

or services needed to create value for its stakeholders. Through the operation of one or more processes, the health-care organization (as a business) can deliver value to its three primary stakeholders (patients, providers, and payers) (Figure 3.3).

$$Value = Outcomes\,(Benefits) - Resources\,(Costs)$$

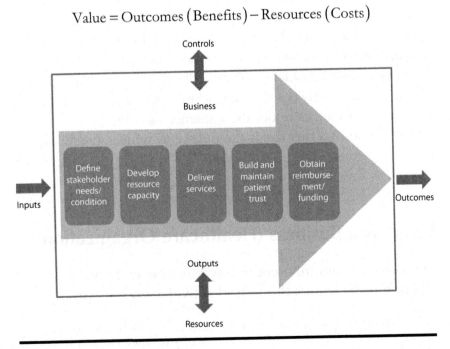

Figure 3.3   Value as a business.

Value as a Program

A program is a process for delivering value to stakeholders by implementing change. The program outcome is a measurable stakeholder benefit created by a new capability because of the program outputs (deliverables). Critical to the program design is the use of a Value Realization Framework to manage programs appropriately to deliver measurable outcomes. Both the program and business are linked through value delivery (Figure 3.4).

$$\text{Program Value} = \text{Program Benefits} - \text{Program Costs}$$

Program Investment Appraisal

The financial value of an intended program is determined by Discounted Cash Flow (DCF), Return on Investment (ROI), Net Present Value (NPV), Internal Rate of Return (IRR), Total Cost of Ownership (TCO), and Payback Period (PP) analysis. NPV and IRR can produce conflicting results due to NPV returning an absolute value of a program over time versus an IRR metric. As an example, one program may have a larger NPV and another a higher IRR, also referred to as yield. This is

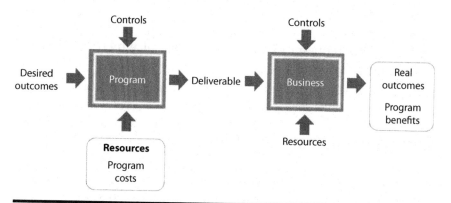

Figure 3.4   Value as a program.[6]

attributed to the amount of cash flow in a given period of time. Normally, NPV is favorable for large-scale programs that will deliver late benefits (outcomes), and IRR favors programs with smaller investment costs and faster positive cash inflows. The DCF valuation is critical in Value Management for evaluating programs because it quantifies the timing of resultant value.

Discounted Cash Flow (DCF)

DCF quantifies value by ignoring non-cash accounting manipulation, notably depreciation, and accounts for the time value of money. The time value of money recognizes that a dollar today is worth more in the future due to investment at an interest rate, or that when borrowed, money will incur an interest rate. In Value Management, it is desired that the value arrived at through DCF analysis is higher than the current cost of investment. The concept is similar to the ancient saying, "a bird in the hand" versus "how many birds are there in the bush …". To compute the present value, the following equations are presented.

$$\text{Present Value} = \text{Cash Flow} \times \text{Discount Rate}$$

$$\text{Discount Rate} = 1 / \left(1 + \frac{r}{100} \right) n$$

Note:

- r (as a percentage) is the interest rate at which the dollar could be invested or the cost of borrowing
- n is the year number for the program in the cash flow

Return on Investment (ROI)

ROI is the ratio of net benefits divided by the total investment. A higher ratio means that the project's net benefits are higher than the investment and the project is judged to be less risky.

In the private sector, ROI is a helpful tool because the best option has a higher ROI metric.

$$ROI = \left(\text{Gain from Investments} - \text{Cost of} \frac{\text{Investment}}{\text{Cost}} \text{Investment} \right)$$

As an example, IF the total estimated cost of a new Electronic Health Record (EHR) system is $3 million over 5 years and during that time an estimated $4 million dollars will be saved through improved clinical workflows and process improvements, THEN the net gain is $1 million. The ROI is then calculated by dividing the $1 million net gain by the $3 million EHR investment cost, which results in an ROI of 33%.

Estimated Savings of $4 million – $3 million EHR

= $1 million Net Gain

$1 million Net Gain ÷ $3 million EHR Investment Cost = 33% ROI

Net Present Value (NPV)

NPV provides today's monetary value of a program and is the present value of all future cash flows minus all cash outflows. Many times, a project requires upfront investment and is more expensive in time value of money terms compared to future benefits. Looking at cash flows over time ensures that all cash flows are made equivalent. Sometimes a project may have a positive cash flow, but because of a large upfront investment cost and the long time it takes to accumulate benefits, it may actually have negative NPV savings. High NPV savings indicate that the project can deliver a real bottom-line impact to the organization. NPV also quantifies the payback period and provides an absolute value of a program's value over time.

Internal Rate of Return (IRR)

IRR is the discount rate at which the present value of future cash inflows equals cash outflows. A higher interest rate compared to competitive projects means that the project has a higher return and generates more effective interest on the investment. The method of calculation involves a series of guesses, but when comparing projects, is one of the most effective metrics in selecting the best comparative project. IRR is a metric related to ROI and provides the interest rate at which the program would have a zero NPV.

Payback Period (PP)

PP is a formula used for determining the timeframe needed for the project to yield a positive cumulative cash flow, which is typically specified in months. The calculation of PP enables a break-even point to be determined. A break-even point is when the total cost of the investment and total dollar return or revenue are equal, or when there is no net loss or gain. The PP starts by comparing cumulative costs versus cumulative benefits by month from the beginning of a project until the point when the cumulative benefits exceed the cumulative costs. A short PP on a project is usually a sign of less risk.

$$\text{Payback Period} = \frac{\text{Required Investment}}{\text{Net Annual Cash Flow}}$$

As an example, the total estimated cost of the EHR is $3 million over 5 years. It is assumed that this includes all of the one-time setup and sustainment costs. IF these costs are planned to be paid annually over 5 years, THEN the $3 million is divided by 5 years ($600,000 per year). IF a $4 million gain (savings/revenue) is assumed over 5 years, THEN the monthly gain should be $800,000. To calculate the net gain or differences between the expenditures and savings, $800,000 is subtracted from $600,000, equaling $200,000 as the net annual cash inflow. Lastly, to calculate the PP, the $3 million investment is divided by the net annual cash inflow of $200,000 to determine that it will take 15 months to pay back the investment. A shorter PP is normally better if all other product features remain equal.

Total Cost of Ownership (TCO)

TCO is a tally of not just the purchase cost of the solution, but all of the solution's costs over its lifecycle. This includes the upfront costs to plan, customize, integrate, and deploy the solution; running costs including support, management, facilities, and maintenance; and the retirement cost at the end of the solution's useful life.

Program Value Linkage (PVL)

PVL is the alignment of program CSFs, KRIs, and actionable KPIs. PVL is achieved through the precise linkage between program deliverables and benefits (outcomes). This correlation can best be achieved by linking program plan deliverables and each milestone to a specific desired outcome, which provides a dynamic NPV and IRR report. The validity of the linkage is determined by the specificity of the outcome, for example, a reduction in the business cost base or an increase in revenue directly aligned to a program deliverable that enables the benefit. Activity-Based Cost Management (ABC/M) provides cost assignment using cost drivers. The methodology can also be adapted to provide revenue drivers.

The portfolio is the sum of an organization's investment (or segment thereof) in the changes required to achieve its strategic objectives. Within the portfolio are various programs to facilitate the accomplishment of an objective. Each program is responsible for coordinating and overseeing projects related to delivering a specific business capability in order to support strategic objectives. As part of each program, the individual projects deliver at least one or more outputs (deliverables) in accordance with the business case and project plan. Both programs and projects are concerned with the cost, schedule, scope, resources, risks, and quality of products delivered. The overall program deliverables provide new or latent business capabilities that successfully meet intended stakeholder outcomes. The common thread through portfolios, programs, and projects is value (Figure 3.5).

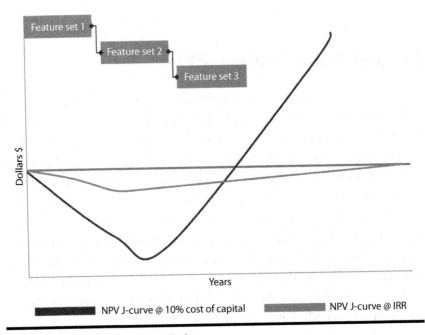

Figure 3.5 Program value linkage.

Use Case: Physical Therapy Consultation Management

To better understand the concepts, methodologies, and tools in this book, the same use case example will be used. This situational example focuses specifically on physical therapy consultations and referrals with a special emphasis on how this new capability can contribute to improved quality of care for U.S. federal employees.

The hypothetical U.S. Department of Federal Affairs (FA) has been chosen because of its commitment to starting new initiatives and programs to improve healthcare services for federal employees by improving technology programs such as the implementation of a "New Consultations Management for Physical Therapy" project, which will be released in the new EHR system.

The use case scenario is as follows:

Mr. Campbell has scheduled an appointment with his primary care provider (PCP), Dr. Tivoli, because he has pain in the neck, tenderness, stiffness, and loss of movement in the neck after a traffic accident and has specific concerns about whiplash. Dr. Tivoli searches on the terms of whiplash and is presented with prerequisite information and additional questions to help decide if proceeding with a traumatology consultation is appropriate. Dr. Tivoli decides to go forward with ordering the traumatology consult, and selects the whiplash protocol and completes her note for this consultation request, which will go on the patient's care plan. This protocol selection initiates a cervical x-ray for Mr. Campbell. This x-ray will go on Mr. Campbell's care plan as one of his tasks. Once the x-ray is complete, the Advanced Practice Nurse (APN) in traumatology will receive the request for service and will triage Mr. Campbell based on his need. She will create a task for the Medical Support Assistant (MSA) who will be responsible for scheduling Mr. Campbell's appointment. Three days after her visit with Mr. Campbell, Dr. Tivoli checks the status of Mr. Campbell's traumatology consultation and sees that it has been scheduled for next week. The following week, Mr. Campbell shows up for his appointment with Mr. Ting. Mr. Ting conducts the cervical MRI scanning and makes a diagnosis of whiplash. Mr. Ting prescribes nonsteroidal anti-inflammatory drugs (NSAIDS) for pain relief and refers Mr. Campbell to physical therapy for rehabilitation. Mr. Campbell chooses to receive a physical copy of his care plan today. Later in the week, when Dr. Tivoli is reviewing her blue clinic patient panel, she sees Mr. Campbell's condition has been diagnosed and is being treated. She has a few extra minutes so she gives him a call to see if the medication is improving his condition. After her conversation with Mr. Campbell, she annotates his updated status in his care plan.

Improving timely, coordinated access to services for federal employees is a top priority of the FA's modernization effort for EHRs. Inefficiencies and breakdowns in the referral process from primary to specialty care has been a persistent challenge across healthcare organizations. Barriers to effective referrals, or consultations, have been reported.

For example, Conley et al. noted that more than one in four consultations did not contain a clear clinical question, illustrating poor communication between clinicians.[7] Similarly, Gandhi et al. found several "communication breakdowns" in consultation management, including the timeliness of information from either the PCP or specialist, a lack of clarity in the note content from the PCP, and the specialist's lack of sufficient information in the initial consultation request.[8]

In the FA, when a PCP decides to initiate a consultation request, he/she enters the request in the EHR (the current EHR Frontend System in FA), oftentimes via a template that was designed by the specialty service provider or clinic. When the "receiving" specialist or staff member logs into the EHR, he/she is immediately notified about the new consultation request via a computerized view alert. The specialist can then deny the consultation or schedule the patient for an appointment. Once the specialist has seen the patient, the provider is expected to create a written assessment in an EHR note, ensure that it is attached to the original consultation request, and then sign the note. At this point, the note becomes available to the PCP to view in the EHR. However, this consultation process in the FA often breaks down.[9] For example, a common communication breakdown involves missing information in the original consultation request entered by the PCP, at least from the perspective of the specialist. Another common one involves the PCP not receiving a notification when the consultation has been completed.[10]

Gaps in the delivery of care for federal employees, a lack of easy-to-use reporting structures to assess the status of consultation requests, and workflow barriers to consultation referrals have been identified as the main problems in the current Consultations Management system (Figure 3.6).

Based on the literature, new EHRs provide consultation value by offering the following improvements:

■ The ability for the provider to track the status of the consultation request submitted
■ The ability for others to track the status of a specialist's action on the consultation request
■ An alert when the consultation is completed or has not been acted on
■ A clear explanation why a consultation request was cancelled

Cervical/thoraccic radiculopathy

Urgency

Acute or rapidly progressing weakness		☐

Prerequesites

MRI or myelogram completed within 6 months	Details	☐
Physical therapy	Details	☑
Physical exam	Details	☐

Figure 3.6   Consultations Management functionality.

Example of Value as a Program for Consultations Management

Coming back to measuring value as a program, and more specifically to the program value linkage, we can use the example use case to demonstrate a correlation between EHR evolution, including Consultation Management capabilities, deployment, and federal employee's satisfaction.

Later in Chapter 8, the "Common Operating Picture" demonstrates how advanced business analytics techniques enable the Value Management Office to objectively show how the EHR modernization program delivers value for all perspectives of health outcomes (Figure 3.7).

Summary of Key Points to Remember

The learning outcomes from this chapter that are important to remember include the following points:

■ Why are the healthcare perspectives outcomes on a Balanced Scorecard important?
A Value Scorecard for Healthcare Delivery Organizations consists of six outcome perspectives: clinical, financial, process improvement, employee satisfaction, patient satisfaction, and learning and growth. Each of the six outcomes when in complete alignment provides measurable value across the entire organization.

■ What is value as an equation?

$$\text{Value Equation} = \text{Outcomes}\left(\text{Benefits}\right)/\text{Costs}\left(\text{Inputs}\right)$$

■ How does an organization link value as a program in a health outcomes setting?
Determining value as a program prior to investment consists of validating the linkage of outcomes and their

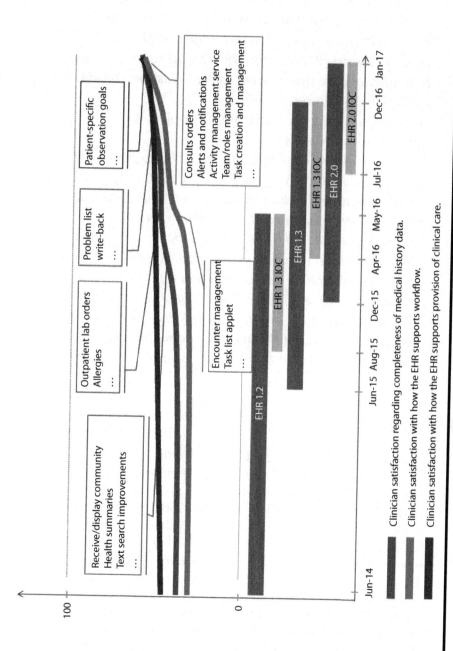

Figure 3.7   Example: EHR consultation management program value linkage.

cost, for example, a reduction in the business cost base or an increase in revenue directly related to a program deliverable that enables the benefit. The financial value of an intended program is determined by DCF, ROI, NPV, IRR, TCO, and PP analysis. The clinical value is aligned to quality of care and patient safety measures (based on condition or episode of care).

■ What if each program or Health IT project had value defined from the start?

Defining value at the beginning of each program or IT project enables the prediction of value such as quantifiable improvements in health outcomes and associated costs. This can best be achieved by linking program plan deliverables and each milestone to a specific desired outcome, which provides a dynamic NPV and IRR report. IT capability must also be linked to a clinical outcome in order to demonstrate value. Therefore, it is important to map the user perspective KPIs and technical KPIs to the CSFs. This demonstrates that the IT capability being built is making a measurable change in business performance.

References

1. Parmenter, D. 2007. *Key Performance Indicators (KPI): Developing, Implementing, and Using Winning KPIs.* New Jersey: John Wiley and Sons.
2. United Nations Development Program. 2002. Handbook on monitoring and evaluating for results. Evaluation Office, NY.
3. Kaplan, R. S. and Porter, M. E. 2011. The big idea: How to solve the cost crisis in health care. *Harvard Business Review.* Available at: https://hbr.org/2011/09/how-to-solve-the-cost-crisis-in-health-care. Accessed February 21, 2016.
4. Kaplan, R. S. and Norton, D. P. 2000. *The Strategy-Focused Organization: How Balanced Scorecard Companies Thrive in the New Business Environment.* Boston, MA: Harvard Business School Press.

5. Kaplan, R. S. and Norton, D. P. 1996. *The Balanced Scorecard: Translating Strategy into Action*. Boston, MA: Harvard Business School Press.
6. Davies, R.N. and Davies, A. J. 2011. *Value Management Translating Aspirations into Performance*. Burlington, VT: Goward Publishing Company.
7. Conley, J., Jordan, M., and Ghali, W. A. 2009. Audit of the consultation process on general internal medicine services. *Qual Saf Health Care*. 18(1):59–62.
8. Gandhi, T. K., Sittig, D. F., Franklin, M. et al. 2000. Communication breakdown in the outpatient referral process. *J Gen Intern Med*. 15(9):626–631.
9. Hysong, S. J., Esquivel, A., Sittig, D. F. et al. 2011. Towards successful coordination of electronic health record based-referrals: A qualitative analysis. *Implement Sci*. 6:84.
10. Saleem, J. J., Russ, A. L., Neddo, A. et al. 2011. Paper persistence, workarounds, and communication breakdowns in computerized consultation management. *Int J Med Inform*. 80(7):466–479.

Chapter 4

Value Management Office

Learning Objectives

After reading this chapter, the reader will be able to answer the following questions:

- Why is it important for organizations to create a Value Management Office (VMO)?
- What is the concept, mission, and vision of a VMO?
- How do management dashboards and performance score-cards provide value?
- What if organizations do not establish a VMO?

The Concept

The VMO serves as a center of excellence for determining evidence-based outcome measurements. The VMO is designed to facilitate the creation of value-based care models and ultimately improve patient care. The office also supports information technology (IT) governance by evaluating business case investments and projected benefits to link people, processes, and technology. A VMO is different from a Project Management Office (PMO) because it combines elements from project management, IT, clinical outcomes, and value-based management.

Organizational leaders and project managers encounter many issues that may cause them to be unsuccessful in delivering value to achieve desired organizational outcomes. The identification and measurement of key metrics can help improve and realign organizational resources to optimize value.

The VMO raises awareness of project issues and provides leaders with insight on what corrective actions can be taken to ensure that projects align with strategic initiatives and generate maximum value (Figure 4.1).

As a result, the VMO covers a wider business scope than typical PMOs. The VMO is a business function, designed to

Major issues in projects	Key levers on which to focus
• Poor alignment to business strategic plan • Disconnection between business and IT changes • The struggle to accept lack of capabilities in the organization • Projects have overreached the competencies of the department • Derogation of individual competencies as a result of reduced training budgets • Poor partnership relations with third parties • Poor use of business and IT resources (especially the key ones) • Piecemeal approach/solutions • Organizaion change capability • Change driven by IT solutions • Involved departments' autonomy • Ownership of "as is" and "to be" operating models	• Formal statement of the strategic plan • Unambiguous goals • Single accountability • Integrating multiple departments • Delivery effectiveness • Productivity monitoring • Budget continuous follow-up • Image • Customer satisfaction • Reporting and communication • Measurement of the results • Technical capacities • Impact on people, processes, and technology

Figure 4.1 Common project issues.[1]

oversee corporate governance, organizational change, quality, compliance, and process management. The VMO should look at every organization activity, and be able to clearly articulate why it is being done, whom it is being done for, what value it provides, and whether it is a business necessity. A VMO leads in defining the "value story."

The VMO acts as a single conduit for the organizational transformation where it can evaluate the impact of change from any initiative within the organization and how changes align with each other (or not) and prioritize accordingly. This helps to minimize the risk of change overwhelming the business and the problem of multiple changes competing for the same resources (Figure 4.2).

The VMO is different from a Program or Project Management Office because it generates integrated value among all evaluated initiatives (Figure 4.3).

Mission and Vision

Mission: To establish and lead processes to enable the Healthcare Delivery Organization (HDO) to evaluate projected and realized strategic, operational, and financial benefits from major business process changes and enterprise initiatives.

Vision: To apply value management as a way of doing business to ensure the efficient deployment of capital, improved clinical outcomes, and the achievement of strategic, operational, and financial objectives.

Role of the Value Management Office

The role of the VMO is to collaborate with agencies and enterprise initiative stakeholders to

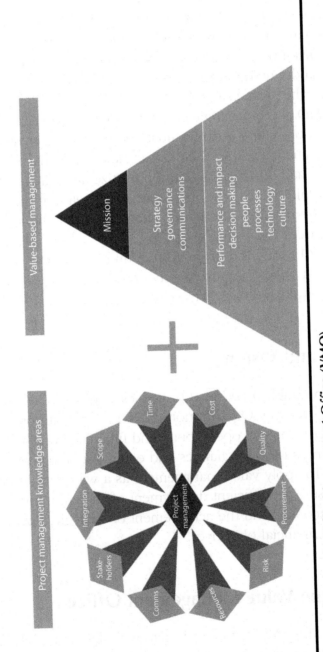

Figure 4.2 Elements of a Value Management Office (VMO).

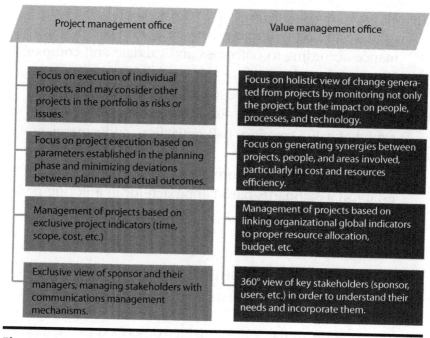

Figure 4.3 VMO versus PMO.

1. Integrate a Value Realization Framework (VRF) to deliver expected outcomes.
2. Estimate projected benefits to build out the "value story" and business case.
3. Identify, select, define, and coordinate the approval of measurable Critical Success Factors, Key Results Indicators, and User Perspective and Technical Key Performance Indicators.
4. Support the creation of a Common Operating Picture (COP) to get insights on what needs to be improved to achieve better outcomes.
5. Identify process changes and the support for the development of Value Improvement Plans needed to achieve desired outcome-oriented results and user value.
6. Define the strategic guidelines.
7. Build and manage the portfolio, define investment priorities, monitor risks, and implement projects.

8. Monitor and report projected versus actual benefits to validate and refine the business case. Evaluate performance according to outcomes and validate and compare benchmarks.

9. Reevaluate strategy, strategic objectives, and achieved versus expected returns. Establish investment strategies aimed at value creation, risk mitigation, and synergies between projects.

10. Create and maintain enterprise reference metrics, which establish a standards-based approach for monitoring performance and outcomes across the organization.

Governance and Staffing of the Value Management Office

In order to perform the VMO activities described previously, three organizational levels with different roles coordinate and collaborate with the same purpose of transforming the organization into a value-driven HDO.

The Value Management Governing Board is established to advise the VMO and make key decisions that affect the organization. This body also reviews and approves the content proposed by the VMO and sponsors the adoption of the Value Management methodologies and tools.

The Value Management Team will be the core office performing all the activities described previously. This multidisciplinary team combines all the different outcome perspectives and contributing factors to value within the HDO. The VMO will also be supported by a series of resources that provide expertise when required and assist with analyses or subject matter input to specific requests by the VMO.

In Figure 4.4, three different levels show how these roles operate and what is required within each level. However, it is up to each healthcare organization to decide how to configure, resource, and support the VMO.

	Role	Frequency	Proposed composition
Value management governing board	• Advise and take key decisions • Review and approve key results indicators • Ensure awareness of key stakeholders • Demonstrate involvement/commitment of leadership	Monthly	• HDO chief medical officer • HDO chief information officer • HDO chief financial officer • HDO program executive(s) • HDO chief transformation officer
	• Review and approve critical success factors	Quarterly	
Value management office (team)	• Drive project on a daily basis • Manage budget and project plan • Report to value management • Review and approve key performance indicators	Weekly or biweekly	• VMO director • Project manager • Lead clinician • IT manager • Quality team representative • Admin. representative • Nurse representative • Business analyst • Finance representative
	• Publish value outcomes	Quarterly	
Project support resources	• Provide expertise when required • Support discrete analyses/provide subject matter input to specific questions	Ad hoc basis (as needed)	• *e.g.,* IT expert, data analyst, statistician, other business analysts, etc.

Figure 4.4 Value management governance and staffing.

Benefits of the Value Management Office

The VMO provides benefits across the following dimensions:

- *Enhanced portfolio performance review*: By conducting periodic portfolio and project analysis, the VMO is able to determine the overall health of each, identify portfolio gaps, recommend projects to meet needs, and support in rebalancing the portfolio.
- *Project evaluation according to strategic objectives*: The VMO's Value Realization Framework measures project alignment and value and quantifies how each project contributes to organizational goals during execution and after completion.
- *Improved decision making*: The reports generated by the VMO provide timely and insightful knowledge to stakeholders and enable improved decision making across all levels of the organization.
- *Portfolio synergies*: By monitoring the overall portfolio, the VMO can improve alignment between projects and strategic objectives and generate synergies across an organization's portfolio.
- *Insights on technical impacts and constraints*: The VMO assesses how planned and completed projects will impact an organization's technical systems and identifies technical constraints that may inhibit progress toward achieving strategic objectives.
- *Improved cost allocation accuracy*: The VMO enables the accurate allocation of costs for projects in planning or monitoring phases.
- *Decreased risk exposure*: The early identification and mitigation of risk increases the value derived from the portfolio and offers greater flexibility and control over investment funding.
- *Custom implementation and model to match needs*: The VMO allows for full or partial implementation and can tailor its process and templates to meet the unique needs of an organization and its operational units.

Value Management Office Deliverables

The VMO collaborates with clinical quality and financial offices (not just from a process point of view) to provide five key deliverables:

1. Defined clinical outcome metrics
2. Defined program outcome metrics
3. Defined IT investment outcome metrics
4. Time-Driven Activity-Based Costing for each clinical outcome
5. New payment models (e.g., bundled payments)

In addition to these five key deliverables, the VMO shall produce management dashboards and performance scorecards to contribute to the overall COP (Figure 4.5).

Management Dashboards

Management dashboards are typically arranged to track the workflows in the business processes of the HDO. Graphically, users may see the high-level processes and then analyze more granular low-level data.

Specialized dashboards may track corporate functions, such as clinical outcomes, patient satisfaction, process efficiency, operations, security, IT, programs and project management, patient relationship management, and other departmental aspects.

The success of management dashboard projects often depends on the metrics that were designated for monitoring. Key Results Indicators and Key Performance Indicators, balanced scorecards, and performance figures are some of the types of content that are appropriate to include on management dashboards.

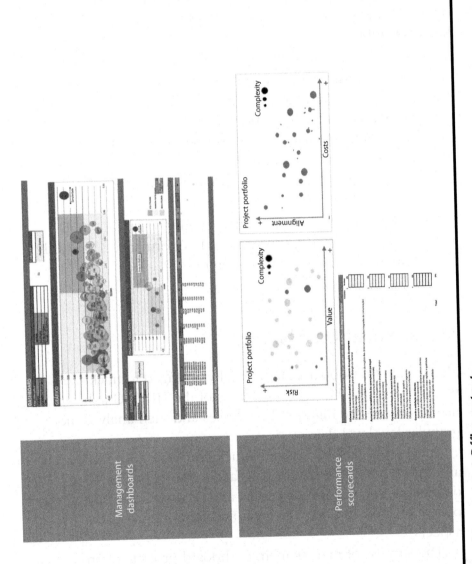

Figure 4.5 Value Management Office outputs.

Management dashboards allow managers to monitor the contribution of the various departments in their healthcare organization. The benefits of using digital dashboards include[2]:

- Visual presentation of performance measures
- Ability to identify and correct negative trends
- Ability to measure efficiencies/inefficiencies
- Ability to generate detailed reports showing new trends
- Ability to make more informed decisions based on collected business intelligence
- Alignment of strategies and organizational goals
- Ability to save time compared to running multiple reports
- Ability to gain total visibility of all systems instantly
- The quick identification of data outliers and correlations

Performance Scorecards

The management dashboard is often confused with the performance scorecard. The main difference between the two is that a management dashboard indicates the status at a specific point in time. A scorecard, on the other hand, displays progress over time toward specific goals.[3]

Summary of Key Points to Remember

The learning outcomes from this chapter that are important to remember include the following points:

- Why is it important for organizations to create a VMO? *A VMO provides core expertise and processes in developing outcome-oriented metrics both horizontally and vertically across an organization. Utilizing a standards-based framework to develop value-based outcomes for six strategic perspectives holistically empowers organizations.*

Outcomes also empower patients, clinicians, and payers and will impact the future healthcare delivery landscape in three distinct ways:

1. *Patients shall choose the providers for their care based on outcome value scores.*
2. *Clinicians shall be data-informed to make targeted improvements and learn.*
3. *Payers shall measure return on investment and direct patients to high-value providers.*

If

$$\text{Value} = \text{Outcomes (Benefits)}/\text{Costs (Inputs)},$$

then the value story attempts to provide patients with a safe and quality health outcome relative to the cost of achieving those outcomes. A VMO can help tell the value story.

■ What is the concept, mission, and vision of a VMO?
The VMO serves as a center of excellence for determining evidence-based outcome measurements. This center of excellence can facilitate the creation of value-based care models, support IT governance by evaluating business case investments, and highlight benefits to link people, processes, and technology. The mission of a VMO is to establish and lead processes to enable the Healthcare Delivery Organizations (HDO) to evaluate projected and realized strategic, operational, and financial benefits from major business process changes, and enterprise initiatives. The vision of a VMO is to apply value management as a way of doing business to ensure efficient deployment of capital, improved clinical outcomes, and achievement of strategic, operational, and financial objectives.

■ How do management dashboards and performance scorecards provide value?

Both management dashboards and performance score-cards are important tools to holistically understand an organization's performance and the value it is providing to patients, providers, and payers. These tools also provide transparency and tell a "value story" of an organization's positive impact on patients' lives and health outcomes.

■ What if organizations do not form a VMO?
Establishing a VMO is not creating another layer of bureaucracy, but rather leverages subject matter expertise (people), standards for developing outcomes (processes), and analytics to inform decision making (technology) to measure and predict value-based outcomes. Organizations that fail to establish such an office or adopt a process for value realization shall face uncertainty in an increasingly competitive and demanding market to demonstrate value.

References

1. Crawford, J. 2013. Building an effective change management organization. CreateSpace Independent Publishing Platform.
2. Briggs, J. 2013. Management reports and dashboard best practice. Target Dashboard.
3. Burkhow, J. 2011. Dashboards versus scorecards. *Data Enthusiast.*

Chapter 5

Value Realization Framework

Learning Objectives

After reading this chapter, the reader will be able to answer the following questions:

- Why is the Value Realization Framework important to Healthcare Delivery Organizations (HDOs)?
- What is the definition of a Critical Success Factor? Key Results Indicator? Key Performance Indicator? How does an organization apply Value Management?
- How does an organization apply the Value Realization Framework?
- What if an organization does not define their desired outcomes?

Need for a Framework

The current state of measuring and monitoring strategic initiatives and financial or clinical outcomes is disjointed and complex. The Value Realization Framework can help HDOs become more technologically driven with a focus on evidence-based outcomes, high accountability, and increased organizational performance. Implementing the Value Realization Framework is beneficial to all stakeholders and the public as demands for more transparency can show that healthcare organizations are providing improved care to their patients.

For this reason, the Value Management Office (VMO) and the Value Realization Framework provide the methodology to align the HDO's mission, vision, and values with improved evidence-based outcomes to patients. This methodology seeks to ensure that decisions regarding HDOs' Health Information Technology Programs are supported with data to improve service delivery, product delivery, information security, and fiscal management.

Figure 5.1 shows how the framework is structured, taking into consideration the following components: the healthcare organization's mission/vision/values, the underlying strategies and initiatives, six strategic outcomes (learning and growth, employee satisfaction, patient satisfaction, financial improvement, clinical improvement, and process improvement), concrete Critical Success Factors (Organization Goals), measurable Key Results Indicators (Program Outcomes), and objective Key Performance Indicators (Actions), both technical and user perspective.

The Value Realization Framework is central to the VMO and provides the main process components for ensuring that the strategies, initiatives, and programs accomplished by the HDO are providing value in all the different perspectives. It has been argued that "measuring the full set of outcomes is also essential in order to reveal the connections between care processes or pathways and patient results."[1]

The underpinning of the Value Realization Framework is to provide both horizontal and vertical alignment for the vision of success within an organization and to use the methodology to achieve the desired outcomes. Sustained success rests on employees, patients, and infrastructure—the learning, growth,

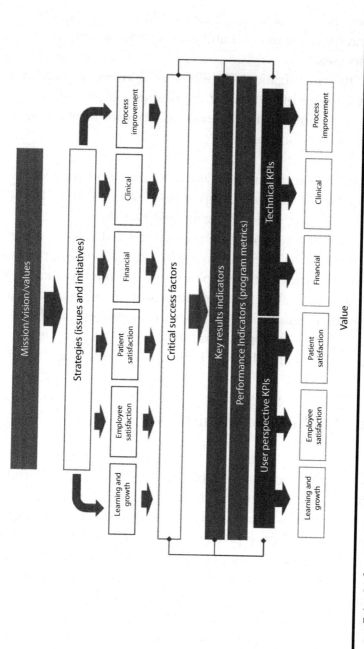

Figure 5.1 Value Realization Framework.

and performance measurement perspectives. Three key questions can be asked to ensure alignment is on track:

- Does the healthcare organization have employees with the required skills and attitudes to drive its internal processes?
- Are the organization's facilities, equipment, and technology capable of producing the desired outcomes?
- Is the organization delivering quality care for its patients, including education?

Kaplan and Norton note that the foundation for effective processes lies in the core competencies of employees, the technology in use, and the organization's culture.[2]

The following sections will provide more detail on applying this framework. In "Steps in the Value Realization Framework," details will be provided to explain how the framework is used in combination with other tools such as Lean Six Sigma, Lean, Business Intelligence and Analytics in the process of identifying, selecting, developing, and measuring the Key Results Indicators (KRIs) and the Key Performance Indicators (KPIs).

Value Equation for Healthcare

As Michael Porter describes in the article "What is value in healthcare?," "Outcomes are inherently condition-specific and multidimensional. For any medical condition, no single outcome captures the results of care. Cost refers to the total costs of the full cycle of care for the patient's medical condition, not the cost of individual services. To reduce cost, the best approach is often to spend more on some services to reduce the need for others."[3]

In the same article from Harvard Business Review, Porter states that "outcomes are the results of care in terms of patients' health over time. They are distinct from care processes or interventions designed to achieve the results, and from biologic indicators that are predictors of results. However, discomfort, timelines, and complications of care are outcomes, not process measures, because they relate directly to the health status of the patient. Patient satisfaction with care is a process measure, not an outcome. Patient satisfaction with health is an outcome measure."*

As illustrated in the Value Realization Framework, six healthcare perspectives of outcomes are defined to align with describing value in healthcare.

1. *Learning and growth*: Promoting a knowledge-based culture of medical best practices and standards in order to improve the operations, performance, and outcomes throughout the organization so that it continues to be a world-class healthcare center of excellence
2. *Employee satisfaction*: Providing pathways for business and IT professionals, clinicians, and physicians to serve patients in models that are more effective, efficient, sustainable, and conducive to restoring and preserving professional satisfaction
3. *Patient satisfaction*: Providing medical care and services with respect, compassion, and empathy by exceeding the needs and expectations of patients and their family members
4. *Financial*: Providing cost-effective care to patients while maintaining the quality of care and services
5. *Clinical*: Providing the best quality medical care to patients without error and harm to return the patient to a state of comfort and peace
6. *Process improvement*: Improving efficiency in completing all tasks required for the patient's medical condition at the HDO facilities

The achievement of the six outcome perspectives creates a quantifiable value-based healthcare system by improving

---

* Page 2 supplement to Porter, M. E. 2010. What is value in health care? *N Engl J Med*. 363:2477–2481.

patient outcomes and reducing cost, which when combined increase value (Figure 5.2).

If the VMO is properly implemented and used, the Value Realization Framework will determine if the organizations' programs and initiatives are creating tangible value across the organization's six main outcomes perspectives: Learning and Growth (LG), Employee Satisfaction (ES), Patient Satisfaction (PS), and Financial (F), Clinical (C), and Process Improvement (PI). This Value Realization Framework, inspired by Kaplan and Norton's work on Balanced Scorecards, can be successfully implemented because it starts and ends with a focus on the "core values" of any HDO.

To measure the value, outcomes for a HDO will be defined as the weighted addition of all the categories previously described.

$$\text{Outcomes} = \text{PS} \times (\text{Patient Satisfaction KRIs}) + \text{ES}$$

$$\times (\text{Employee Satisfaction KRIs}) \, \text{C} \times (\text{Clinical KRIs}) + \text{F}$$

$$\times (\text{Financial KRI}) + \text{LG} \times (\text{Learning and Growth}) + \text{PI}$$

$$\times (\text{Process Improvement KRIs})$$

Note:

PS, ES, C, F, LG, and PI are weights that can be customized depending on the priorities of the healthcare organization

After applying the Value Realization Framework, the Value Equation that was provided in Chapter 3 will be represented in the following way:

$$\text{Value} = \text{Outcomes} \, [\text{PS} \times (\text{Patient Satisfaction KRIs}) + \text{ES}$$

$$\times (\text{Employee Satisfaction KRIs}) + \text{C} \times (\text{Clinical KRIs}) + \text{F}$$

$$\times (\text{Financial KRIs}) + \text{LG} \times (\text{Learning \& Growth}) + \text{PI}$$

$$\times (\text{Process Improvement KRIs})] / \text{Costs} \, [\text{of the Initiatives}]$$

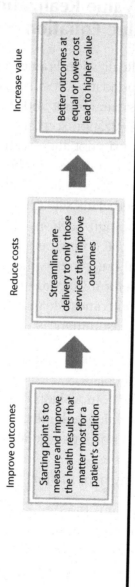

Improve outcomes

Starting point is to measure and improve the health results that matter most for a patient's condition

Reduce costs

Streamline care delivery to only those services that improve outcomes

Increase value

Better outcomes at equal or lower cost lead to higher value

Figure 5.2 Value from outcomes.

Note:
   PS, ES, C, F, LG, PI are weights that can be customized depending on the priorities of the healthcare organization

Application of the Value Realization Framework and Value Equation

To implement the Value Realization Framework, the HDO must first begin with its core foundation, focusing on its mission, vision, and values. This is paramount and should be disseminated throughout the organization so that there are no isolated strategies or initiatives that do not align with the "core."

When the entire HDO is focused on the core foundation, the remaining parameters of the Value Realization Framework can be properly developed. This will allow the leaders of the organization to take meaningful action, backed by valid data, to improve the six HDO categories/perspectives of outcomes.

Measuring meaningful outcomes is the starting point for value-based healthcare reform. According to the International Consortium for Health Outcomes Measurement, there are five reasons why outcome measurement is essential[4]:

■ Outcomes define the goals of the organization and its accountability to patients.
■ Outcomes inform the composition of integrated care teams.
■ Outcomes highlight value-enhancing cost reduction.
■ Outcomes motivate clinicians to collaborate and improve together.
■ Outcomes enable payment to shift from volume to results.

The next step after establishing the core and the initiative is to define the remaining components of the Value Management Framework: Critical Success Factors (CSF), measurable Key Results Indicators (KRI), measurable Performance Indicators (PI), and actionable Key Performance Indicators (KPIs), as shown in Figure 5.3.

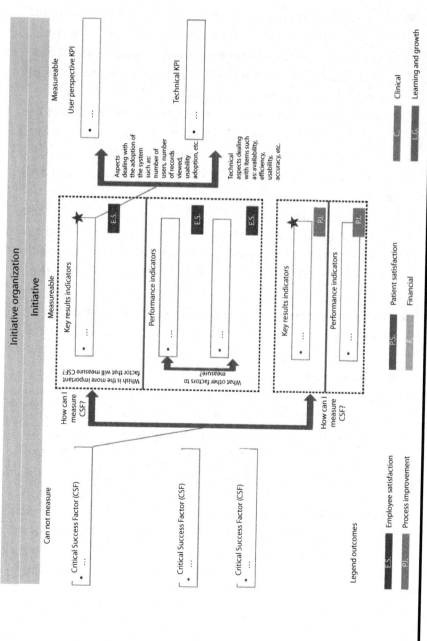

Figure 5.3 Value Realization Framework application.

In order to provide answers to the components discussed earlier, it is important to understand the following concepts:

- *Critical Success Factors (CSFs)*: These refer to "the handful of key areas where an organization must perform well on a consistent basis to achieve its mission."* CSFs are strongly related to the mission and strategic goals of the healthcare organization and its projects. Whereas a healthcare organization's mission and goals focus on the aims and what is to be achieved, CSFs focus on the most important areas and get to the very heart of both what is to be achieved and how the healthcare organization will achieve it.
- *Key Results Indicators (KRIs)*: These "measure the results from the business actions, which are critical in tracking progress and defining success."[5] KRIs exist to tell healthcare organization stakeholders and senior leaders if the organization is operating well.
- *Performance Indicators (PIs)*: These measure the efficiency or productivity by comparison with an agreed standard or target and are considered essential in delivering high quality.
- *Key Performance Indicators (KPIs)*: These "measure the actions and events that lead to a result and are critical to the success of the business as their data is crucial in creating strategies and aligning goals."[5] While KRIs are important in determining if end goals have been met, they cannot help the healthcare organization achieve or improve on its goals; they are simply benchmarks (which are still crucial to any healthcare organization's definition of success). KPIs focus on the actions that lead to the results; they provide information that is critical in creating

---

* Carnegie Mellon definition of Critical Success Factors. From Caralli, R. A. 2015. The critical success factor method: Establishing a foundation for enterprise security management.

strategies and aligning goals that can further or hinder the organization's success. KPIs are the metrics used to measure the performance of the CSFs—they are the metrics that dissect success.

Using the framework, one will be able to create a chart with each of the components described previously. Each initiative is unique and will focus on one outcome and compose its CSFs, KRIs, PIs, and KPIs according to that initiative. Nevertheless, one can have various outcomes tied to one initiative. Figure 5.4 and Table 5.1 illustrate how different indicators can be identified at each level (CSF, KRI, or KPI) for each category/perspective of outcomes.

The numbers listed in Figure 5.4 correspond to an individual row with examples in Table 5.1. The purpose of Table 5.1 is to demonstrate how an organization can achieve both vertical and horizontal alignment. This alignment shapes the Common Operating Picture, which is discussed in Chapter 8.

In the following section, a more specific example demonstrates how this framework can be applied to one specific use case.

Application of the Framework to Consultations Management

The use case example introduced in Chapter 3, "Physical Therapy Consultations Management in FA," is presented to illustrate how the Value Realization Framework can be used for one initiative within the HDO.

As the initiative has already been established, the first step will be to define the CSFs. CSFs are objective statements measured by the achievement of results (KRIs), and are the key areas in which an organization must perform well in order for

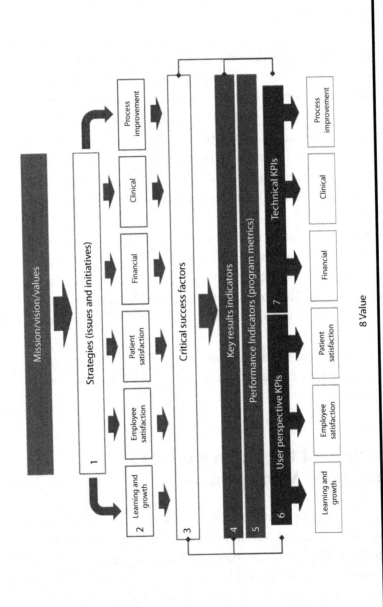

Figure 5.4   Value Realization Framework process steps example.

Table 5.1   Metrics for Different Levels and Perspectives of Outcomes

Any healthcare initiative, either strategic or tactical, or clinical, operational or technical, might have a focus in one of the perspectives of outcomes (e.g., patient safety or improving clinician engagement), but is always going to impact on all the perspectives of outcomes in a direct or indirect manner.
As an example of initiative, the "**Development and Deployment of a new Electronic Health Record System**" in the organization is presented below:

Initiatives	Clinical Outcomes	Financial Outcomes	Process Improvement	Learning and Growth	Employee Satisfaction	Patient Satisfaction
Critical Success Factors	Health status achieved; Process of Recovery; Sustainability of Clinical Outcomes	More cost-effective care; Reduced variation in cost and utilization between internal HDO and external community care for patients with similar conditions	Patients and physicians experience; Average wait times for consultation	Defined processes to set learning agenda and capture, distill, apply, and share medical knowledge; Creating a culture of continuous improvement	Physicians following standard guidelines; Physician Attrition due to dissatisfaction; and satisfaction from medical services	Quick and easy eligibility, appointment, scheduling and referral, and processes; Patient satisfaction

(Continued)

Table 5.1 (Continued)   Metrics for Different Levels and Perspectives of Outcomes

Initiatives	Clinical Outcomes	Financial Outcomes	Process Improvement	Learning and Growth	Employee Satisfaction	Patient Satisfaction
Key Results Indicators	Reduced quality of care; Reduced adverse drug events; Synchronized consultation	Case-adjusted revenue, costs, utilization, and cost effectiveness; Managed litigations	Reduced variation in practice across physicians and regions; Complexity reduction in care coordination	Role-based training programs and their participation; Leveraging existing knowledge	Provider knowledge about medical history, allergies, and medications; Effective communications to improve performance	Improved quality of coordinated care; Accommodation of patient preferences
Performance Indicators	Reduced number of readmissions; Reduced length of stay; Reduced excesses; Reduced costs	Claims processing speed and accuracy; Significant decreases in medication costs	Physician patient consultation time; Patient wait times; Patient external provider experience	Number of additions to the knowledgebase; Number of users of the knowledgebase	Consultation effectiveness and consultation efficiency; Collaboration with medical care	Physicians keeping appointments; Patient involvement in health

(Continued)

Table 5.1 (Continued)   Metrics for Different Levels and Perspectives of Outcomes

Initiatives	Clinical Outcomes	Financial Outcomes	Process Improvement	Learning and Growth	Employee Satisfaction	Patient Satisfaction
User perspective KPI	Physician availability for patients on desired date; Faster and easier referral scheduling	Patient billing accuracy; Minimizing patient contributions; Utilization of assets	Patient end-to-end care process (Scheduling to discharge processes)	Instituting award and recognition programs for collaboration	Employee satisfaction score; Employee experience with medical users	Patient experience with multiple faculties and providers
Technical KPI	Number of tickets opened by user regarding performance or functionality of the system	Reimbursement cycle time and accuracy; Procurement payment cycle time	Monitoring cycle times and wait times for care; Throughput of each process step	Online training programs to advance skills of patients in cutting edge communication technologies and programs	Access to number of patients; Reducing no shows and number of reschedules	Number of patients scheduled remotely; Number of patients with active online participation
Value elements	Overall patient wellness and enthusiastic participation	Care-based cost optimization	Streamlined operations—bottlenecks eliminated	Promoting employee learning and growth	Provider satisfaction and experience	Patient satisfaction and experience

the strategy, program, or initiative to succeed. For example, CSFs for this use case might be to

■ Improve efficiency in the Consultation Management Process
■ Improve access to consultations
■ Improve clinician satisfaction with the new consultations feature
■ Improve patient satisfaction with consultations for physical therapy

The next step will be to define measurable KRIs for the CSF. In order to do that, a number of PIs are identified for the CSF. These indicators will help answer the question "How can I measure a CSF?" in a way that is consistent with the Value Realization Framework and related to the six perspectives of outcomes. Once that is done, picking out the KRIs should be easier because they are the most important outcomes with which to measure the CSF.

As illustrated in Figure 5.5, the example shows how KRIs can be created for one CSF and focuses on the "employee satisfaction" perspective (although the same process could be applied for any of the other outcomes perspectives).

The third step is to define the KPIs that are tied to the KRI. User perspective KPIs deal with aspects related to the adoption of the system such as number of users, number of records viewed, usability adoption, and user satisfaction. Technical KPIs deal with aspects such as availability, efficiency, usability, and accuracy (Figure 5.6).

Finally, to ensure that the right indicators are chosen, one must define how these indicators will be measured. For example, in the case of the KRI, the method used to gather data (positive/negative results) will be a survey given to physical therapists, whereas for a KPI, a user usability testing method will be used to get the System Usability Score (SUS) (Figure 5.7).

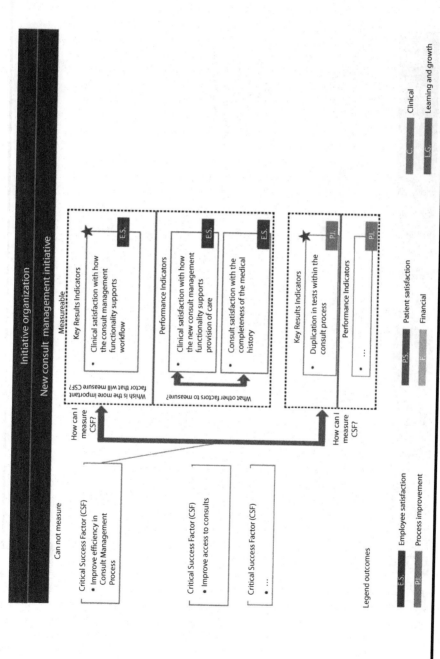

Figure 5.5 Use case example applying KRI and PI to CSF.

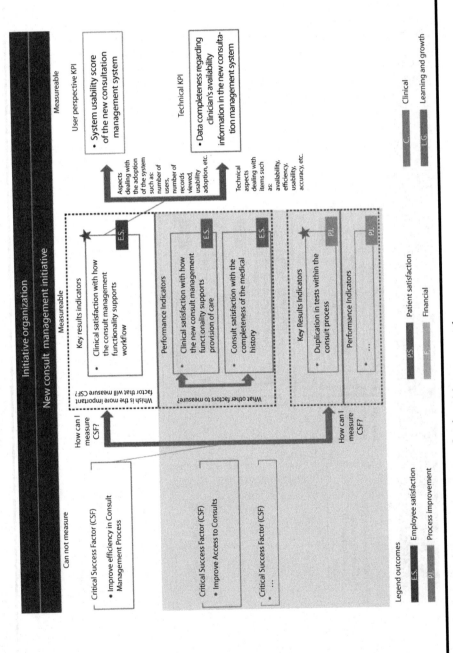

Figure 5.6 Technical KPIs for Consultation Management.

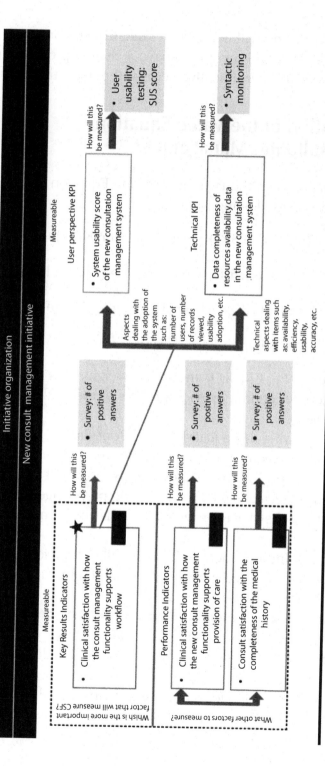

Figure 5.7 Indicators measurement.

In the end, one will complete a table like the one in Table 5.2 for physical therapy to have a clear approach to measuring the value of an initiative across all perspectives.

Application of the Value Equation to Consultation Management

As stated earlier, the Healthcare Value Equation can be represented by the following formula:

$$\text{Value} = \text{Outcomes}\,[\text{PS} \times (\text{Patient Satisfaction KRIs}) + \text{ES}$$

$$\times (\text{Employee Satisfaction KRIs}) + \text{C} \times (\text{Clinical KRIs}) + \text{F}$$

$$\times (\text{Financial KRIs}) + \text{LG} \times (\text{Learning \& Growth}) + \text{PI}$$

$$\times (\text{Process Improvement KRIs})]\,/\,\text{Costs}\,[\text{of the Initiatives}]$$

Where PS, ES, C, F, LG, and PI are weights that can be customized depending on the priorities of the healthcare organization.

When applying this equation to the Consultation Management example, the outcomes are simplified by the following KRIs in each outcome perspective. Hypothetically, each KRI has changed (increased or decreased) by the following percentages one year after the Consults Management Initiative has been initiated:

- Clinical: Improvement in basic mobility functioning—2%.
- Financial: Cost reduction in duplicate consultations that are finally cancelled—5%.
- *Process improvement*: Reduction of unnecessary steps to complete high-value clinical activities—10%.
- *Learning and growth*: Increase in provider adoption of technology—5%.
- *Employee satisfaction*: Improvement in clinical satisfaction with the Electronic Health Record (EHR) support workflow—5%.

Table 5.2 Metrics for Consultations Management

Initiatives	Consultations Management Feature in the EHR Program					
Outcomes	*Clinical*	*Financial*	*Process Improvement*	*Learning and Growth*	*Employee Satisfaction*	*Patient Satisfaction*
Critical Success Factors	Improve patient consultations for physical therapy	Increase features delivered on time within budget and meeting quality standards	Improve efficiency within the consultations process	Increased adherence to specialty care plans by primary clinicians without need for consultations	Improve clinician satisfaction with new consultations feature	Improve patient satisfaction scores with access to physical therapy care
Key Results Indicators	Improvement in basic mobility functioning	Cost reduction in duplicate consultations that are finally cancelled	Variability of care; unnecessary Steps to complete high value clinical activities	Provider adoption of technology	Clinical satisfaction with the EHR support workflow	Specialty SHEP Score Q6— In the last 6 months, when you contacted this provider's office to get an appointment for care you needed right away, how often did you get an appointment as soon as you needed?

(Continued)

Table 5.2 (Continued)   Metrics for Consultations Management

Consultations Management Feature in the EHR Program

Initiatives							
Outcomes	Clinical	Financial	Process Improvement	Learning and Growth	Employee Satisfaction	Patient Satisfaction	
Performance indicators	30-day readmission rate following discharge from physical therapy	Cost reduction in duplicate tests within the consultations process	Percent appointments completed <=30 days from preferred date for physical therapy	Number of training courses planned versus conducted (by location)	Clinical satisfaction with EHR support and provision of care	Percentage of no-shows at physical therapy appointments	
User Perspective KPI	Reduction of adverse drug events within the physical therapy consultations process	Costs incurred in sustainment of legacy systems for Consults Management	Time required (90th percentile) to complete a consultation request	System Usability Score (SUS) of the new consultations management functionality	User satisfaction with the new consultations management functionality	PCMH SHEP Score Q18—Wait time includes time spent in the waiting room and exam room. In the last 12 months, how often did you see this provider within 15 min of your appointment time?	

(Continued)

Table 5.2 (Continued) Metrics for Consultations Management

Initiatives	Consultations Management Feature in the EHR Program					
Outcomes	*Clinical*	*Financial*	*Process Improvement*	*Learning and Growth*	*Employee Satisfaction*	*Patient Satisfaction*
Technical KPI	Availability of records (uptime); Accuracy of records (data quality); Efficiency of records (transaction times)	Number of defects per user acceptance criteria	IT support performance = (Number of IT support requests within SLA)/(Total number IT support requests) in standard hours of operation	Number of clinical decision support and consultation management process rules triggered that relate to care plans for patients	Service level effectiveness = (Surveyed users with >= 90% satisfaction)/(Total number of surveyed users)	Use of MyFA .gov and patient-facing portals for consult-related patient activities. Rate of patient engagement transactions
Value elements	Patient wellness	Value for money	Streamlined operations	Technology adoption	Provider satisfaction	Patient satisfaction

Source: Haley, S. M. and Fragala-Pinkham, M. A. 2006. Interpreting change scores of tests and measures used in physical therapy. *Phys. Ther.* 86(5), 735–743, 2006.

Note: Numerator: the number (or proportion) of a clinician's patients in a particular risk-adjusted diagnostic category who meet a target threshold of improvement in basic mobility functioning. Denominator: all patients in a risk-adjusted diagnostic category with a mobility goal for an episode of care. Cases to be included in the denominator could be identified based on ICD-9 codes or alternatively based on CPT codes relevant to treatment goals focused on basic mobility function.

■ Patient satisfaction: Improvement in PCMH SHEP Q6 (get an appointment for care when needed right away)—3%.

Note: Normally, several KRIs would be combined for each outcome perspective; in this case, in order to facilitate the understanding of the example, assume there is only one KRI per outcome perspective.

$$Value = [PS \times (3\% \text{ improvement in patient satisfaction}) + ES$$

$$\times (5\% \text{ improvement in employee satisfaction}) + C$$

$$\times (2\% \text{ improvement in clinical outcomes}) + F$$

$$\times (5\% \text{ improvement in financial outcomes}) + LG$$

$$\times (5\% \text{ improvement in learning and growth outcomes}) + PI$$

$$\times (10\% \text{ improvement in process improvement outcomes})]$$

$$/ Costs (\text{of the Consults Management Initiative})$$

Once the outcomes have been measured, the benefit from each outcome is determined and compared with the cost invested in the initiative to quantify the value. Advanced analytics techniques for healthcare are introduced later in this book, and can be used to calculate the financial benefits associated with each outcome.

To illustrate the process, the rationale is provided to correlate each outcome and its impact on value.

Approach to Quantifying the Value

Step 1: For each KRI, identify the outcome improvement (benefit) and the rationale associated with it. These measures have to be tangible and care must be taken to identify the associated performance measures.

The outcomes and benefits associated with the KRI's are:

1. *Improvement in basic mobility functioning:* Effective treatment reduces the number of hospitalization days.
2. *Cost reduction in duplicate consultations that are finally cancelled:* Reassigns the resources to other activities that would be waiting if the consultation were not cancelled enough time in advance.
3. *Variability of care and unnecessary steps to complete high-value clinical activities:* Standardization reduces the number of steps to perform the task and there is consistency across hospitals.
4. *Provider adoption of technology:* Faster technology adoption improves the efficiency and effectiveness of clinicians providing care to patients.
5. *Clinical satisfaction with EHR support workflow:* Clinical satisfaction reduces clinician attrition and increases their engagement, providing better care to patients.
6. *Get appointment for care when needed:* Delayed appointments aggravate the situation and increase the cost of providing care.

Step 2: Identify the current situation (as is) associated with the performance metrics identified in step 1. For example, to improve the outcome of basic mobility functioning, if the mobility is obtained faster, the number of days in hospital will be reduced, thus saving money.

The next step is to identify the number of days a patient is in the hospital (A) before the consultation management capability. This step is followed by identifying the percentage reduction in the hospital days associated with a 2% improvement in basic mobility functioning (5% in this example). Finally, the benefit is calculated by multiplying this figure by the cost of one day of savings as shown in Table 5.3.

Table 5.3 Value Calculation in Dollars

Outcome	Benefits	Before Consult Management Capability	Benefit with Consult Management Capability	After Consult Management Capability
Basic mobility functioning	Reduction in the # of days of hospitalization	X days in hospital	5%	X * (1%–5%) * Cost of one day of hospitalization
Cost reduction in duplicate consultations	Reduction in the # of duplicate consultations	X duplicate tests scheduled per patient	10%	X * (1%–10%) * Average cost of test*Number of patients
Reduction in variability of tests	Reduction in the # of steps to complete consultation process	X number of steps	15%	X * (1%–15%) * Average cost of performing a step of the workflow

(Continued)

Table 5.3 (Continued)   Value Calculation in Dollars

Outcome	Benefits	Before Consult Management Capability	Benefit with Consult Management Capability	After Consult Management Capability
Provider adoption of technology	Reduction in the # of minutes saved/patient; Reduction in the # of errors per patient	X minutes saved/ patient Y number of errors patient/ year	20% 10%	X * (1%–20%) * Cost of saving 1 min of time + Y * (1%–10%) * Y * Average cost of error
Clinical satisfaction (nurse and physician satisfaction)	Reduced attrition Improved patient care and thereby satisfaction	X number of clinicians leaving FA Y # of extra patients	1% 1%	X * (1%–10%) * Cost searching for and hiring a replacement Y * 1% * Average revenue generated/patient
Get appointment for when care is needed	Reduction in the number of days to schedule a patient	X number of days to get appointment	20%	X * (1%–20%) * Average cost of delay

Step 3: Conduct research and identify the actual values for all the variables. When conducting research, care must be taken to ensure the credibility of the source and the applicability of the results. Sometimes transformations are needed to get the number in the form we need. For example, if we know the average salary of the physician, we need to add benefits and divide by the number of days and hours to get the average cost of physician/hour. For the consultation process, all the actual numbers from the research are as follows:

1. Number of days of hospitalization = 8
2. Cost of one day of hospitalization = $1400
3. Number of days on sick leave = 21
4. Cost of one day of worker compensation = $550
5. Number of duplicate tests performed = 4
6. Average cost of performing a test = $120
7. Number of steps in the workflow = 20
8. Average cost of performing a step of the workflow = $400
9. Average time spent on patients by care providers = 22 min
10. Average cost of saving physician time/hour = $143
11. Number of errors identified/patient/year = 0.01%
12. Average cost of an error conducted by the clinician = $500
13. Number of clinicians at the hospital = 800
14. Average cost of searching for and hiring a replacement = $10,000
15. Total revenue of the hospital = $20 million
16. Total number of patients seen in a year = 6667
17. Average revenue generated/patient = $300
18. Average number of days to schedule = 14
19. Average cost of delay in providing care = $500

Step 4: In this step, all the values are substituted for variables to get the total value of the consultations capability as indicated below:

■ Savings from reduced hospitalization =
  8 × 5% × $1400 = $560/patient = $560K/year

- Savings from duplicate tests $= 2 \times 10\% \times 140 = \$28/$ patient $= \$28K/year$
- Savings from process streamlining $= 20 \times 15\% \times \$400 = \$120/$patient $= \$120K/year$
- Savings from physicians' time saved $= 22 \times 20\% \times \$143 = \$629/$patient $= \$629K/year$
- Savings from fewer physician errors $= 1000 \times 0.01 \times 5000 = \$50K/year$
- Savings from reduced attrition of physicians $= 800 \times 1\% \times \$10,000 = \$80K/year$
- Savings from additional people accommodated $= 1,000 \times 1\% \times 12,000 = \$120K/year$
- Savings from reduced delay in care $= 14 \times 20\% \times 50 = \$1400/$patient $= \$140K/year$

Therefore, the total benefits (quantified value) from improving the consultations capability would be $1.7 million per year.

These financial gains can be applied to the previous Value Equation in addition to the cost information of the initiative. As a result, the organization would be able to report the Value of the Consults Management Initiative.

If the cost of the initiative is $1.5 million, then the value is $(1.727/1.5) = \$1.15$ million, with an ROI of $(0.227/3) = 15.13\%$ (a good return on a one-year project). Other financial measures can be calculated for Internal Rate of Return (IRR), Net Present Value (NPV), Payback Period (PP), and Total Cost of Ownership (TCO).

Note: Assume that all the variables are equally distributed and have the same coefficient.

In this particular example, data collection for KRI measurement may begin (baseline measure) at any point at the start of a new Consults Management Initiative. Once data collection begins, it is recommended that it continues annually for as many years as is feasible.

Annual data collection is intended to provide information for comparing outcomes across providers. A 2-month window is recommended for collecting these measures. (Annual measures collected between 10 and 14 months from the base-line or the previous time point will be suitable.)

In this book, the timing of data collection is left for the HDO to decide.

Summary of Key Points to Remember

The learning outcomes from this chapter that are important to remember include the following points:

■ Why is the Value Realization Framework important to HDOs?
Measuring and monitoring strategic initiatives across six outcome perspectives is essential for a HDO to focus on evidence-based outcomes that matter most to the patient, provider, and payer. The Value Realization Framework provides the basis for achieving and predicting outcomes while also minimizing costs.

■ What is a CSF? KRI? KPI? Moreover, how do they apply to Value Management?
How do KRIs and KPIs apply to Value Management? Remember, the VMO is an umpire of sorts, so let's use a baseball analogy. An easier way to look at KPIs and KRIs would be to think of the HDO as a sports team. The general manager is interested in the overall wins and trophies that a team has accumulated (KRIs), similar to the payers and HDO leadership. The coach, however, is more interested in how the players are performing and the advanced statistics that show them where the team can improve (KPIs), similar to management in the HDO. In this scenario, the HDO senior leadership is concerned with KRIs, while the coach/management is more occupied with KPIs. Both sets of metrics have a definite purpose regarding the

success of the team, but the two are used and looked at in two entirely different ways.

■ How does an organization apply the framework?
A3 Thinking is recommended. Through a process-driven approach, first define the business problem in order to properly develop a CSF. The next step will be to define measurable KRIs for the CSF. Each KRI (outcome result) must be measurable and repeatable to be meaningful. Follow-on tasks include the development of PIs and KPIs. The importance of applying the Value Realization Framework process cannot be understated. Applying it enables a HDO to transition from the antiquated fee-for-service model to a fee-for-value system. In a value-based system, payers will insist on paying a fixed price per diagnosis and hence over-staying is a cost to the hospital, not the payer. In the current fee-for-service environment, shorter stays can also be equated with loss of revenue, which can create a conflict of interest resulting in our broken healthcare system.

■ What if an organization does not define their desired outcomes?
Obviously, everyone wants to achieve their outcomes on the first go, but realistically this is not possible. Sometimes, the best lessons are learned by doing. Shortcomings identify areas for process improvement, which is the main benefit of the Value Realization Framework. The framework provides both vertical and horizontal insight into how the organization is delivering value and provides invaluable information for decision makers. Demonstrating incremental improvement and transparency enables organizations to tell a value story that resonates with those they serve.

References

1. Porter. M. E. 2010. Measuring health outcomes: The outcome hierarchy. *N Engl J Med*. 363:2477–2481. (10.1056/NEJMp1011024) Appendix 2.
2. Kaplan, R. S. and Norton, D. P. 2000. *The Balanced Scorecard: Translating Strategy into Action*. Boston: Harvard Business School Press. p. 175.
3. Porter, M. E. 2010. What is value in health care? *N Engl J Med*. 363:2477–2481.
4. International Consortium for Health Outcomes Measurement. 2015. Available at: www.ichom.org.
5. Parmenter, D. 2007. *Key Performance Indicators (KPI): Developing, Implementing, and Using Winning KPIs*. New Jersey: John Wiley and Sons.

Chapter 6

Steps in the Value Realization Framework

Learning Objectives

After reading this chapter, the reader will be able to answer the following questions:

- Why is it important to follow a process toward defining value?
- What are the three outputs from Task 3: Build a hierarchy of Critical Success Factors (CSFs)?
- How do Key Performance Indicators (KPIs) help organizations?
- What if the success is not defined upfront?

Process Overview

It is important that Healthcare Delivery Organizations (HDOs) use a collaborative framework for developing a dashboard for monitoring value and generating reports in a way that results in action. As demonstrated before with the "Consultation Management for Physical Therapy" use case, the Value Realization Framework (Figure 6.1) supports a process for providing the organization's leadership with an actionable monitoring and reporting methodology to make informed decisions.

As described earlier in this book, the Value Realization Process begins with the creation of a programs' CSFs. The CSFs are identified and developed by the business owners with the support of the Value Management Office (VMO). Once the CSFs are created, the Key Results Indicators (KRIs) are identified to measure the outcomes and results considered essential to the desired health outcome and the program's success. The organization's Enterprise Reference Metrics, which are based on standards applicable to all programs, are used to identify user perspective KPIs and technical KPIs (leading indicators) for each of the program's systems and projects.

After the KPIs have been developed, the most essential ones are selected for each of the organization's systems and products and mapped back to the program's CSFs that were created in the beginning of the Value Realization Process. Before the indicators are applied to a program's systems and products, they are vetted and approved by the VMO governing board.

The last part of the process is the development of the program's dashboard that will monitor and report whether or not the KPIs and KRIs are achieving their targets. Baselines and goals will need to be established for every indicator in order to implement the Value Improvement Plan for every outcome that needs to be enhanced.

This Value Realization Process involves multiple workstreams and stakeholders who execute the various tasks. The VMO serves as the anchor, providing support and guidance throughout the entire process.

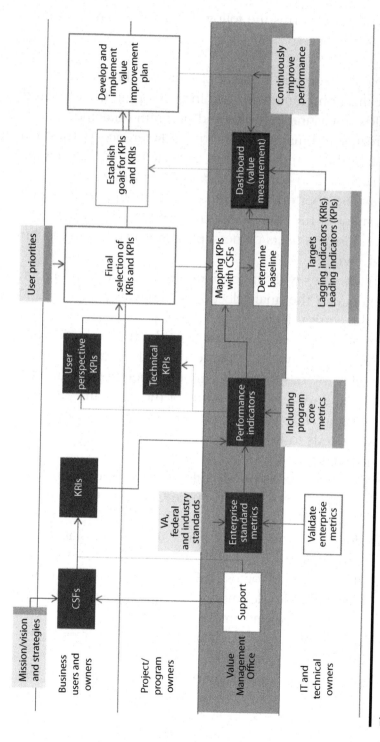

Figure 6.1 Value realization process.

The VMO performs the following tasks within the Value Realization Process:

- Provides support in the application of the Value Realization Framework and in developing the CSFs and KRIs (measurable health and program outcomes).
- Creates and maintains Enterprise Reference Metrics, which establish a standards-based approach for monitoring performance and outcomes across the organization.
- Develops performance indicators that support the development of the user perspective and technical KPIs with the business users/owners, program owners, and technical owners.
- Collaborates with the business users/owners and program owners for the final selection of the user perspective KPIs and technical KPIs.
- Provides the mapping linkage of the final selection of user perspective KPIs and technical KPIs to the CSFs.
- Creates the dashboard (Common Operating Picture) to track and report on the status of the KRIs and KPIs critical to the HDO achieving its mission to get insight on what needs to be improved in order to achieve better outcomes.
- Supports the creation of "value stories" and business cases based on insight from the Common Operating Picture (COD).
- Evaluates outcome performance and validates it compared to benchmarks.
- Evaluates the outcomes reported in the dashboard and supports the development of a Value Improvement Plan for the required outcomes.
- Supports the reevaluation of strategic objectives and achieved versus expected returns.
- Supports the coordination of the final metrics that will be incorporated into the program/initiative dashboard for approval by the governing board.

The business users and owners perform the following tasks:

- Develop the CSFs and KRIs with the support of the VMO.
- With the support of the VMO, develop technical KPIs that measure the user's experience in executing daily business activities and functions using IT systems and products, with an emphasis on reliability, efficiency, and accuracy.
- Collaborate with the technical owners and the VMO for the final selection of user perspective KPIs for projects and systems.
- Jointly with the project/program and technical owners and with the support of the VMO, establish goals and baselines for the selected indicators (KRIs and KPIs).
- Lead the development of a Value Improvement Plan for the outcomes related to KRIs.

The project/program owners perform the following tasks:

- With the support of the VMO, develop technical KPIs that measure the technical performance of information technology (IT) systems and products to ensure that they are functioning properly, as this has an indirect impact on the frontend user experience.
- Collaborate with business users/owners and the VMO for the final selection of user perspective KPIs and technical KPIs for the organization's projects and systems.
- Lead the development of a Value Improvement Plan, mostly for the outcomes related to KPIs.

The technical owners perform the following tasks:

- Provide validation and approval of the Enterprise Reference Metrics and targets that set the performance standards for the user perspective KPIs and technical KPIs.
- In the following sections, more detail is provided for the several steps that comprise the Value Realization Process.

Some of these steps will be supported by the utilization of tools and methodologies, such as Lean Six Sigma, Business Intelligence, or Business Analytics, that facilitate the identification of CSFs, KRIs, and KPIs.

As shown in Figure 6.2, the Value Realization Process is mainly focused on the following four steps:

Step 1: Critical Success Factors

It is imperative that CSFs be determined in advance of the performance measures. The creation of CSFs is subjective in nature and requires engaged leadership during this subjective exercise. CSFs are derived after the business problem has been identified and a problem statement has been created. Success cannot be defined without first understanding the problem. The effectiveness and usefulness of the CSFs is dependent on collaborative analysis and acceptance. Five key tasks have to be followed for identifying CSFs.

- *Task 1: Establish a value management working group.* This group shall include senior leadership who will answer the fundamental question, "What does success look like?"
  Only through collaboration and engaged leadership can we truly define success.
- *Task 2: Review all the strategic documents in the organization.* This information is used to develop the CSFs. Ensure that the proposed CSFs address all six of these performance perspectives:
  - Clinical
  - Financial
  - Patient satisfaction
  - Employee satisfaction
  - Process improvement
  - Learning and growth

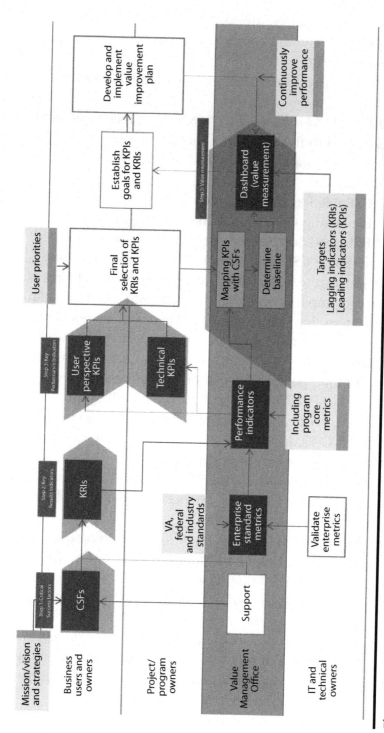

Figure 6.2   Value realization process main steps.

Note: These perspectives comprise the "Balanced Scorecard" and are essential in analysis and the determination of value.

Perspective focuses on what is valuable and what is not.

- *Task 3: Build a hierarchy of CSFs.* One technique is to select two to five[1] CSFs that include
  - Strategy mapping (A cascade matrix is an effective method)
  - CSF relationship mapping
  - Evaluating CSFs against the number of the six Balanced Scorecard perspectives that are impacted

Note: Some CSFs will naturally cover more than one perspective (e.g., the timely appointment scheduling of patients impacts nearly all the perspectives). This is an indication that it is a core CSF. The CSFs are good when they are contributing to several perspectives but also focused enough so that the strongest relationship with one unique perspective can be easily identified.

Core CSFs define the path to value realization.

A checklist can be applied to assess the quality of the defined CSFs; in Table 6.1, some of the main questions within the checklist are provided.

As demonstrated in Figure 6.3, a good CSF is related to many different outcomes perspectives as they influence and contribute to each other.

- *Task 4: The value management working group and governing board conduct a formal review of CSFs.* The successful outcome of this review is to approve CSFs.

  People can agree to disagree, but in the end, explicit CSF approval removes the "fog of war."
- *Task 5: Communicate CSFs to employees and stakeholders.* Once the final CSFs have been agreed on, communicate them to all management and staff. This is essential for creating a common understanding and purpose.

  Communicate, communicate, and communicate!

Table 6.1 Critical Success Factors Analysis Checklist

1. Have Critical Success Factors (CSFs) been defined for your organization?	☐ Yes	☐ No
2. If so, have the CSFs been recently reviewed to confirm relevance?	☐ Yes	☐ No
List your organization's current CSFs and indicate if they make the top five CSFs.	**In top 5 CSFs**	
	☐ Yes	☐ No
	☐ Yes	☐ No
	☐ Yes	☐ No
	☐ Yes	☐ No
3. List possible additional CSFs that require further analysis.		

(Continued)

Table 6.1 (Continued)   Critical Success Factors Analysis Checklist

4. How do your top 5 CSFs cover the six perspectives of performance?

Critical Success Factor	Clinical	Financial	Process Improvement	Employee Satisfaction	Patient Satisfaction	Learning and Growth
Example: Patient satisfaction with time for getting appointments			✓	✓	✓	
Example: Reduction in duplicate prescriptions		✓	✓	✓		
Example: Improved quality of life for lower joint surgeries	✓	✓		✓	✓	

5. Have the top five CSFs been discussed with employee representatives?	☐ Yes	☐ No
6. Do the top five CSFs cover the following traditional issues organizations face?	☐ Yes	☐ No

CSF for Clinical Outcomes

Example: Patient-centered—Providing care that is respectful of and responsive to individual patient preferences, needs, and values to ensure that patient values guide all clinical decisions	☐ Yes	☐ No

(Continued)

Table 6.1 (Continued) Critical Success Factors Analysis Checklist

Example: Timeliness—Reducing wait time and harmful delays for both those who receive care and those who give care	☐ Yes	☐ No
	☐ Yes	☐ No
CSF for Process Improvement		
Example: Safe and healthy workplace	☐ Yes	☐ No
Example: On-time completion and on-budget measurements	☐ Yes	☐ No
	☐ Yes	☐ No
CSF for Finance		
Example: Growth in revenue and product mix (new products, new applications, new customers and markets, new relationships, new product and service mix, new pricing)	☐ Yes	☐ No
Example: Cost reduction/productivity improvement (reduce unit cost and procedures, improve channel mix, reduce operating expenses)	☐ Yes	☐ No
	☐ Yes	☐ No
CSF for Patient Satisfaction		
Example: Quality of Life—Improved functionality and/or reduced pain	☐ Yes	☐ No
Example: Increased repeat business (increased percentage of patient retention)	☐ Yes	☐ No
	☐ Yes	☐ No

(Continued)

Table 6.1 (Continued) Critical Success Factors Analysis Checklist

CSF for Learning and Growth		
Example: Developing strategic skills within management	☐ Yes	☐ No
Example: Improved alignment of individual and organizational goals	☐ Yes	☐ No
	☐ Yes	☐ No
CSF for Employee Satisfaction		
Example: Retention of key staff	☐ Yes	☐ No
Example: Increase in employee satisfaction	☐ Yes	☐ No
	☐ Yes	☐ No

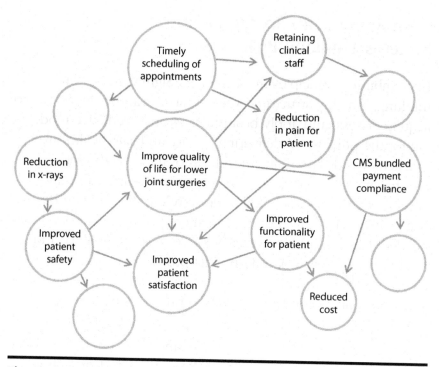

Figure 6.3   Outcomes correlation.

Step 2: Key Results Indicators

In the process of identifying and selecting KRIs and KPIs, it is recommended to apply Lean Six Sigma methodologies and tools. It is recommended that an A3 thinking approach be used to identify goals and metrics that contribute to one specific business problem or specific patient condition. Cause and effect diagrams, Pareto diagrams, and care delivery value chain diagrams are also recommended as the most appropriate tools to make correlations in the value analysis.

In the following section, short definitions of these tools are provided for use with the Value Realization Process.

Combining Lean Six Sigma and Systems Thinking Processes

By combining principles from Lean Six Sigma and systems thinking, a highly structured value strategy can be developed to acquire, assess, and apply best practices and predictive modeling for the purpose of delivering quality and safe healthcare that achieves desired outcomes. Each of these methodologies has various tools that have proven useful in healthcare and other sectors. A detailed understanding of them can be challenging—from a value management perspective, not all are needed. It is up to each organization to weigh the utility and pros or cons of each based on what problem or initiative it is trying to solve and build its own toolkit. It is recommended that a general value management toolkit consist of the following:

- Six Sigma is an extremely disciplined process that assists organizations in focusing on developing and providing near perfect services and/or products. The word "sigma" is a statistical term that measures how far a given process deviates from perfection. The key principle behind Six Sigma is that if you can measure how many "defects" you have in a process, you can systematically determine how to eliminate those and approach "zero defects."
- A3 thinking is a standards-based approach to problem solving that requires organizations to analyze the root causes of a problem before testing possible solutions. A3 provides a clear one-page summary that consolidates a large amount of information into an understandable format using a visual display. The A3 approach is applicable at various levels of organizational improvement work, including
  1. Strategic planning (transformational plan of value stream analysis)
  2. Rapid improvement capability
  3. Focused unit-based problem solving and improvement

■ Cause and effect diagrams (sometimes called fishbone diagrams or Ishikawa diagrams) are used to fully understand the issue and to identify possible causes. The "effect" is the problem you are working on, for example "waiting time" (a specific component of access to care).

If the cause of the delay is understood, the solution can be better implemented. The cause and effect diagram categories are materials, methods, equipment, environment, and people and the effect is written as a problem statement. Determining the causes is accomplished by asking "Why?" until you have reached a level of detail that can be measured. The diagram has a variety of benefits, which include:

 – It helps teams understand that there are many causes that contribute to an effect.
 – It graphically displays the relationship of the causes to the effect and to each other.
 – It helps to identify areas for improvement.

■ The Pareto diagram is named after a nineteenth-century Italian economist, Vilfredo Pareto, who conducted a study in Europe on wealth and poverty. Pareto found that wealth was concentrated in the hands of the few and poverty in the hands of the many. The Pareto Principle is founded on the unequal distribution of things in the world. It is the law of the "significant few versus the trivial many," and provides a rule of thumb which states that "20% of the problems have 80% of the impact." The 20% of the problems are the "vital few" and the remaining problems are the "trivial many." From a quality point of view, this diagram was introduced by J. M. Juran as an instrument for the classification of quality problems:

1. Major problems: There are few, but their results are quite important.
2. Secondary problems: There are a great deal of minor problems, but their results are limited.

The Pareto diagram is a statistical technique used in decision making. It is a good tool to use when the process investigated produces data that is broken down into categories and it can be counted for the number of times each category occurs. A Pareto diagram puts data in a hierarchical order, which allows the most significant problems to be corrected first. This methodology can be used to design medical processes in order to identify defects and aid in the development of a system that reduces the risk of medical care. One place where it is useful is at the start of a project to help define the scope.

A Pareto chart has the following objectives:

1. To separate the few major problems from the many possible problems so efforts can focus your improvement efforts
2. To arrange data by priority or importance
3. To determine which problems are most important using data, not perceptions

The benefits of using a Pareto Diagram are:

■ It enables efficient problem solving by the identification and ranking of the main causes of faults according to their importance
■ It sets priorities for process improvement efforts for increased readiness, patient or clinician needs, suppliers, and investment opportunities
■ It illustrates where to focus efforts

Healthcare value chain analysis is another tool in the toolkit used to understand how each activity contributes to care delivery and outcomes. The tool is often applied to business lines or units, and not the organization as a whole. A HDO can use value chain analysis to determine how to improve quality or lower costs by connecting patients to the right services based on their need and predicted health benefit. Value chain analysis combined with clinical care pathways and propensity modeling yields tangible benefits in delivering value-based care at the right time, right place, and for the right patient.

Porter popularized the term value chain in academic circles to refer to the entire production chain from the input of raw materials to the output of the final product consumed by the end user.[2] This chain is called a value chain because each link in the chain adds some sort of value to the original inputs. However, the use of value chains for healthcare lacks standardization and requires a coordinated effort between hospitals and providers. Integrated delivery networks are needed to share knowledge and best practices in order to deliver the greatest value at the lowest cost.

An example template is provided to illustrate the relationship to the user story regarding Mr. Campbell. This template is a useful tool for depicting the cycle of care for a specific medical condition in order to identify the set of clinical outcome dimensions at each tier. It also depicts where and when measurements should occur and guides outcome and process improvement efforts. The measures chosen for each clinical outcome dimension should reflect five considerations:

■ Select measures that best capture the particular outcome from the perspective of the patient and medical science.
■ All other things being equal, the selection of standard and tested measures shall improve validity and facilitate comparison across hospitals and providers.
■ Measures should minimize ambiguity and judgment in scoring to ensure the accuracy and consistency of results.
■ Patient surveys should be utilized to measure outcomes such as functional status and discomfort that reflect patients' realities and are difficult for outside parties to measure.

Provider surveys should be utilized to measure outcomes, such as Electronic Health Record (EHR) workflow and clinical decision support satisfaction, and reflect provider realities.

The care delivery value chain illustrates the full care cycle and all stakeholders or units involved in Mr. Campbell's care (Table 6.2).

Table 6.2   Care Delivery Value Chain Example

Informing and engaging	Importance of weight reduction, exercise, nutrition	Discuss meaning of diagnosis, prognosis, benefits, and risks specific for the patient	Setting realistic expectations, importance of nutrition, weight, vaccinations, and home preparation	Discuss realistic expectations for recovery, importance of rehabilitation and post-surgery risk factors	Importance of adhering to rehabilitation and discuss longitudinal care plan	Importance of exercise and maintaining a healthy weight
Measuring	Specific symptoms and functions (e.g., WOMAC scale), overall health (e.g., SF-12 scale)	Loss of cartilage, change in function and overall health	Baseline health status and fitness for surgery (e.g., ASA score)	Blood loss, operating time, complications	Measure any infections, joint-specific symptoms and function, inpatient length of stay, and ability to return to normal activities	Measure specific symptoms and functions, weight gain or loss, missed work, and overall health

(Continued)

Table 6.2 (Continued) Care Delivery Value Chain Example

Accessing	Primary care office	Specialty office	Specialty office	Operating room and recovery room	Nursing facility	Specialty office
	Physical therapy	Imaging facility	Pre-op evaluation center	Specialty surgery center	Physical therapy clinic, home	Primary care office
	Monitoring/preventing	Diagnosing	Preparing	Intervening	Recovering/rehabbing	Monitoring/managing
Care delivery	Monitor (conduct PCP exam and refer to specialists if necessary)	Imaging (MRI and x-rays as required), assess injury	Overall preparation (conduct home assessment)	Anesthesia (administer general, epidural, or regional)	Surgical (immediate return to OR if needed)	Monitor through regular consultations
	Prevent (prescribe anti-inflammatory medicines, recommend exercises, and set weight loss targets if required)	Clinical evaluation (review patient medical history and imaging, perform physical exam, and recommend treatment plan)	Surgical preparation (perform surgery, run blood labs, conduct pre-op exam)	Surgical procedure (determine approach, insert device, complete procedure)	Medical (monitor coagulation)	Manage (prescribe prophylactic antibiotics when needed, set long-term exercise plan, revise if necessary)

(Continued)

Table 6.2 (Continued)   Care Delivery Value Chain Example

			Pain management (prescribe preemptive pain medicine)	Living (provide daily living assistance [shower, dressing]), track risk indicators (fever, swelling, other)	
				Physical therapy (daily or as required and duration)	

Source: Porter, M. 2013. The strategy that will fix health care. *Harvard Business Review.* Available at: https://hbr.org/2013/10/the-strategy-that-will-fix-health-care.[13]

As referenced earlier, A3 Reports are one-page analyses used for documenting the necessary information needed for progress reporting and decision making for one specific business problem. A3 is a structured problem solving and continuous improvement approach, first employed at Toyota and typically used by Lean manufacturing practitioners.[3] It provides a systematic approach to problem solving.

The A3 Report got its name from placing all problem solving elements on a ISO A3 sheet of paper. This is where the process got its name. The process is based on the principles of PDSA (Plan-Do-Study-Act) (Figure 6.4).

A3 reports condense the information to a single page and visually communicate it to the reader using graphs, charts, and bullet points. A3 one-page reports typically include the following elements[4]:

■ *Background*: A brief description of the problem, highlighting the importance to the organization and the measures used.
■ *Current situation*: Visual depictions of the problem under consideration.
■ *Analysis*: The analysis performed to determine root cause(s).

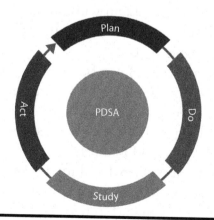

Figure 6.4   PDSA.

- *Goal*: A visual depiction of what the situation and outcomes would need to be so that the problem would not occur.
- *Recommendations*: The solution that will be (or has been) implemented.
- *Implementation plan*: Tasks, start dates, duration, responsibilities, and completion status.
- *Follow-up*: Post-implementation measures to ensure solution benefits are maintained.
- *Results report*: Charted progress to plan with implementation in a dashboard or report.

All these elements are included in a one-page report as shown in Figure 6.5.

As seen in Figure 6.5, the first part of the process (left components—background, current situation, analysis, and goal) is focused on understanding the problem and the goal and outcomes that are expected in order to solve the problem. On the other hand, the second half of the process (right components—recommendation, implementation plan, follow-up, and results report) is focused on the solution and its implementation.

When defining KRIs and KPIs, several A3 reports may be created for each CSF (depending on the business problems that are contained within it). Therefore, each A3 report addresses one business problem within the CSF, and helps with the identification and selection of the KRIs and KPIs for the selected CSF (Table 6.3).

The checklist in Table 6.3 can be used to guide the application of the PDSA methodology and the A3 report on problem solving. The checklist in combination with the A3 report should be used along with the following steps within the Value Realization Process (Table 6.4).

It is recommended that A3 Thinking be performed by working groups with a high level of specialization in the selected business problem and in the different perspectives of outcomes. One subject matter expert will lead each

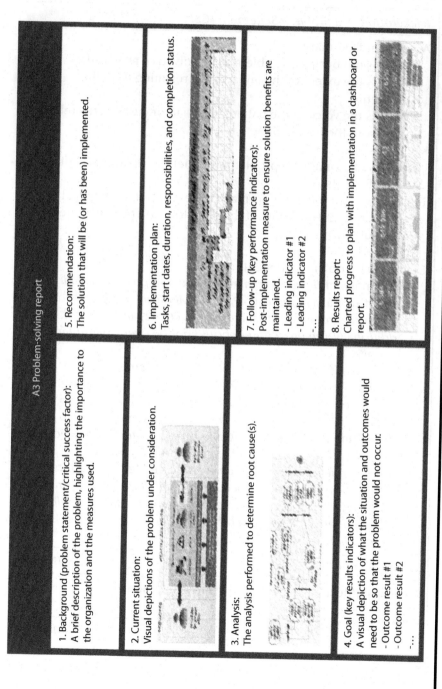

A3 Problem-solving report

1. Background (problem statement/critical success factor):
A brief description of the problem, highlighting the importance to the organization and the measures used.

2. Current situation:
Visual depictions of the problem under consideration.

3. Analysis:
The analysis performed to determine root cause(s).

4. Goal (key results indicators):
A visual depiction of what the situation and outcomes would need to be so that the problem would not occur.
- Outcome result #1
- Outcome result #2
- ...

5. Recommendation:
The solution that will be (or has been) implemented.

6. Implementation plan:
Tasks, start dates, duration, responsibilities, and completion status.

7. Follow-up (key performance indicators):
Post-implementation measure to ensure solution benefits are maintained.
- Leading indicator #1
- Leading indicator #2
- ...

8. Results report:
Charted progress to plan with implementation in a dashboard or report.

Figure 6.5   A3 problem-solving report.

Table 6.3   Project Charter + A3 Thinking Checklist

Background and Problem Statement (CSF)

Assessment Questions:
1. What is the business problem to be solved or analyzed?
2. What is the extent of the impact/pain resulting from the problem?
3. What is the voice of the patient, clinician or customer(s) telling you about the problem?

Key Tasks:
Use the background and problem statement to define the Critical Success Factor(s).

Toolkit: Problem statement format: (1) Description of the ideal scenario; but (2) The reality of the situation; (3) The consequences for the audience.

Example #1 Problem Statement:
- *Description of the ideal scenario: In order to provide outstanding patient care at a minimal cost, Acme Medical Hospital needs diagnostic procedures that are safe, accurate, and efficient. Additionally, the procedures should not be overly painful for the patient.*
- *But the reality of the situation is: Currently, Acme Medical Hospital's main diagnostic tools are CAT scans and myelograms (spinal taps). The CAT scan fails to make clear diagnoses 65% of the time. When the CAT scan fails, clinicians must resort to the myelogram. While the myelograms are accurate, this procedure is very painful and sometimes dangerous for the patient.*
- *The consequences for the audience: If Acme Medical Hospital continues to do the two procedures, it will jeopardize overall efficiency, quality of care, and earnings potential. This could also lead to patients choosing another hospital or provider with more advanced facilities.*

Team: [Name]	Leader: [Name]

Members: [Must have names to ensure accountability for deliverables.]

(Continued)

Table 6.3 (Continued) Project Charter + A3 Thinking Checklist

Current Situation

Assessment Questions:
1. Is the current condition clear and logically depicted in a visual manner?
2. Does the current condition frame the business problem accurately?
3. Is the problem quantified in some manner or is it too qualitative?

Key Tasks:
1. Describe the current state by listing:
- <u>Who</u> is involved? Who is affected by the problem?
- <u>What</u> is going wrong? What are the baseline metrics?
- <u>When</u> (day of week, time of day, shift) is it happening?
- <u>Where</u> (location, department, team) is it happening?
- <u>How</u> does the process work?

2. Draw a high-level process map of the current state process
- Define each step in the process and the wait between steps.
- Identify value and non-value steps.
- If relevant, estimate the time and distance for each step.
- Highlight the problems that occur at each step.

Toolkit: Pareto chart, process map diagram.

Scope

- Process start (First step in process, e.g., register the patient)
- Process stop (Last step in process)
- In scope (Facility, hospital, ward, patient group, work shift, etc.)
- Out of scope (Facility, hospital, ward, patient group, work shift, etc.)

Analysis

Assessment Questions:
1. Has cause and effect been demonstrated or linked in some manner?
2. Is there evidence of "5 Whys" thinking about the true cause?
3. Have all relevant factors been considered? (People measurement, methods, equipment, environment and machine)

Key Tasks:
Use a problem analysis tool to show cause and effect relationships.
Toolkit: 5 Whys, fishbone diagram.
Note: Root cause analysis assists in the development of comparative benchmarks

(Continued)

Table 6.3 (Continued)   Project Charter + A3 Thinking Checklist

Future State Goals (Key Results Indicators)
Assessment Questions: 1. What value-based outcomes are expected and for what reason? 2. When can improvement be expected? 3. How will you measure the improvement? **Key Tasks:** 1. Determine the desired Key Results Indicators (KRIs) 2. Ensure monitoring systems are available for measurement and reporting purposes Tools: Value management CSF checklist

working group. The Value Management Meeting Template (Appendix III) can be used to guide the meetings of the working groups.

As demonstrated in the checklist in Table 6.3, the KRIs are developed in the "goal" step, when the VMO in coordination and collaboration with the project/program business users and owners proposes a sct of key results and outcomes (for several of the outcomes perspectives previously described) that can be measured and are actionable according to SMART criteria (specific, measurable, attainable, relevant, and time-bound) (Figure 6.6).

When a dollar sign is placed with a number, it is converted into a result indicator (e.g., daily sales are a result of activities that have taken place to create the sales). The KPI lies deeper down. It may be the number of visits from or contacts with the key customers who make up the most profitable part of the business.[5]

The KPIs and KRIs should be linked to each other. Often, these indicators are referred to as "leading" and "lagging" indicators, demonstrating a cause and effect relationship. There should be a distinct thread that is monitored and reported to management, which is essential in creating a meaningful Common Operating Picture. Measures that are reported quarterly or annually by definition cannot be "key" to your business

Table 6.4   A3 Thinking (PDSA)

Plan – Do – Study – Act

PLAN—Recommendation

Assessment Questions:
1. Do the countermeasures link to the root cause of the problem?
2. Who specifically is responsible for doing what and when?
3. What is the monitoring plan and performance or progress indicators?

Key Tasks:
1. Conduct a brainstorming session and list as many potential countermeasures as possible.
2. Identify an effective countermeasure that directly addresses the root cause.
3. Delegate responsibility for each specific countermeasure.

Toolkit: Create a monitoring and reporting plan that states how and when metrics will be collected (weekly, monthly).

Countermeasure	Reason (expected impact)	Metric	Expected result
The change	How will it help? Which root cause?	How you'll measure	From X to Y

Note: Countermeasures become the actionable Key Performance Indicators (KPIs) to determine if success will be achieved.

DO—Implementation Plan

Assessment Questions:
1. What are the tasks required to prepare and test each countermeasure?
2. How many PDSA cycles will you run before you reach conclusions?
3. How long is each cycle and when will each be completed?

Key Tasks:
1. Select the most practical and effective countermeasure.
2. Create a clear and detailed action plan.
3. Implement quickly.

Toolkit: Action plan and Gantt chart.

(Continued)

Table 6.4 (Continued)   A3 Thinking (PDSA)

Task	Who	When
1. What will be done to prepare or run the test?	Who is responsible?	By date?

STUDY—Experiments

Assessment Questions:
1. Is anything jeopardizing patient safety? (If so, stop the experiment!)
2. Is anything jeopardizing quality of care? (If so, closely monitor to ensure no impact)
3. As a result of implementation, is anything immediately impacting financial outcomes negatively?

Key Tasks:
1. Describe the changes made in each PDSA cycle.
2. Execute the implementation plan and measure the KPIs and KRIs.
3. Monitor progress.

Toolkit: Run chart, control charts, and IT-related dashboards.

ACT—Follow-up (Key Performance Indicators)

Assessment Questions:
1. How does the system actually behave with the countermeasure(s) (experiment)?
2. Was the goal/target level of performance achieved? If not, why not?
3. If performance has not improved, then why? What was missed?

Key Tasks:
1. Study the results with each team.
2. Report findings to stakeholders.
3. Capture lessons learned from each cycle.

Toolkit: Monitoring reports and run charts.

Cycle	Results	Analysis

(Continued)

Table 6.4 (Continued)   A3 Thinking (PDSA)

ACT—Result Report
Assessment Questions: 1. Accept: If you achieved the goal or as close to it as you think is feasible, what is your plan to monitor, sustain, and spread the improvement? 2. Adapt: If the goal was not achieved, why not (root cause analysis)? What will you change in the next cycle to address the root cause and get to your goal? Add this to your Plan, then Do, Study, and Act again. 3. Abandon: If after multiple cycles of testing you have still not achieved the target, you conclude the selected countermeasures are not appropriate or effective for the problem at hand. **Key Tasks:** 1. Document the new process and set as new standard. 2. Share the new standard through training, education, and deployment. 3. Continue to monitor and report on results. **Toolkit:** Standard operating procedures, change management plan.

if you are monitoring after the fact. Therefore, KRIs and KPIs must be current/future versus past-oriented measures.

Ten tasks are performed to identify the right KRIs that measure the achievement of goals.[6] This process starts by identifying the objectives of the business problem and the final metrics definition. Data-driven decision making is a key feature of the VMO.

- *Task 1: Target goals.* Define all the goals for the problem selected (within the CSF).
- *Task 2: Ask questions.* Define the questions that need to be answered to ensure goals are achieved. Perform an in-depth analysis of what it will take to achieve the target goals.
- *Task 3: Identify metrics.* Determine all the indicators that will answer the questions. After an organization discusses what is important to achieve, the next step is to choose

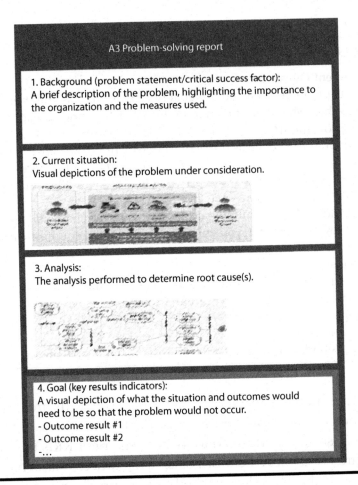

Figure 6.6   KRIs in the A3 report.

specific performance measures, understanding that the delivery of care involves a number of systems and processes. Performance measures serve as indicators for the effectiveness of those systems and processes.

■ *Task 4: Select key results.* From the list of metrics previously identified, select and approve the ones that are key for achieving the goals. Two to five KRIs per CSF at any given time is recommended by ITIL.[6]

Several recommendations are provided for the selection of the KRIs.[7]

- Measure what is important based on the evaluation of the organization's community, population, and priorities.
- Measure what is required to meet funding or contractual expectations (These first two considerations often overlap. Agencies supporting or funding a healthcare organization may require specific performance measures.)
- Include staff in the measure selection process as staff will be involved in the actual implementation of measurement and improvement activities. Buy-in from staff significantly facilitates these steps.
- Use existing measures if possible.
- Consider using several measures of different types related to different outcomes perspectives. For example, diabetes care may best be evaluated by including
  • Frequency of evidence-based testing (process improvement)
  • Patient blood pressure control (clinical)
  • Patient satisfaction as diabetes care delivery evolves (patient satisfaction)
  • Calculation of co-pays regarding clinical monitoring of diabetes care (financial)

■ *Task 5: Assess the measures.* When evaluating the selected KRIs, the group has to consider the characteristics of good performance measures and the Institute of Medicine framework[8] in addition to the SMART criteria. According to the Desirable Attributes of a Quality Measure by the Agency for Healthcare Research and Quality (AHRQ), the KRIs can be grouped into three broad conceptual areas[9] within which narrower categories provide more detail: (1) importance of a measure; (2) soundness of a measure; and (3) feasibility of a measure.

1. Importance of the Measure
- *Relevance to stakeholders*: The topic area of the measure is of significant interest and financially and

strategically important to stakeholders (e.g., patients, clinicians, purchasers, public health officers, and policy makers).
- *Health importance*: The aspect of health that the indicator addresses is important as defined by high prevalence or incidence and/or has a significant effect on the burden of illness (i.e., effect on the mortality and morbidity of a population).
- *Potential for improvement*: There is evidence indicating a need for the measure.
- *Susceptibility to being influenced by the program/initiative*: The results of the measure relate to actions or interventions that are under the control of the program for which performance is being measured.
2. Soundness
- *Explicitness of evidence*: The evidence supporting the measure is explicitly stated.
- *Strength of evidence*: The topic area of the measure is strongly supported by the evidence.
- *Reliability*: The results of the measure are reproducible for a fixed set of conditions irrespective of who makes the measurement or when it is made; reliability testing is documented.
- *Validity*: The measure truly measures what it purports to measure; validity testing is documented.
- *Comprehensible*: The results of the measure are understandable for the user who will be acting on the data.
3. Feasibility
- *Explicit specification of numerator and denominator*: A measure should usually have explicit and detailed specifications for the numerator and denominator; statements of the requirements for data collection are understandable and implementable.
- *Data availability*: The data source needed to implement the measure is available and accessible within the timeframe for measurement.

■ *Task 6: Establish a baseline and target for the KRIs.* Once performance measures are chosen, the organization collects the baseline data for each measure.

Baseline data is a snapshot of the performance of a process or outcome that is considered normal, average, or typical over a period of time and reflects existing care systems. Determining the baseline involves calculating the measure. As the HDO assesses where it is before embarking on a quality improvement (QI) program, it often finds that its data reflects a lower-than-desired performance level. This should not cause concern, but rather provide the opportunity to focus QI efforts to improve performance.

■ *Task 7: Standardize definitions.* Agree to standard definitions for the entities and their measured attributes.[10]

■ *Task 8: Choose a measurement function* (high-level calculations), and *establish a measurement method* (detailed calculations). Determine the mechanism or method to calculate the metric. Break down the metric into its lowest level base measures. Specifically, it is important to record the following for each measure[10]:
  – Data source
  – Collection method
  – Frequency of data collection
  – Standardized time to collect data as applicable
  – A detailed record of staff responsible for measurement and other aspects of the measurement process

■ *Task 9: Define decision criteria.* Determine how the measurements will be used.

■ *Task 10: Define reporting mechanisms.* Decide how to report the KRIs.

Once the KRIs have been defined, the following template table (based on the Template of Measure Attributes provided by AHRQ[11]) should be completed for each KRI (Table 6.5):

Table 6.5   Key Results Indicators Attributes Template

Title	Identifies the title of the intended measure.
Source(s)	Identifies the complete bibliographic source(s) for the intended measure as suggested by the measure submitter(s).
Measure Domain	
Critical Success Factor	Identifies the Critical Success Factor for which the KRI is being used.
Business problem	Describes the business problem for which the KRI will be used to measure its objectives. Identifies the aspect of health to which the measure refers, such as a structural feature, a condition, a process, a health outcome, and/or a patient or population characteristic.
Primary outcome perspective	Classifies the major focus of the measure according to the outcomes perspectives.
Secondary outcome perspective	Identifies the secondary focus of the intended measure according to the outcomes perspectives (if applicable).
Brief Abstract	
Description	Provides a concise statement of the specific outcomes of health, the target population, providers, setting(s), and time period that the intended measure addresses.
Rationale	Identifies the rationale that briefly explains the importance of the KRI (i.e., why it is used).
Evidence for rationale	Identifies citation(s) submitted by the developer related to the rationale for the measure.
Denominator description	Provides the *general* specifications of any descriptive component that is the basis for inclusions and exclusions in the denominator.

(*Continued*)

Table 6.5 (Continued)   Key Results Indicators Attributes Template

Numerator description	Provides the *general* specifications of any descriptive component that is the basis for inclusions and exclusions in the numerator.
Evidence Supporting the Measure	
Additional supporting information needed for the measure	Describes additional characteristics for the intended measure supplied by the developer, including the clinical component, environment, and public health issues (e.g., incidence/prevalence, burden of illness, costs, etc.).
Evidence of need for additional supporting information for the measure	Identifies citation(s) supplied by the developer documenting evidence concerning the intended measure.
Extent of measure testing	Describes the extent of testing of the measure specifications, including reliability and/or validity testing.
Evidence for extent of measure testing	Identifies citation(s) documenting measure testing as described in the extent of measure testing field.
National Guideline Clearinghouse link	Identifies link(s) to guideline summary(s) in the National Guideline Clearinghouse™ (NGC) where the measure was developed from an evidence-based guideline.
State of Use of the Measure	
State of use	Identifies the status of the intended measure regarding its use within the past 3 years by health-related organizations.
Current use	Specifies the current use(s) of the intended measure.
Application of the Measure in its Current Use	
Measurement setting	Specifies the settings for which the intended measure was developed.

(Continued)

Table 6.5 (Continued)   Key Results Indicators Attributes Template

Statement of acceptable minimum sample size	Indicates whether the intended measure defines a minimum sample size for the denominator.
Professionals involved in delivery of health services	Specifies the professional(s) involved in delivering the services addressed by the intended measure.
Data Collection for the Measure	
Case finding period	The time period that is searched to determine if a case/event is potentially eligible in the denominator.
Denominator sampling frame	Specifies the specification for selecting cases/events potentially eligible for inclusion in the denominator, from which a more restrictive sample of cases is sometimes selected.
Denominator (index) event or characteristic	Identifies the event or characteristic that defines eligibility for inclusion in the denominator group.
Denominator time window	The denominator time window is associated with the denominator index event and classifies the time period in which occurrences identified as potentially eligible for inclusion in the denominator are reviewed to determine whether they are finally included.
Denominator inclusions/exclusions	Describes the specific inclusion and exclusion criteria used to refine the denominator.
Numerator inclusions/ exclusions	Describes the specific inclusion and exclusion criteria used to refine the numerator.
Numerator search strategy	Identifies the type of situation that isolates cases for inclusion in the numerator.
Data source	Identifies the data source(s) necessary to implement the intended measure.

(Continued)

Table 6.5 (Continued)   Key Results Indicators Attributes Template

Instruments used for the measure	Identifies all instruments, such as a standardized survey instrument or flow sheet, used in implementing the intended measure.
Computation of the Measure	
Measure for specifying disaggregation	Describes whether the intended measure can be disaggregated based on alternative approaches to splitting the denominator or numerator.
Basis for disaggregation	Describes the variant specifications of denominator or numerator.
Scoring	Identifies the method used to score the intended measure.
Interpretation of score	Classifies interpretation of score according to the desired value.
Description of allowance for patient or population factors	Describes the analytic considerations made for the intended measure based on the patient or population factors and characteristics.

The following checklist can be applied to assess the quality of the defined KRIs and whether the recommended process was correctly followed (Table 6.6).

Step 3: Key Performance Indicators

The KPIs are identified and selected when developing the right side of the A3 report. This side of the analysis is focused on the solution and its implementation. More specifically, the follow-up section is completed with measurement criteria for monitoring the success of the implementation plan.

The KPIs are focused on measuring what success looks like from the solution and the way it is implemented. The focus is on the user experience. KPIs include measures related to the

Table 6.6 Key Results Indicators Assessment Checklist

Background and Problem Statement (CSF)		
1. Has the CSF been identified?	☐ Yes	☐ No
2. Has the business problem for the CSF been identified?	☐ Yes	☐ No
3. Has the impact from the problem been clearly defined?	☐ Yes	☐ No
4. Have the patient and users described the problem?	☐ Yes	☐ No
Current Situation		
1. Has the current condition been clearly and visually illustrated (using fishbone and/or Pareto diagrams)?	☐ Yes	☐ No
2. Does the current condition frame the business problem accurately?	☐ Yes	☐ No
3. Is the problem quantifiable or is it too qualitative?	☐ Yes	☐ No
Analysis		
1. Have the causes of the conditions been identified through a deep analysis including asking the patients and users?	☐ Yes	☐ No
2. Have the causes and effects been linked to the business problem in a graphical manner?	☐ Yes	☐ No
3. Have all relevant factors been considered? (People measurement, methods, equipment, environment, and machine)	☐ Yes	☐ No
4. Have the five main causes been identified?	☐ Yes	☐ No
5. List the main causes of the business problem.		

(*Continued*)

Table 6.6 (Continued) Key Results Indicators Assessment Checklist

Goals				
1. Have several indicators been identified for the main causes?			☐ Yes	☐ No
2. Have the expected results been defined?			☐ Yes	☐ No
3. List the main goals defined:				
4. Does each KRI comply with the following characteristics?				
For each KRI	**1. Importance of the Measure**			
		Relevance to stakeholders	☐ Yes	☐ No
		Health importance	☐ Yes	☐ No
		Potential for improvement	☐ Yes	☐ No
		Susceptibility to being influenced by the program/ initiative	☐ Yes	☐ No
	2. Soundness			
		Explicitness of evidence	☐ Yes	☐ No
		Strength of evidence	☐ Yes	☐ No
		Reliability	☐ Yes	☐ No

(Continued)

Table 6.6 (Continued) Key Results Indicators Assessment Checklist

		Validity	☐ Yes	☐ No
		Comprehensibility	☐ Yes	☐ No
	3. Feasibility			
		Explicit specification of numerator and denominator	☐ Yes	☐ No
		Data availability	☐ Yes	☐ No
5. For each KRI, has the threshold and the target been specified?			☐ Yes	☐ No
6. For each KRI, has the measurement method been specified?			☐ Yes	☐ No
7. For each KRI, has the baseline data been collected?			☐ Yes	☐ No
8. For each KRI, has the template been completed?			☐ Yes	☐ No

adoption of and user satisfaction with the new or modified systems and how the system performance is improving user satisfaction (Figure 6.7).

For this reason, two types of KPIs are identified in this phase:

1. *User perspective KPIs*: These KPIs measure the user's experience executing daily business activities and functions using IT systems and products, which influences system adoption by users.
2. *Technical KPIs*: These KPIs measure the IT system's technical performance and products. Measurements ensure that systems are working properly and have an indirect impact on the frontend user experience, with an emphasis on reliability, efficiency, and accuracy.

The technical KPIs are based on the application of international and enterprise standards for monitoring

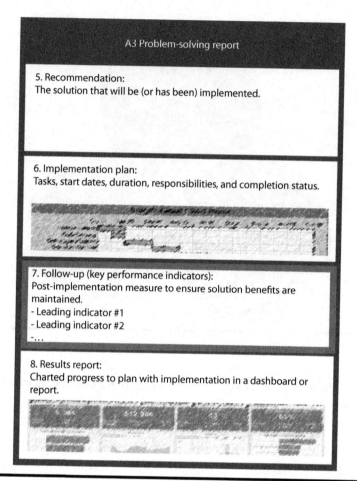

Figure 6.7 KPIs in the A3 report.

systems performance. More detail about these standards is provided in Figure 6.8.

All of these indicators relate to the primary concern of stakeholders with strategic issues and give a clear picture of how the program is performing in relation to these issues. A KPI should inform what action is needed and tie to a specific system or individual. Selected KPIs should affect most of the core CSFs and at least one perspective to show both vertical and horizontal alignment.

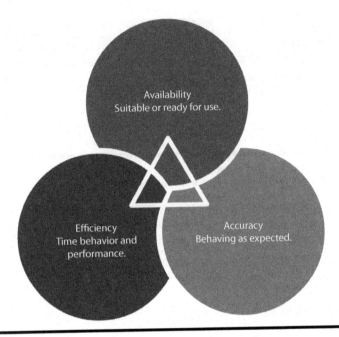

Figure 6.8 Technical dimensions for user experience.

The process for developing technical KPIs is comprised of the following tasks:

- *Task 1: Review CSFs and KRIs and identify the main IT systems or features that are contributing to their success.* The KPIs are "leading indicators" for the key results and CSFs. Before suggesting new performance indicators, it is important to understand the most important systems and features that contribute to the business goals as stated in the A3 report's definition of the business problem. This step is also completed through the A3 analysis "recommendation" section.
- *Task 2: Review the Enterprise Reference Metrics.* Apply the standards created for the organization and identify users' perspective and technical metrics that are relevant to the selected systems or features determined in the previous step.
- *Task 3: Select KPIs.* In coordination with the project/program technical owners, select the users' perspective and

technical metrics that are key to following up on the success of the solution and its implementation. For instance, if the business problem is oriented to improve clinical outcomes, the accuracy of clinical history data provided to users might be the key to achieving better clinical outcomes. Alternatively, if the business problem is focused on improving one clinical or administrative process and its efficiency, then the time behavior of the system becomes a key consideration.

■ *Task 4: Assess the KPIs through the SMART criteria.* In a similar manner to KRIs, KPIs need to be evaluated to ensure that they are valid. The SMART criteria provided in the appendix of this book can be used for this purpose.

■ *Task 5: Map the KPIs to the KRIs and CSFs.* The KPIs need to contribute to the business outcomes in order to demonstrate their relevance.

■ *Task 6: Endorse the KPIs.* This stage involves the endorsement of the metrics by the organization's business and technical leadership team for correctness, applicability, and use.

■ *Task 7: Provide detail for the KPIs.* For each KPI, research is conducted to identify the acceptable performance and desired performance based on the systems requirements. The rationale for a particular KPI is documented along with its relevance. After completing the definition, the next step is to identify the measurement approach and the data required to test the metric. The references are documented for validity and ease of future KPI customization.

The form in Table 6.7 must be completed for each KPI at the end of this process.

The checklist in Table 6.8 can be applied to assess the quality of the defined KPIs and whether the recommended process was correctly followed.

Table 6.7 Detail Table per KPI

Title	Identifies the title of the measure.
Business Domain	
Critical Success Factor	Identifies the CSF that the KPI uses.
Business problem	Describes the business problem for which the KPI will be used.
Key Results Indicators	Classifies the major KRIs within the CSF that this KPI is contributing to.
Brief Abstract	
Description	This will describe the objective of the KPI and explain how the KPI links to the associated CSF and KRI.
Rationale	Identifies the rationale that briefly explains the importance of the KPI (i.e., why it is used).
Denominator description	Provides the *general* specifications of any descriptive component that is the basis for inclusions and exclusions in the denominator.
Numerator description	Provides the *general* specifications of any descriptive component that is the basis for inclusions and exclusions in the numerator.
System Relationship	
IT system	The identification of the "as is" and "to be" systems and the system points of contact (PoCs) that were engaged in providing inputs on defining the KPIs and setting their goals.
IT capability description	The description of the IT system capabilities or features that have been selected for defining the KPI and setting its goals. A brief description of the expected behavior of the capability is provided.
Enterprise Reference Metric	The title of the generic reusable standard metric that lays the foundation in developing the title of the KPI.

(*Continued*)

Table 6.7 (Continued)   Detail Table per KPI

State of Use of the Measure	
State of use	Identifies the status of the KPI regarding its use within the past 3 years.
Current use	Specifies the current use(s) of the measure.
Measurement mechanism	Specifies the mechanisms currently in place to measure the KPI.
Data Collection for the Measure	
Measurement specification	This will compose the measurement plan that will detail the calculation method, i.e., determine the numerator and the denominator for the KPI and the testing protocols to test the KPI in the test environment.
Data source	Identifies the data source(s) necessary to implement the measure. The identification of IT systems and databases that contain all the data elements that need to be collected in order to perform the KPI calculation.
Tools used for measurement	Identifies all instruments used in implementing and measuring the KPI.
Computation of the Measure	
Threshold	The benchmarks used to measure and evaluate the KPIs against "acceptable performance standards." The thresholds can be either set by guidance provided by the Enterprise Reference Metrics or created independently for the selected system if the Enterprise Reference Metrics do not provide any guidance.
Goal/Target	The benchmarks used to measure and evaluate the KPIs against final "targets." The targets can be either set by guidance provided by the Enterprise Reference Metrics or created independently for the selected system if the Enterprise Reference Metrics do not provide any guidance.
Scoring	Identifies the method used to score the KPI.
Interpretation of score	Classifies the interpretation of score according to the desired value.

Table 6.8   Key Performance Indicators Checklist

Recommendation		
1. Do the recommended countermeasures link to the root causes of the problem (mapping required)?	☐ Yes	☐ No
2. Are the countermeasures clearly defined (all components are identified and described)?	☐ Yes	☐ No
3. Do business owners confirm that countermeasures will impact on the root causes of the business problem?	☐ Yes	☐ No
Implementation Plan		
1. Are all the tasks and elements within each countermeasure clearly defined and planned?	☐ Yes	☐ No
2. Are all the stakeholders involved in each activity clearly described?	☐ Yes	☐ No
3. Is there a clear mapping between the activities and the countermeasures?	☐ Yes	☐ No
Followup (Key Performance Indicators)		
1. Can the adoption of the countermeasures be measured?	☐ Yes	☐ No
2. Have several metrics for measuring the adoption of the countermeasures been identified?	☐ Yes	☐ No
3. Can the performance of the countermeasures be measured?	☐ Yes	☐ No
4. Have several metrics for measuring the performance of the countermeasures been identified?	☐ Yes	☐ No
5. Have the key indicators been identified both for adoption and performance?	☐ Yes	☐ No
6. Have the key indicators been mapped to key results?	☐ Yes	☐ No

(Continued)

Table 6.8 (Continued)   Key Performance Indicators Checklist

7. List the main indicators selected for adoption (user perspective KPIs):					
8. List the main indicators selected for performance (technical KPIs):					
9. Does each KPI comply with the following characteristics?[14]					
For each KPI	S	**Specific**	Metrics should be specific. They should be outlined in a clear statement of precisely what is required, describing the result that is desired in a way that is detailed, focused, and well-defined.	☐ Yes	☐ No
	M	**Measurable**	Measurement is very important because it will enable you to know whether an objective has been achieved. Therefore, include a measure to enable organizations to monitor progress and to know when the objective has been achieved.	☐ Yes	☐ No

(Continued)

Table 6.8 (Continued)   Key Performance Indicators Checklist

	A	**Achievable (or agreed)**	An indicator can be said to be achievable if the necessary resources are available or similar results have been achieved by others in similar circumstances. Design objectives to be challenging, but ensure that failure is not built into objectives. Metrics should be agreed by managers and employees to ensure commitment to them.	☐ Yes	☐ No
	R	**Realistic (or relevant)**	The concepts of "realistic" and "achievable" are similar and this may explain why some use the term "relevant" as an alternative. Focus on outcomes rather than the means of achieving them.	☐ Yes	☐ No
	T	**Time-bound**	It is necessary to set a date or time by which the objective should have been accomplished or completed and this contributes to making objectives measurable. Therefore, agree on the date by which the outcome must be achieved.	☐ Yes	☐ No

(Continued)

Table 6.8 (Continued)   Key Performance Indicators Checklist

10. For each KPI, has the threshold and the target been specified?	☐ Yes	☐ No
11. For each KPI, has the measurement method been specified?	☐ Yes	☐ No
12. For each KPI, has the baseline data been collected?	☐ Yes	☐ No
13. For each KPI, has the template been completed?	☐ Yes	☐ No

Source: Chartered Management Institute (CMI). 2014. Setting smart objectives. Available at: www.managers.org.uk/knowledge-bank/smart-objectives.

A3 Thinking with Consultation Management for Indicators Identification

In the following table, the consultation management example is used to demonstrate how to apply A3 thinking and reporting in combination with the cause and effect diagram and the Pareto chart. For this example, the focus is specifically on the problem regarding access to care for patients that have been referred to a specialist (Table 6.9).

Step 4: Value Measurement

The details about how to measure and monitor value are provided in the "Common Operating Picture" and "How to Measure Value" chapters. In these sections, several alternatives for measurement and providing information to the decision makers are provided. Management techniques such as Balanced Scorecard, Lean Six Sigma, Business Intelligence, and Analytics can support decision making through better access to information.[12]

Table 6.9 A3 Thinking for Consultations Management

A3 Problem-Solving Report
Background (CSF: Improve Access to Consultations)
Improving timely, coordinated access to services for federal employees is a top priority of the EHR program.
Inefficiencies and breakdowns in the referral process from primary to specialty care have been a persistent challenge across the FA. Barriers to effective referrals or consultations have been reported that deteriorate access to care for federal employees, a lack of easy-to-use reporting structures to assess the current status of consultation requests, and workflow barriers to consultation referrals have been identified as the main problems in the current Consultations Management system.
Current Situation
A cause and effect diagram is used for showing the analysis of the current business problem.

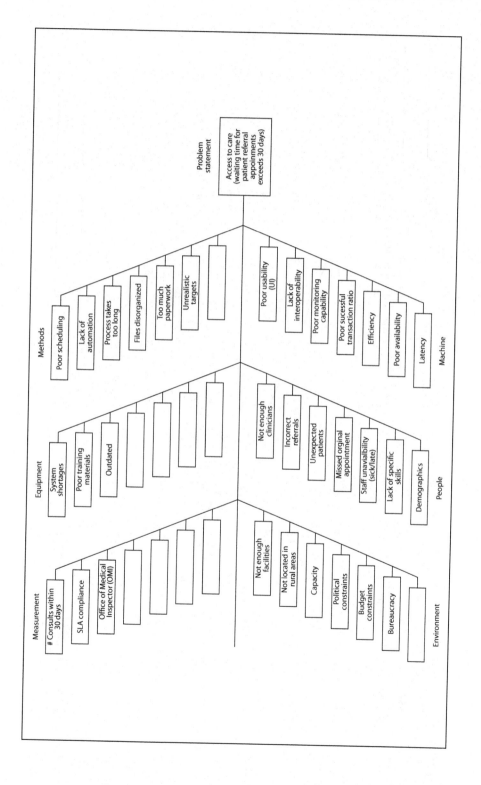

Analysis

A Pareto chart is used for showing the main root causes that are contributing to the problem.

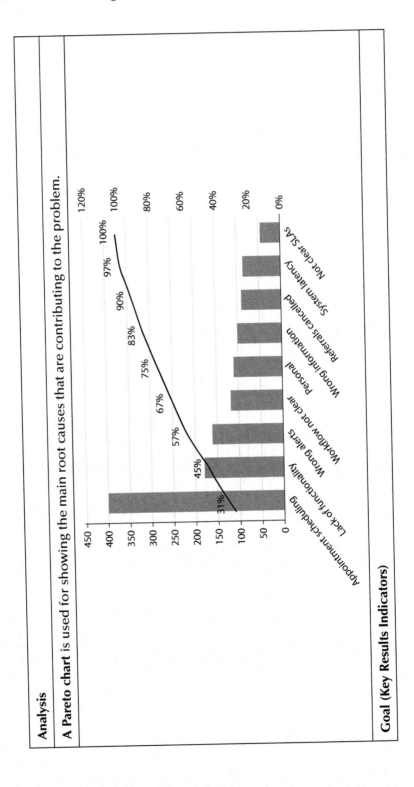

Goal (Key Results Indicators)

Outcomes that would need to be achieved so that the problem does not occur:
Cost reduction in duplicate consultations that are finally cancelled
Referrals according to service level agreements
Clinical satisfaction with the EHR support workflow
Get an appointment for care when needed right away

Recommendation

The new EHR system will need to improve prerequisite management through standardization and the automation of service level agreements and consultation management processes. It will support the improvement of management and the tracking of consultations at patient and population levels with the addition of more granular consultation statuses and reporting tools. The new system will be based on the utilization of task-based communication and management tools to manage consultations.

The new EHR provides consultation value by facilitating the following:

- The ability of the provider to track the status of the consultation request he/she submitted
- The ability for others to track the status of a specialist's action on the consultation request
- Sending an alert when the consultation is completed or has not been acted on
- Offering a clear explanation why a consultation request was cancelled

Implementation Plan

The implementation plan for the new EHR in which the new Consultations Management features will be included:

EHR 2.0	12/1/15	12/27/16	12/1/15	1/31/17
EHR 2.0 IOC entry	7/13/16	7/13/16	7/13/16	
EHR 2.0 IOC exit	10/18/16	10/18/16	10/18/16	
EHR 2.0 enterprise availability	12/22/16	12/22/16	12/22/16	
EHR 2.0 deployment patterning (January 2017)	12/23/16	12/23/16	12/23/16	
EHR 2.0 FOC complete	12/27/16	12/27/16	1/31/17	1/31/17

7/13
△ 10/18
△ 12/22
△ 12/23
△△ 1/31

Follow-Up (Key Performance Indicators)

Some indicators that have been selected as key for measuring the performance of the solution and its implementation are:

- Costs incurred in the sustainment of legacy systems for Consultations Management
- Time required (90th Percentile) to complete a consultation request from primary care
- System Usability Score (SUS) of the new Consultations Management functionality
- User Satisfaction with the new Consultations Management functionality
- Accuracy of records of available resources for making referrals (uptime)
- Number of defects per user acceptance criteria

Results Report

A visual dashboard needs to be created to report on the KRIs and KPIs to support informed decision making. The dashboard must reflect how new Consultations Management and clinician satisfaction with the new functionality are contributing to a reduction in wait times for accessing specialty care from a referral by primary care.

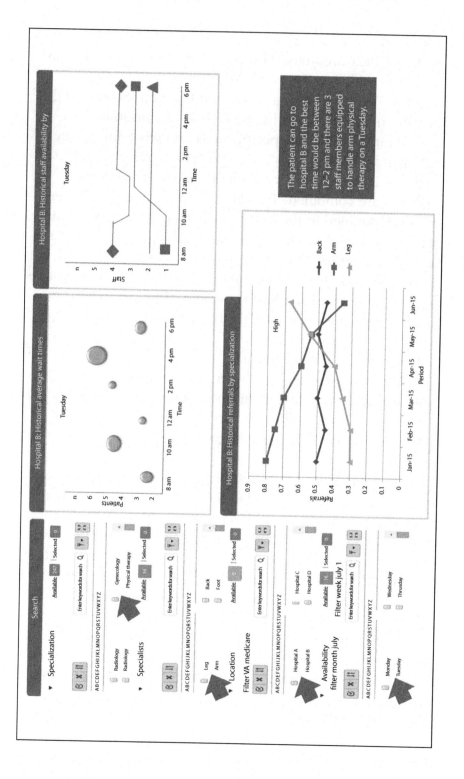

From a process standpoint, the selected KRIs and KPIs are being measured based on the measurement information already provided in the previous steps.

Central to Lean Six Sigma and the Balanced Scorecard is measurement. By measuring outcomes, organizations can focus their attention on specific areas and what affects key outcome-oriented metrics.

In the Balanced Scorecard methodology, multiple perspectives are combined. Typically, these include the six perspectives outlined in the Value Realization Framework. This provides a simple model of the value creation process for any healthcare organization.

By continuously evaluating the key indicators, the measures become essential to the HDO's success. The key indicators can accomplish a range of activities and tasks:

- Provide a change agenda
- Translate the strategy to operational terms
- Link and align the organization around its strategy
- Make strategy everyone's job
- Make strategy a continuous process

Business Intelligence and Analytics provide the technology and methodological foundation for measurement. Both areas involve creating value for the organizations based on data, or more precisely, facts. From a modern business-value perspective, corporations use Business Intelligence and Analytics to enhance decision-making capabilities for managerial and clinical processes, and to ensure critical information is used effectively.

Based on the information provided through the measurement and through comparison with baseline and target goals defined for each indicator, decision makers are able to decide whether the outcomes and performance of the program and systems are sufficient.

If the organization is satisfied with the current level of outcomes and performance, it may then

- Acknowledge and celebrate the success
- Check performance periodically to ensure that the underlying systems involved in performance continue to function satisfactorily
- Consider another performance measure

If the healthcare organization's outcomes and performance are less than desired, then it may establish a performance improvement plan in coordination with the VMO.

Summary of Key Points to Remember

The learning outcomes from this chapter that are important to remember include the following points:

- Why is it important to follow a process toward defining value?
  The Value Realization Framework supports a process for providing the organization's leadership with an actionable monitoring and reporting methodology to make informed decisions. Following a standards-based process ensures that things are not missed and that desired value is attained.
- What are the three outputs from Task 3: Build a hierarchy of Critical Success Factors?
  - *Strategy mapping (A cascade matrix is an effective method)*
  - *CSF relationship mapping*
  - *An evaluation of CSFs against the number of the six Balanced Scorecard perspectives they impact*

■ How do Key Performance Indicators help organizations?
KPIs "measure the actions and events that lead to a result, and are considered to be critical to the success of the business as their data is crucial in creating strategies and aligning goals."[12] KPIs should be reflected on a Balanced Scorecard and monitored daily (or at a minimum weekly). If not, they are not really KPIs. Often referred to as leading indicators, KPIs provide executives with timely information in order to make adjustments and track progress toward achieving a target. KPIs are the metrics used to measure the performance of the CSFs; they are the metrics that dissect success.

■ What if the success is not defined upfront?
A governing board (decision makers) must approve both the CSFs and indicators prior to program start or value measurement. This approval process ensures that there is a shared understanding and vision for what success looks like. In the event that success is not defined, the likelihood of not achieving desired outcomes increases at a faster rate and can lead to higher costs and poorer quality of care provided. The main idea is to define and approve CSFs and measurable outcomes before resources are committed.

References

1. ITIL. 2011 edition. Continual Service Improvement, Section 5.5.1. London: TSO.
2. Porter, M. E. 1980. *Competitive Strategy*. New York: Free Press.
3. Debashis, S. 2010. The A3 problem solving way. Available at: https://www.processexcellencenetwork.com/lean-six-sigma-business-transformation/columns/the-a3-problem-solving-way-an-introduction. Accessed November 10, 2016.
4. A3 Report. MoreSteam. Available at: www.moresteam.com/lean/a3-report.cfm. Accessed November 10, 2016.

5. Parmenter, D. 2010. *Key Performance Indicators (KPI): Developing, Implementing, and Using Winning KPIs.* New Jersey: John Wiley and Sons.

6. Westfall, L. 12 steps to useful software metrics. *The Westfall Team.* pp. 1–13. http://www.westfallteam.com/Papers/12_steps_paper.pdf. Accessed October 15, 2016.

7. U.S. Department of Health and Human Services Health Resources and Services Administration. 2011. Performance management and measurement. Available at: www.hrsa.gov/quality/toolbox/508pdfs/performancemanagementandmeasurement.pdf. Accessed November 15, 2016.

8. Institute of Medicine. 2001. Envisioning the national health care quality report. Washington, DC: National Academies Press.

9. National Quality Measures Clearinghouse. 2015. Desirable attributes of a quality measure. Available at: www.qualitymeasures.ahrq.gov/tutorial/attributes.aspx.

10. Westfall, L. 2009. *The Certified Software Quality Engineer Handbook.* Milwaukee, WI: ASQ Quality.

11. National Quality Measures Clearinghouse. 2015. Template of measure attributes. Available at: www.qualitymeasures.ahrq.gov/help-and-about/summaries/template-of-measure-attributes.

12. Nelson, G. S. 2010. *The Healthcare Performance Dashboard: Linking Strategy to Metrics. http://support.sas.com/resources/papers/proceedings10/167-2010.pdf.*

13. Porter, M. E. and Lee, T. H., MD. 2013. The strategy that will fix health care. *Harvard Business Review.* Available at: https://hbr.org/2013/10/the-strategy-that-will-fix-health-care. Accessed October 12, 2016.

14. Chartered Management Institute (CMI). 2014. Setting smart objectives. Available at: www.managers.org.uk/knowledge-bank/smart-objectives. Accessed October 12, 2016.

Chapter 7

Outcome Metrics

Learning Objectives

After reading this chapter, the reader will be able to answer the following questions:

- Why is it important to measure the six perspectives of healthcare?
- What are the six focus areas of healthcare?
- How does an organization measure clinical outcomes?
- What if an organization does not measure patient and employee satisfaction?

Clinical Outcomes

The term "clinical outcomes" is defined as the results of care in terms of a patient's health measured over time. The primary reason for measuring and managing clinical outcomes performance is to drive quality improvement. Every initiative taken to improve quality and outcomes in health systems has as its starting point some understanding of what is meant by "quality." Without this understanding, it would be impossible to design the interventions and measures used to improve results.* According to Porter, author of *Measuring Health Outcomes: The Outcome Hierarchy*, "Outcomes are the true measures of quality in healthcare. Understanding the outcomes achieved is also critical to ensuring that cost reduction is value enhancing. Thus, outcome measurement is perhaps the single most powerful tool in revamping the healthcare system. Yet systematic and rigorous outcome measurement remains rare or nonexistent in most settings."[1]

The dialogue about an organization's priorities should include the community assessment, the organization's strategic plan and quality management plan, and similar strategic documents.[1]

Any healthcare organization needs to consider critical opportunities for improvement from the patient's perspective. For an in-depth overview of some critical areas from the patient's perspective, refer to "Crossing the quality chasm: A new health system for the twenty-first century" by the Institute of Medicine's Committee on Quality of Health Care in America.

This report highlights six focus areas of care, which are also consistent with the definition of quality of healthcare by the World Health Organization:

- *Safety*: Avoiding injury to patients from the care that is intended to help them
- *Effective*: Providing services based on scientific knowledge to all who can benefit and refraining from providing services to those not likely to benefit (avoiding underuse and overuse)
- *Patient-centered*: Providing care that is respectful of and responsive to individual patient preferences, needs, and

---

* World Health Organization. 2006. Quality of care: A process for making strategic choices in health systems. Available at: http://www.who.int/management/quality/en/.

values to ensure that patient values guide all clinical decisions

- *Timely*: Reducing waits and delays for both those who receive and those who give care
- *Efficient*: Avoiding waste, in particular the waste of equipment, supplies, ideas, and energy
- *Equitable*: Providing care that does not vary in quality because of personal characteristics, such as gender, ethnicity, geographic location, and socioeconomic status

Outcome Measures in Perspective

Measuring clinical outcomes is central to assessing the quality of care. Outcome measures can be very useful in quality improvement programs by pointing out the areas in which intervention could improve care.* More specifically, "Outcomes should be measured for each medical condition covering the full cycle of care, including acute care, related complications, rehabilitation, and reoccurrences. It is the overall results that matter, not the outcome of an individual intervention or specialty (too narrow), or a single visit or care episode (too short). For example, if a surgical procedure is performed perfectly but a patient's subsequent rehabilitation fails, the outcome is poor."[2]

Outcomes can include a vast range of health states: mortality; physiologic measures such as blood pressure; laboratory test results such as serum cholesterol; patient-reported health states such as functional status; and symptoms may all be used as outcome measures. Outcome measures in different contexts, such as quality improvement, public reporting, and incentive programs, can be controversial because inferences

---

* Agency for Healthcare Research and Quality. June 2015. Selecting health outcome measures for clinical quality measurement. Available at: www.qualitymeasures.ahrq.gov/tutorial/HealthOutcomeMeasure.aspx.

from health states regarding quality are sometimes difficult to make. Interpretations may differ regarding the degree to which a specific clinical outcome is attributable to the antecedent healthcare received by a patient as opposed to other factors, including some that are unrelated to healthcare. For instance, determinants of outcomes after a heart attack include patient age, gender, severity of coronary artery occlusion, and prior heart attacks as well as other complicating conditions, such as hypertension, diabetes, or obesity. In addition, a variety of healthcare services can be major determinants of or contributors to an outcome. For heart attack outcomes, these could include services delivered by emergency medical technicians in the field, emergency room teams, inpatient and cardiac catheterization laboratory staff, and rehabilitation professionals. Attributing outcomes after a heart attack to specific healthcare services or to specific providers in a context such as this proves challenging.[2]

Defining Outcome Dimensions and Measures

Outcomes should be measured by the patient's medical condition or primary care patient segment, and not by procedure or intervention. The outcome should reflect the full cycle of care for the patient's condition. Each medical condition will have its own set of outcome measures that will vary according to the patient population. An outcome dimension may involve one or more specific measures and will depend on the range of available treatments, complications, and the duration of care.

According to Porter, "The outcome dimensions chosen should be important to the patient. Engaging patients and their families in defining this importance is an invaluable step, through focus groups, patient advisory councils, or other means."[3]

As Porter proposed in "The strategy that will fix health care,"[4] the full set of outcomes for any medical condition can be arranged in a three-tiered hierarchy (see Table 7.1). The top tier of outcomes is generally the most important, with lower-tier outcomes reflecting a progression of results contingent on success at higher tiers. As shown in Table 7.1, each tier of the hierarchy contains two broad levels, each of which involves one or more distinct outcome *dimensions*. Outcome dimensions capture specific aspects of patient health.

- *Tier 1 Health status achieved or retained*: This tier focuses on the initial patient outcome that determines whether a patient can return to a functional status and survive in the most severe conditions. This is measured over a period of 1 to 5 years depending on the severity of the condition.
- *Tier 2 Process of recovery*: The recovery tier focuses on the patient's journey back to a functional status. This includes time to recovery, treatment processes, and all interventions involved to overcome the medical disease or condition. The second tier is where issues with discomfort, retreatment, short-term complications, and errors can be found.
- *Tier 3 Sustainability of health (post-recovery)*: The sustainability tier focuses on allowing the patient to live a fully functional life without the interruption of recurrences or the development of new medical illnesses.

Measuring Clinical Outcomes

Most current outcome measurements focus on the immediate results of a treatment for a patient condition rather than the overall success of the full life cycle of care. The preponderance of hospital measurements tends to be process driven as opposed to outcome driven and less centered on the dimensions most important to the patient. It is recommended that Healthcare Delivery Organizations (HDOs) create a Value Management Office to gather the most accurate information

Table 7.1   The Outcome Measures Hierarchy

Tier 1 Health status achieved or retained	
Survival	Example: Hip Replacement • Mortality rate (inpatient)
Degree of health or recovery	• Time to begin treatment • Time to return to physical activities • Time to return to work
Tier 2 Process of recovery	
Time to recovery	• Time to begin treatment • Time to return to physical activities • Time to return to work
Disutility of care or treatment process (e.g., diagnostic errors, ineffective care, treatment-related discomfort, complications, adverse effects)	• Delays and anxiety • Pain during treatment • Length of hospital stay • Infection • Pulmonary embolism • Deep-vein thrombosis • Myocardial infarction • Need for reoperation • Delirium
Tier 3 Sustainability of health	
Sustainability of health or recovery Nature of recurrences	• Maintained functional level • Ability to live independently • Need for revision or replacement
Long-term consequences of therapy(e.g., care-induced illnesses)	• Loss of mobility due to inadequate rehabilitation • Risk of complex fracture • Susceptibility to infection • Stiff knee due to unrecognized complications • Regional pain syndrome

Source: From Rogers, E. 2003. *Diffusion of Innovations* (5th Edition). New York: Simon and Schuster.

Note: Ibid.

for clinical outcome measurement and evaluation. This is best achieved when using a system where patients, healthcare professionals, and healthcare providers work together to ensure that it can be used to improve services, treatment, and quality of care.*

Three kinds of clinical outcomes can be differentiated depending on the implementation, interpretation, and reporting by a rater of a patient assessment—a rater being a patient, clinician, or non-clinician observer[5]:

- Patient-reported outcome assessments have the patient as rater and rely on patient-provided responses to questions that are directly captured, without any interpretation or judgment on the part of anyone else. An example is a patient's self-report on a pain scale from 0 (no pain) to 10 (worst possible pain).
- Clinician-reported outcome assessments have a clinician as rater. An example would be a clinician-reported rating scale on the severity of a patient's depression (mild, moderate, or severe).
- Observer-reported outcomes have as rater someone other than the patient or clinician, someone who need not have specialized healthcare professional training.

Clinical outcomes are usually derived from evidence-based clinical guidelines. Some examples of this type of indicator (improvement in basic mobility functioning, readmission rate following discharge from physical therapy, or reduction of adverse drug events within the physical therapy consultations process) are provided in Chapter 5 within the section on Consultations Management in physical therapy. It is important to note that generalized outcomes, such as readmission rates, hospital infection, or mortality rates, are too broad to conduct

---

* Amplitude. 2016. Putting the patients at the heart of clinical outcomes. Available at: http://amplitude-clinical.com/.

a suitable evaluation of a providers' care that is meaningful to a specific patient. Such generalized measurements fail to provide concrete value to patients, providers, and payers and limit an organization's process improvement efforts. Focusing on the wrong things well still equates to failure.

Measurement allows for an assessment of an important outcome of care for a designated population of patients, and is a proxy for understanding the effectiveness of the underlying systems of care. Just as there are evidence-based care guidelines for many conditions, there are also established measures that indicate how effectively guidelines are translated to practice.

National organizations carefully consider these measures. Examples of general sources for clinical measures include[5]

■ *Healthcare Effectiveness Data and Information Set (HEDIS®)*: This is a tool used by more than 90% of America's health plans to measure performance on important dimensions of care and service. HEDIS® is developed and maintained by the National Committee for Quality Assurance (NCQA). Altogether, HEDIS® 2015 consists of 83 measures across five domains of care.*

Some of the metrics included in HEDIS® could be used for our example on physical therapy:
   – Effectiveness of care: Weight assessment and counseling for nutrition and physical activity for children/adolescents
   – Effectiveness of care: Use of imaging studies for low back pain
   – Access/availability of care: Adult access to preventive/ambulatory care
   – Measures collected through Medicare Health Outcomes Survey (HOS): Fall risk management or physical activity in older adults

* HEDIS® Measures. 2015. Available at: www.ncqa.org/HEDISQualityMeasurement/HEDISMeasures.aspx.

■ *AHRQ National Quality Measures Clearinghouse*™*: The National Quality Measures Clearinghouse (NQMC™) is a public resource for evidence-based quality measures and measure sets. NQMC™ also hosts the HHS Measures Inventory. The NQMC™ is sponsored by the Agency for Healthcare Research and Quality (AHRQ) to promote widespread access to quality measures by the healthcare community and other interested individuals. The NQMC™ mission is to provide an accessible mechanism for obtaining detailed information on quality measures, and to further their dissemination, implementation, and use in informing healthcare decisions.

Within the NQMC™, there are also interesting measures that could be used for our example:

– Physical functional status: A change score in patients' mobility following physical therapy intervention as assessed using the Outpatient Physical Therapy Improvement in Movement Assessment Log (OPTIMAL) Instrument.[†]

■ *National Quality Forum (NQF)*: These endorsed measures are evidence-based and valid, and, in tandem with the delivery of care and payment reform, they help

– Make patient care safer
– Improve maternity care
– Achieve better health outcomes
– Strengthen chronic care management
– Hold down healthcare costs

New directions are further strengthening how people engage with the healthcare community to drive quality improvements.

---

* National Quality Measures Clearinghouse™ (NQMC). Available at: www.ahrq. gov/cpi/about/otherwebsites/qualitymeasures.ahrq.gov/index.html.
[†] American Physical Therapy Association: Professional Association. 2012. Measure Summary. Available at: www.qualitymeasures.ahrq.gov/content.aspx?id=26749&search=Physical+Therapy+Modalities.

NQF is helping the U.S. Department of Health and Human Services to establish a portfolio of quality and efficiency measures for use in reporting on and improving healthcare quality.*

Coming back to an earlier example, sample measures from the 2016 Physical Therapy/Occupational Therapy Preferred Specialty Measure Set could be used:[†]

- *Communication and care coordination*: Pain assessment and follow-up: Percentage of visits for patients aged 18 years and older with documentation of a pain assessment using a standardized tool(s) on each visit AND documentation of a follow-up plan when pain is present
- *Patient safety*: Falls risk assessment: Percentage of patients aged 65 years and older with a history of falls who had a risk assessment for falls completed within 12 months
- *Communication and care coordination*: Functional deficit: Change in risk-adjusted functional status for patients with neck, cranium, mandible, thoracic spine, ribs, or other general orthopedic impairments: Percentage of patients aged 18 or older that receive treatment for a functional deficit secondary to a diagnosis that affects the neck, cranium, mandible, thoracic spine, ribs, or other general orthopedic impairment in which the change in their risk-adjusted functional status is measured

■ *Centers for Medicare and Medicaid Services Clinical Quality Measures*: Clinical quality measures (CQMs) are tools that help measure and track the quality of healthcare services provided by eligible professionals, eligible

---

* National Quality Forum. Available at: www.qualityforum.org/story/About_Us.aspx.
† Center for Medicare and Medicaid Services. 2016. Physical Therapy/Occupational Therapy Preferred Specialty Measure Set. Available at: www.cms.gov/medicare/quality-initiatives-patient-assessment-instruments/pqrs/measurescodes.html.

hospitals, and critical access hospitals within our healthcare system. These measures use data associated with providers' ability to deliver high-quality care or relate to long-term goals for quality healthcare. CQMs measure many aspects of patient care including*

- Health outcomes
- Clinical processes
- Patient safety
- Efficient use of healthcare resources
- Care coordination
- Patient engagements
- Population and public health
- Adherence to clinical guidelines

Measuring and reporting CQMs helps to ensure that the healthcare system is delivering effective, safe, efficient, patient-centered, equitable, and timely care.

Centers for Medicare and Medicaid Services (CMS) CQMs also recommend similar measures for adults that can be applied to the example cited earlier:

- Use of imaging studies for low back pain
- Preventive care and screening: Body mass index (BMI) screening and follow-up
- Closing the referral loop: Receipt of specialist report

■ *International Consortium for Health Outcomes Measurement (ICHOM)*: ICHOM is a nonprofit organization that seeks to "…unlock the potential of value-based healthcare by defining global standard sets of outcome measures that matter to patients for the most relevant medical conditions and by driving adoption and reporting of these measures worldwide to enable learning, choice, and competition on value" (2012). Twelve national registries and 60 international organizations have already aligned with or expressed the intent to measure outcomes

---

* CMS.gov. Clinical quality measures basics. Available at: www.cms.gov/regulations-and-guidance/legislation/ehrincentiveprograms/clinicalqualitymeasures.html.

according to ICHOM standard sets. ICHOM plans to launch benchmarking among the community of value innovators in 2016.

ICHOM members approach outcome measurement in a different manner, with a special focus on patient value rather than the process, the specialty, or the intervention. The following principles for outcome measurement are recommended by Porter[6] and supported by this book:

- Outcomes should be measured by medical condition or primary care patient segment (not by procedure or intervention).
- Outcomes should reflect the full cycle of care for the condition.
- Outcomes are always multidimensional and should include the health results most relevant to patients.
- Measurements must include initial conditions/risk factors to allow for risk adjustment.
- Outcome measures should be standardized to enable comparison and learning.

Very often, clinical outcome measures use processes of care or services as "proxies" for patient's health states. For example, the 30-day hospital readmission rate is sometimes referred to as an outcome measure; the underlying theory is that readmission reflects a change in health state. In reality, readmissions can occur for many reasons other than the health state of the patient. A high readmission rate may indicate that the patient's health has deteriorated, or it could indicate another issue, such as a lack of caregivers in the home or a misjudgment about the discharge destination at the time of discharge. A high rate of readmissions could reflect poor care during the first admission, or superior care leading to a sicker population on average at discharge. Such measures may be considered "proxies for health outcomes"[6] but they are not the real outcomes for patients.

For this reason, in the Consultation Management example, "improvement in basic mobility functioning" was the selected

KRI, that is, the outcome for patient's health, and "30-day readmission rate following discharge from physical therapy" was the KPI for this specific initiative.

Financial Outcomes

When measuring the financial health of a HDO, just like any other business, HDOs must have a sharp focus on financial performance. If a HDO cannot manage and control their financials, the organization will not be viable, especially in the new era of doing more with less. HDOs need to have an awareness of how they are performing in the essential financial performance areas: profitability, cash flow, liquidity, capital structure, age of physical buildings, and plants.[7]

There are several unique factors that impact a HDO's financials:

- *Location*: Urban, suburban, rural
- *Size*: Community, network, academic medical center
- *Payer mix*: Medicare, Medicaid, managed care, self-pay
- *Tax status*: For profit, not for profit

All HDOs need to be concerned with the performance of the essential financial performance areas so that they can achieve the core objectives that should be a top priority for all HDOs[8]:

- Revenues and expenses must be in balance, but ideally revenues should exceed expenses.
- Resources must be available to deliver the healthcare services and fund daily operations.
- The entity must be able to replenish or renew itself so that it can invest in new facilities and technology to meet future healthcare needs.

The margins that a HDO receives from its revenues and expenses are paramount, with particular emphasis on the patient care margin. While HDOs might have multiple sources of revenue, the margin on patient care is the core of the business. The patient care margin is the driving factor in financing daily operations, expanding the services provided to the community, and having reserves set aside for emergencies and hardships.[8]

Measuring Financial Outcomes

The following types of financial KRIs are commonly used for measuring value from the financial outcome perspective:

- Profit[9]
  - *Operating margin (%)*: Total operating revenues minus total operating expenses, divided by total operating revenues
  - *Excess margin (%)*: Total operating revenues plus non-operating revenues minus total operating expenses divided by total operating revenues plus non-expenses, divided by total operating revenues plus non-operating operating revenues
- Cash flow and liquidity
  - *Cash flow margin (%)*: Cash flow from operations, divided by total operating revenues plus non-operating revenues
  - *Debt service coverage ratio (X)*: Net increase in unrestricted net assets plus depreciation and interest expense, divided by interest expense (net of deferred financing) plus principal payments
  - *Days cash on hand*: Unrestricted cash and investments, divided by daily cash operating expenses (total operating expenses less depreciation/amortization expenses)
  - *Cushion ratio (X)*: Unrestricted cash and investments, divided by maximum future annual debt service

■ Capital
  - *Debt financing (%)*: Total assets minus unrestricted net assets, divided by total assets
  - *Long-term debt to capitalization*: Long-term debt, divided by long-term debt plus unrestricted net assets
■ Physical plant
  - *Accumulated depreciation*: Accumulated depreciation divided by gross property, plant, and equipment.
  - *Capital expenditures as percent of depreciation expense (%)*: Annual expenditures on property, plant, and equipment, divided by depreciation expense.

Cost of Care

Since the model for healthcare reimbursement is changing and becoming unpredictable, moving away from fee-for-service toward bundled payments, medical homes, and incentive payments, many HDOs focus on managing cost as their top priority to improve the patient care margin.

Four cost categories affect every HDO:

■ *Fixed cost:** A cost that does not change with an increase or decrease in the number of goods or services produced. Fixed costs are expenses that must be paid by a company, independent of any business activity.
■ *Variable cost:*† A corporate expense that varies with production output. Variable costs are those that vary depending on a company's production volume; they rise as production increases and fall as production decreases.

---

* Investopedia. Fixed cost (2016). http://www.investopedia.com/terms/f/fixedcost. asp. Accessed October 15, 2016. Variable cost. (2016). http://www.investopedia. com/terms/v/variablecost.asp. Accessed October 15, 2016. Direct cost. (2016). http://www.investopedia.com/terms/d/directcost.asp. Accessed October 15, 2016.
† Ibid.

Table 7.2 Categories of Cost

Categories of Cost	
Direct hospital cost: Fixed	• Buildings • Utilities • Equipment • Information Technology • Labor
Direct hospital cost: Variable	• Medications • Food • Consultations • Treatments • Procedures • Devices • Testing
Indirect cost	• Lost Wages • Diminished worker productivity • Short-term and long-term morbidity • Mortality • Income lost by family members • Time spent by family/friends for hospital visits, travel costs, home care
Intangible cost	• Psychological cost • Pain and suffering • Change in social functioning/daily activities

Note: Adapted from Haddix, A. C and Shaffer, P. A. 1996. Cost-effectiveness analysis. In *Prevention Effectiveness: A Guide to Decision Analysis and Economic Evaluation*. Oxford: Oxford University Press.

■ *Indirect cost*: Indirect costs are those that are not directly accountable to a cost object (such as a project, facility, function, or product).

■ *Intangible cost*: Intangible costs represent a variety of expenses such as losses in productivity, customer goodwill, or drops in employee morale. While these costs do not have a firm value, managers often attempt to estimate the impact of the intangibles (Table 7.2).

Cost of Care in the Patient Life Cycle

The cost categories and variables discussed previously affect patients throughout the life cycle of care. As described before in the "Clinical Outcomes" section, the *outcome hierarchy* sets three tiers of outcomes to be measured along the life cycle of care. If cost can be contained and controlled at "Tier 1: Health status achieved or retained" with high-quality clinical outcomes, it will cause the cost to go down in the other two tiers.[10] This is one reason why operational and volume KPIs are areas of financial importance for any HDO.

According to Dr. Thomas Feeley, it is important for health-care organizations to measure outcomes and costs for every patient.[11] He notes six major obstacles:

- The need to believe that outcome measurement is important: Major focus on process, structure, and guidelines since 2000.
- Important and broad measures based on the condition of the patient.
- Some believe patient-reported outcome measures (PROM) are research tools and not clinical tools.
- PROMs take time for patients to complete: Measures must be tested and validated.
- Manual data collection takes time.
- IT systems are way behind in capturing measures in work flow: Were built as revenue cycle tools.

In April 2016, Dr. Feeley recommended the following for getting started:

- Committed leadership
- A small group of dedicated individuals
- One or two conditions: Paper and pencil

- Recognizing that scaling is important: Work with those who want to improve their outcomes and those who want PROMs
- Recognizing that IT industry outcome measurement is important

MD Anderson, by implementing the value agenda and focusing on measuring outcomes and costs, demonstrated its outcomes beyond clinical trials and justified a higher cost structure. It has also recently negotiated a bundled payment with United Healthcare due to its high confidence in achieving desired health outcomes.*

Time-Driven Activity-Based Costing

As highlighted in the previous two sections, there are growing demands on hospitals' budgets and patient care expenditures. Since there is pressure on hospitals to become more cost efficient, attention is turning to accounting principles that are used in the private sector, such as Activity-Based Costing (ABC).[12]

The hope is that if hospitals start using improved accounting principles, they will be able to collect better data on their budgets and financial outcomes so that they can identify efficiencies and make projections on how changes in patients' demands affect resource requirements.[12]

One of the problems with conventional cost accounting methods is that they sum indirect cost and overhead cost and divide by a universal denominator such as patient days. The problem with this type of accounting is that it assumes an overhead cost per patient day for all types of patients. This method does not factor in important variables such as the

---

* Feeley, T. April 2016. HBS Value measurement presentation. Harvard Business School. Dr. Thomas Feeley lecture.

patient's acuity level, the complexity of the procedure needed for the patient, and the length of stay required for the patient.[13]

While ABC sounds complex, it is essentially a costing methodology that identifies activities in an organization and assigns the cost of each activity with resources to all products and services according to the actual consumption by each.* In recent years, there have been modifications to ABC to account for the shortcomings that did not factor in realistic capacity implications as noted by Robert S. Kaplan and Steven R. Anderson in their Time-Driven Activity-Based Costing (TDABC) article in *Harvard Business Review*.[14]

On implementation of TDABC (Activity-Based Costing factoring in the capacity implications), seven process steps must occur:

> Step 1: Select medical condition and/or patient population to be examined
> Step 2: Define the care delivery value chain
> Step 3: Develop process maps of each activity in patient care delivery; identify the resources involved and any supplies used for the patient at each process
> Step 4: Obtain time estimates for each process step
> (e.g., mental health for Steps 3 and 4; process mapping for mental health)
> Step 5: Estimate the cost of supplying each patient care resource
> Step 6: Estimate the practical capacity of each resource provider, and calculate the capacity cost rate
> Step 7: Compute the total costs over each patient's cycle of care.
> (e.g., mental health for Steps 5, 6, and 7; calculate capacity cost rate)

---

* Activity Based Costing. https://en.wikipedia.org/wiki/Activity-based_costing. Accessed October 17, 2016.

Once a hospital has implemented an ABC system, variance analysis can be used to determine the efficiency in delivering patient outcomes, using the right resources to care for the patient and discharging the patient on time.

A few of the variance measurements that can be monitored include[15]

- Patient variances: Complications or changes related to a patient's health
- Caregiver variances: Nursing and physician variances
- Environmental variances: Caused by equipment breakdown, unavailable beds, scheduling problems, lab delays, and power outages
- Price variances: Caused by paying higher than budgeted prices for supplies, drugs, instruments, and labor
- Efficiency variances: Duplication of work, patient delays, waste, and scheduling issues

With the successful implementation of an ABC system, hospitals will finally have a realistic organizational picture of the cost of care for each type of patient.

Activity-Based Costing for Consultation Management

This approach can now be applied for ABC in our Consultation Management for Physical Therapy example (Table 7.3).

Table 7.3 examines a hypothetical scenario demonstrating the differences between two types of ABC methods and a Conventional Costing method.

In this scenario, an analysis of how to allocate the overhead cost of two clerks to 13 medical specialties is presented. This assumes that all clerks are scheduling referrals for every specialty and the accounting system has only one generic cost bucket for the cost of clerks.

Table 7.3 Activity-Based Costing for Consultation Management

Cost of Clerks focused only on scheduling appointments for referrals

Medical Specialty	Quantity	Unit Time (Min)	Total Time Used (Min)	Cost-Driver Rate	Time-Driven ABC (80% Capacity)	Traditional ABC (100% Capacity)	Non-ABC (Unit Time is Equal)
Physical Therapy	900	25	22,500	$0.33	**$7,500**	$9,302	$11,612
Oncology	700	30	21,000	$0.33	**$7,000**	$8,682	$9,032
Mental Health	400	40	16,000	$0.33	**$5,333**	$6,614	$5,161
Cardiology	320	50	16,000	$0.33	**$5,333**	$6,614	$4,129
Dermatology	320	50	16,000	$0.33	**$5,333**	$6,614	$4,129
Gastroenterology	700	20	14,000	$0.33	**$4,666**	$5,788	$9,032
Gynecology	800	30	24,000	$0.33	**$8,000**	$9,922	$10,322
Hematology	200	40	8,000	$0.33	**$2,666**	$3,307	$2,580
Nephrology	340	20	6,800	$0.33	**$2,266**	$2,811	$4,387
Ophthalmology	600	30	18,000	$0.33	**$6,000**	$7,441	$7,741
Otolaryngology	320	35	11,200	$0.33	**$3,733**	$4,630	$4,129
Rheumatology	400	35	14,000	$0.33	**$4,666**	$5,788	$5,161
Urology	200	30	6,000	$0.33	**$2,000**	$2,480	$2,580
					$64,500	**$80,000**	**$80,000**

For the calendar year, the total cost of clerks = $80,000. Depending on which costing method is used, the $80,000 can be allocated to the 13 medical specialties in different amounts.

The Conventional Costing method only factors in the quantity of units and the number of referrals scheduled, and assumes that each medical specialty requires the same amount of time to schedule a referral appointment. This is somewhat misleading as more complex medical specialties will require more time to schedule referral appointments.

The traditional ABC method factors in units of time. Using this method, the actual total time spent scheduling and processing the referrals for each of the medical specialties can be factored in to the calculation. The benefit of this method is that it provides a more realistic picture of cost when determining the cost of care for each medical specialty.

The TDABC method provides an additional benefit to the traditional ABC method. This method factors in a capacity variable. As an employee or system cannot operate at 100% capacity, unused capacity can be calculated. For clerks, this would be time for breaks, setting up and closing down for the day, and attending team meetings. For systems, this would be downtime for maintenance and repairs.

In Figure 7.1, the difference between the three methods for all types of outpatient referrals is presented.

In this scenario, it is assumed that clerks operate at approximately 80% capacity.[16] By knowing how much time and money is spent on unused capacity, managers can review the data and determine the appropriate actions to take to minimize unused time and money.

If this hypothetical scenario were real, the manager of this department might be willing to allow the clerks to shift to other departments for periods of time so that unused capacity does not go to waste.

The most important thing to note about TDABC is that it is not just a theory, it has already been introduced in many places and has been demonstrated to work. One such study

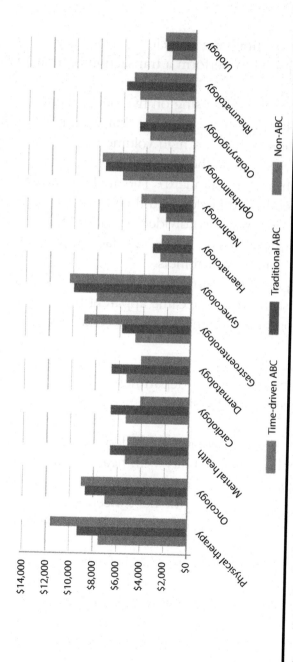

Figure 7.1   Application of activity-based costing models.

was in Belgium. TDABC was executed based on Porter's vision where only two parameters need to be measured.

These two parameters are

1. Unit cost of supplying capacity
2. Time required to perform a transaction or an activity

This was tested by focusing on five departments (out of the nineteen located there). The five that were selected for the study were chosen due to a high volume of patients and growing workload, as well as the fact that most services provided were non-technical (or standard). The analysts took the two parameters needed and calculated them for each of the five departments. Cost was also divided into four main "resource pools" consisting of: (1) secretary; (2) machine; (3) medical material; and (4) cost of cabinets.

Ultimately, once the costs were all calculated and the full results for cost utilization became apparent from applying ABC, the departments witnessed improvements in

1. Operational processes
2. Profitability analysis per department
3. Future investment decisions

Future investment decisions included secretaries being centralized, telephone accessibility with headsets and voice recognition settings, healthy competition and open communication between the different departments concerning possible operational improvements, and different heads' understanding of the different organizational processes.[17]

Another benefit of TDABC unfolds from managers now having control of analyzing and reporting costs. They can do this on an ongoing basis to reveal the true costs of business activities and the time spent doing them. Therefore, they can see the difference between capacity supplied and capacity used.

When the TDABC model has been put in place, it can be updated and changed easily. This is another one of the main differences (and more modern attributes), besides the capacity rate, that separates it from the traditional ABC model. The model can be updated to reflect (A) *new changes in operating conditions.*

This will cause the cost-driver rates to change based on two factors:

1. Changes in prices of resources supplied (i.e., compensation increase or new equipment cost)
2. Shift in efficiency of activity (i.e., quality programs, continued improvement efforts, reengineering, or the introduction of new technology)

The (B) *time equations* also make the models more complex. The time factors allow the model to reflect how order and activity characteristics cause processing times to vary. An example of this would be changing a model for shipping depending on if that product is a special chemical (or the like) that needs to be treated differently from the average product.

In conclusion, TDABC offers a transparent, scalable methodology that is easy to implement and update. It draws on existing databases to incorporate specific features for specific orders, processes, suppliers, and customers. It provides owners and managers with meaningful cost and probability information quickly and inexpensively.[18]

Another company that has applied the TDABC method and witnessed improvements is Lewis-Goetz, a hose and belt manufacturer in Pittsburgh. The owner came to the realization that one of their plants was operating at only 27% of capacity. Rather than attempt to downsize the plant, he kept it, expecting a large contract later that year, so that he did not need to buy up more space and resources.[18]

Porter also points out more benefits to incorporating TDABC into the healthcare system. Ultimately, the improvement in healthcare needs to come from gathering around one common focus, namely increasing value for patients, which is measured by health outcomes achieved per dollar spent.

Porter states that "true reform" will require both

1. Moving toward universal insurance coverage
2. Restructuring the care delivery system

Universal Coverage (6 Steps):

■ Universal coverage is achieved by first changing the nature of healthcare competition. Currently, this is a zero-sum competition environment where health plans compete by subscribing healthier subscribers, denying services, and negotiating discounts. Porter insists that they should be competing on value.

■ The second step is keeping employers in the insurance system. Porter states that there should be encouragement to keep them in by reducing the extra amount they currently pay through higher insurance costs to cover the uninsured and subsidize government programs.

■ The third step is to address the burden on people who have no access to employer-based coverage. He proposes equalizing the tax deductibility of insurance through individuals and then employers.

■ The fourth step is having large statewide or multistate insurance pools to spread risk. For the reinsurance system, equitably spread the cost of insuring Americans with very expensive health problems across both regional pools and employers.

■ The fifth step is income-based subsidies, which will be needed to help lower-income people buy insurance.

■ The concluding step is that everyone must be required to purchase health insurance so no opt-outs, especially by the young and healthy.

Restructuring the Care Delivery System (7 steps):

■ Restructuring the care delivery system is completed by first making the measurement of health outcomes mandatory for every provider (and every medical condition). These outcomes are to be measured over a full cycle of care.

■ The second step in restructuring the care delivery system is to reexamine how to organize delivery/prevention, wellness, and routine health maintenance services.

■ The third step is to reorganize care delivery around medical conditions. This would be based on integrated practice units (IPUs). The IPUs would encompass all skills and services required over the full cycle of care for each medical condition.

■ The fourth step is to have a reimbursement system that aligns everyone's interests with improving value for patients. This would initiate the movement to single bundled payments covering the entire cycle of care for a medical condition (including all providers and services).

■ The fifth step is to require providers to compete for patients based on value at the medical condition level, both within and across state lines. Porter also weighs in that a minimum volume threshold for complex medical conditions may need to be implemented. According to him, this would spur the geographic expansion of specific providers.

■ The sixth step is having all medical/health records changed to an Electronic Medical Record (EMR). They will have value but only if they support integrated care and outcome measurement.

■ The last step for restructuring the system requires that consumers become much more involved in their health and, coinciding with that, their healthcare.

In conclusion, comprehensive reform will require simulta-neous progress in both these areas because they are mutually reinforcing. The big question is whether we can move beyond the reactive and piecemeal approach of the current state to a true national healthcare strategy focused on value.[19]

Measuring Cost of Care Outcomes

HDOs encounter several cost variables in treating patients as highlighted in Table 7.2. While HDOs should be concerned with all costs, as they are all interrelated in the total cost of care, they should focus on KPIs that are within their means of control. These include the fixed and variable costs that relate to the operational and volume aspects of the life cycle of care.

- Operational KPIs[20]: KPIs related to a fixed unit of cost in treating and caring for patients
  - Salary expenses per adjusted admission
  - Supplies expenses per adjusted admission
- Volume KPIs: KPIs related to workload units in treating and caring for patients
  - Total number of patient days
  - Average length of stay
  - Total number of tests
  - Total number of patient visits

While it is difficult to measure the indirect and intangible costs, HDOs can get a good indication of how they are performing in these two categories by considering patient satisfaction.

Reimbursement for Care

Due to recent healthcare policies, the future of healthcare reimbursement is going to be complex and unpredictable. Market forces and patient demands are affecting HDO reimbursement, which will no longer be based on the volume of procedures (the fee-for-service model).

Payers are demanding that healthcare reimbursements be linked to high-quality clinical outcomes. This has prompted the industry to start examining new types of payment models, such as bundled payments, medical homes, and quality-based incentive payments. The U.S. Department of Health and Human Services (HHS), the payers of Medicare and Medicaid, have reported that the agency would like to tie 50% of payments to the new payment models by 2018 and factor quality into 90% of traditional Medicare payments by 2018.[21]

One way to prepare for this transition is with data. By collecting the right data on key aspects of their business, HDOs will be better prepared to deal with external stakeholders, that is, health insurers, government agencies, and patients.

As the demand for high-quality care and outcomes continues to grow, many HDOs will focus on optimizing revenue cycles to new healthcare reimbursement models, and they will likely encounter challenges such as penalties, reimbursements being withheld, or not being reimbursed at all. With these challenges looming, it is imperative that HDOs take steps to ensure that they are maximizing efficient revenue collection.

Bundled payment models are widely being tested and implemented with several leaders in healthcare. As an example, MD Anderson has launched a 3-year pilot with United Healthcare, which includes four bundles based on the treatment plan with a modifier for ≥ two comorbidities and stop-loss for significant outliers. They tracked both outcomes and financial metrics using TDABC versus the old system of Hierarchical Condition Category (HCC) costs (Table 7.4). This bundled payment already yields tangible benefits for patients by simplifying bills and out-of-pocket costs known at the start of treatment. It also prevents insurance coverage from dictating care.

Table 7.4 TDABC versus the Old System of HCC Costs

Financial Tracking	Outcomes Tracking (Head and Neck Only)
TDABC Costs	Survival and quality (speaking, swallowing, and returning to activities)
Charges	Treatment times
HCC costs (old system)	Automated patient-reported outcomes (PROs) using validated symptom tool
FFS reimbursement	Complication of treatment
Bundle reimbursement	Reoccurrence
Before and after the pilot, compare resource utilization	PROs obtained via the MD Anderson Symptom Inventory (MDASI-HN)—responses integrated into EMR
Examine claims management	Incorporate into clinical workflow

Revenue Life Cycle Operations

The revenue cycle includes all clinical and administrative functions that involve documenting, capturing, submitting, and managing insurance claims to collect reimbursement for the healthcare services provided.* This process is essential for all HDOs' departments.

Revenue Cycle Aspects[23]

- *Patient access*: All tasks related to patient scheduling, pre-registration, financial counseling, and patient registration
- *Case management*: All tasks related to utilization management and discharge planning

---

* Oregon Health and Science Institute. Revenue Cycle. Available at: www.ohsu. edu/xd/about/services/patient-business-services/revenue-cycle/.

- *Service documentation*: All tasks related to the charge master, charge capture, coding, and late charges
- *Billings*: All tasks related to the claims editor, bill reconciliation, and contractual adjustments
- *Accounts receivable management*: All tasks related to the cash/explanation of benefits (EOB) posting, third party collections, account write offs, and bad debt
- Customer Services: All tasks related to customer inquiries, issue resolution, and service recovery

Having an efficient HDO revenue cycle is necessary for long-term financial stability. There are reports that indicate that CMS rejects 26% of all claims and up to 40% of claims are never submitted.[22] These two inefficiencies are caused by a variety of factors, such as poor training, lack of communication, and poor workflow processes. With proper KPI measurement and monitoring, these inefficiencies can be greatly mitigated.

Measuring Revenue Cycle Outcomes

The following examples show just a few KPIs that can provide HDOs with valuable information on the efficiency and effectiveness of their revenue cycle processes.

Patient access quality[23]: KPIs which indicate that patient access processes are timely, accurate, and efficient

- *Insurance verification rate* equals the number of verified encounters divided by the number of registered encounters
- *Conversion rate of uninsured patient to payer source* equals the number of total uninsured patients converted to insurance divided by the number of total uninsured discharges and visits

Claims process[23]: KPIs that indicate accuracy in submitting claims to the payers and health insurers

- *Clean claim rate* equals the number of claims from payers that pass edits requiring no manual intervention divided by the total claims accepted into the claims scrubber tool for billing prior to submission
- *Denial–Zero pay* equals the number of zero paid claims denied divided by the number of total claims remitted

Management process[23]: KPIs that indicate revenue cycle efficiency in collecting reimbursement from the payers and the health insurers

- *Days in accounts receivable* equals the gross accounts receivable divided by the average daily net patient service revenue
- *Total uncompensated care* equals the uninsured and uncompensated care (bed debt + charity care + uninsured care discount) divided by the gross patient service revenue

Patient Satisfaction

Patient satisfaction is an important and commonly used indicator for measuring quality in healthcare. Patient satisfaction affects clinical outcomes, patient retention, and medical malpractice claims. It affects the timely, efficient, and patient-centered delivery of quality healthcare. Patient satisfaction is thus a proxy indicator used to measure the success of doctors and hospitals.[24]

Patients' evaluation of care is a realistic tool that provides the opportunity for improvement, enhances strategic decision making, reduces costs, meets patients' expectations, frames strategies for effective management, and monitors the health-care performance of health plans and benchmarks across healthcare institutions.[25–28]

Patients' feedback is necessary to identify problems that need to be resolved for improving health services. Even if patients still do not use this information systematically to improve care delivery and services, this type of feedback triggers a real interest that can lead to a change in culture and patient perception.[29]

In addition, due to healthcare organizations' focus on patient-centered care, patient satisfaction reflects patients' involvement in decision making and their role as partners in improving the quality of healthcare services.[29,30]

There is a significant correlation between measuring patient satisfaction and continuity of care where satisfied patients tend to comply with the treatment and stay with the same health-care providers.[31] Patient satisfaction represents a key marker of health-related behavior.[32]

Improved patient satisfaction not only leads to an enhanced patient experience; it is also associated with improved treatment outcomes. In 2008, researchers demonstrated that improved patient satisfaction was correlated with higher quality hospital care "for all...conditions measured." Work that is more recent has begun to identify exactly how this correlation works. For example, higher patient satisfaction has been associated with reduced readmission rates. Additionally, improved patient satisfaction has been correlated with reduced inpatient mortality, "suggesting that patients are good discriminators of the type of care they receive."[33]

From a financial perspective, patient satisfaction responses constitute 30% of each hospital's score under the federal value-based purchasing system. This score will either increase or decrease a hospital's overall Medicare payments by up to 1% in 2013.[34]

Determinants of Patient Satisfaction

In the increasingly competitive healthcare environment, health-care managers should consider focusing on achieving high or excellent patient satisfaction ratings to improve the quality of service delivery. To accomplish higher ratings, healthcare managers need to define the factors influencing patient satisfaction, which are used to assess the quality of healthcare delivery. To understand various factors affecting patient satisfaction, researchers have explored a range of dimensions of perceived service quality as meaningful and essential measures of patient perception of healthcare quality.[35]

Patient satisfaction is one of the most important goals of any health system. It is often difficult to measure satisfaction and gauge the responsiveness of health systems as it is not only the clinical but also the nonclinical outcomes of care that influence customer satisfaction.[36]

Patient satisfaction depends on a variety of factors such as quality of clinical services provided, availability of medicine, behavior of doctors and other healthcare staff, cost of services, hospital infrastructure, physical comfort, emotional support, and respect for patient preferences.[37] A mismatch between patient expectations and the service received is related to decreased satisfaction.[38] Therefore, assessing patient perspectives gives them a voice, which can make public health services more responsive to people's needs and expectations.*[39]

Swayne, Duncan, and Ginter (2008) described the healthcare value chain in two parts[40]: (1) the service areas (the top half) that deal directly with patients; and (2) the support areas (the lower half) that provide resources to employees interacting with patients. The goal of both parts of the organization is patient satisfaction. Pre-service activities involve researching to determine patient and/or clinician (customers) desires and

---

* World Health Organization. 2000. The world health report 2000: Health systems: Improving performance. Geneva: WHO.

developing a product that fulfills their desires. The point-of-service actions include how the patient is treated and what care has been provided. Actions must focus on the quality of care provided, the timeliness of treatment, and the outcome. After-service actions focus on post-care follow-up activities where a provider contacts a patient to check on his/her post-visit condition. The follow-up activities demonstrate a high quality of care for the patient and show that the provider is truly concerned about their well-being. These after-service actions are critical in gaining and sustaining high patient satisfaction and contributing to better healthcare outcomes (Figure 7.2).

Measuring Patient Satisfaction

Despite the correlation between higher patient satisfaction rates and improved outcomes, the measurement of patient satisfaction remains controversial among many healthcare providers.

Certainly, there are instances in which sound medicine may lead to a lower rate of patient satisfaction; infrequently, satisfaction can correlate, not with high-quality care, but with the fulfillment of patients' prior wishes for their treatment. A good example of this problem is the difficulty in refusing to fill narcotics prescriptions and steering a patient toward alternative pain relief modalities when the physician has good evidence of patient narcotics abuse. While the doctor in this example

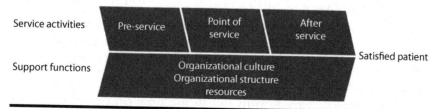

Figure 7.2   Example: EHR program value linkage.

is following good practice guidelines, it is highly unlikely that the patient will have high satisfaction.

Although such cases may be rare, many studies show a deep divide between how patients and doctors view medical care, and thus demonstrate the need to measure patient satisfaction rates.

It is clearly important to understand patient satisfaction results both for patients contemplating treatment options and for payers contemplating coverage decisions. It is important for doctors as well. As the practice of medicine changes, physician fatigue has also become an issue. Of note, there is a high correlation between patient satisfaction with care and provider satisfaction with his/her work. This likely represents a symbiotic relationship between happier, more satisfied patients and happier, more satisfied practitioners. Thus, a focus on patient satisfaction will lead to an improvement in the professional lives of physicians as well as the delivering better treatment results.

Patients and their doctors inevitably view the same episodes of care through different lenses. Therefore, knowledge of patient satisfaction is critical in understanding the patient experience and the effectiveness of treatment. This knowledge helps patients make decisions that are more informed and it helps physicians practice medicine more effectively.

There are two approaches for evaluating patient satisfaction: qualitative and quantitative. The quantitative approach provides accurate methods to measure patient satisfaction. Standardized questionnaires (either self-reported, interviewer-administrated, or by telephone) have been the most common assessment tool for conducting patient satisfaction studies.[41,42] Over the past 20 years, patient satisfaction surveys have gained increasing attention for providing meaningful and essential information for identifying gaps and developing an effective action plan for quality improvement in healthcare organizations.[43]

There is great variation in questionnaires on measuring patient satisfaction. The spectrum includes instruments

provided by private vendors and several public and standardized instruments, such as patient satisfaction questionnaires
and PSQ-18 and consumer assessment health plans (CAHPS).
Such survey instruments have the advantage of good reliability and validity; however, most offer a limited scope of survey
questions.[44]

HCAHPS Survey

The Hospital Consumer Assessment of Healthcare Providers
and Systems (HCAHPS) survey is the first national, standardized, publicly reported survey of patients' perspectives of
hospital care. HCAHPS (pronounced "H-caps"), also known as
the CAHPS hospital survey, is a survey instrument and data
collection methodology for measuring patients' perceptions of
their hospital experience. While many hospitals have collected
information on patient satisfaction for their own internal use,
until HCAHPS, there was no national standard for collecting
and publicly reporting information about patient experiences
of care that allowed valid comparisons to be made across hospitals locally, regionally, and nationally.[45]

The HCAHPS survey asks discharged patients 27 questions
about their recent hospital stay. The survey contains 18 core
questions about critical aspects of patients' hospital experiences (communication with nurses and doctors, the responsiveness of hospital staff, the cleanliness and quietness of
the hospital environment, pain management, communication
about medicines, discharge information, overall rating of hospital, and if would they recommend the hospital).

The HCAHPS survey is administered to a random sample
of adult patients across medical conditions between 48 hours
and 6 weeks after discharge; the survey is not restricted to
Medicare beneficiaries. Hospitals may either use an approved
survey vendor, or collect their own HCAHPS data (if approved
by CMS to do so). HCAHPS can be implemented in four

different survey modes: mail, telephone, mail with telephone follow-up, or active interactive voice recognition (IVR). Hospitals can use the HCAHPS survey alone, or include additional questions after the core HCAHPS items.

CAHPS Clinician and Group Patient-Centered Medical Home (PCMH) Survey

To assess patient experience with the patient-centered medical home model, the CAHPS Consortium developed an expanded version of the clinician and group 12-month survey that incorporated the CAHPS Patient-Centered Medical Home (PCMH) Survey.[46]

The PCMH survey includes standardized questionnaires for adults and children in primary care settings. Although this survey could be used by any physician practice, it is intended to be especially useful for physician practices that have adopted features of a patient-centered medical home.

The PCMH survey produces the same set of patient experience measures as the 12-month survey:

■ Getting timely appointments, care, and information
■ How well providers communicate with patients
■ Helpful, courteous, and respectful office staff
■ Patients' rating of the provider
■ Provider's attention to your child's growth and development (child only)
■ Provider's advice on keeping your child safe and healthy (child only)

It also produces three additional composite measures:

■ Talking with you about taking care of your own health
■ Attention to your mental and emotional health (adult only)
■ Talking about medication decisions (adult only)

In the example of Consultation Management for Physical Therapy, the CAHPS scores PCMH SHEP Q6 (get an appointment for care when needed right away) and PCMH SHEP Q18 (wait time includes time spent in the waiting room and exam room) were used as examples for measuring patient satisfaction.

Process Improvement

A well-managed hospital strives to deliver clinical excellence to their patients and to provide their patients, staff, and guests with an exceptional experience. Throughout the patient care cycle, for example, registration, intake, clinical visit, plan of care discussions, and discharge instructions, there are several activities, interactions, and handoffs involving people, processes, and systems that make up a variety of value streams.

These value streams include patient flow, medical records, medical equipment, or any resource used for patient care. In an ideal world, hospitals want the value streams to be efficient, but just like any process, there can be waste in parts of the value streams.

In the patient care cycle, value must always be seen from the eyes of the patient. Only activities that the patient truly wants, needs, cannot do without, and is willing to pay for should be included. Excessive procedures and the use of expensive diagnostic tests are subject to physician opinion on whether or not they affect a patient outcome. In the United States, excessive testing drives up costs without necessarily providing value for the patient health outcome. Compared to other countries, U.S. providers choose more procedures and tests. This could be attributed to

■ A fear of litigation or malpractice
■ Payment structures that support higher provider salaries if additional tests are conducted, regardless of medical need
■ Patients asking for more services and tests

Regardless of the rationale for increased testing and procedures, there is some amount of waste that can be reduced if providers shift toward a value-based approach for delivering healthcare. This sort of process improvement can minimize cost while simultaneously providing value for the patient.

> Data suggests that the United States does do more tests than other OECD countries. The United States did 100 MRI tests and 265 CT tests for every 1000 people in 2010—more than twice the average in other OECD countries.
>
> **PBS**[47]

Most industry standards place patient care activities in three distinct categories, as described below by the Lean Advancement Initiative Educational Network[48]:

- Value-added activity
  - Transforms patient, material, information, decisions, or risk.
  - The customers want it or understand why it is necessary.
  - The activity is done right the first time; there is no duplication.
- Enabling activity
  - No patient value is created, but is necessary to complete a process in the patient care cycle.
- Non-value-added activity (waste)
  - Consumes resources but creates no value in the eyes of the patient.
  - If this activity is removed, the process can most likely continue.

When the value streams are not efficient, patients get poor service and providers are strained, which likely results in poor quality of care and clinical outcomes. In addition, providers that are strained are more likely to report poor employee satisfaction and HDOs may face significant problems in the recruiting and retention of providers. With reimbursement cuts coming in the near-term, hospitals must eliminate as much waste as possible to avoid providing poor quality of care and clinical outcomes and retain providers.

Bottom line, hospitals are spending more time and resources in finding ways to make the value streams more efficient. Since process reengineering and process improvement can be complex tasks, hospitals are beginning to use operational methodologies from the private sector.

Operational methodologies such as A3 Analysis, a structured problem-solving technique used by Lean practitioners in the private sector, and DMAIC, a core tool used when working on Six Sigma projects, are gaining popularity in the healthcare sector. Essentially, these methodologies seek to provide the most optimal processes for value streams so that they do not erode the performance of the people performing the activities, thus providing the patients with the best quality care with the desired clinical outcomes.

These operational methodologies allow hospitals to dissect both direct and indirect activities. The direct care includes activities such as the time spent transporting the patient, administering drugs, and explaining discharge instructions. The indirect care activities include activities that support the patient's preparation, such as preparing supply trays, medical documentation, and answering phones calls.* Research shows that 80% of the patient care cycle is waste, as found by a study from the University of Iowa Hospitals and Clinics.[49] Using

---

* Kis, G. 2016. Huron Healthcare. Reducing waste in care processes. White paper. Available at: www.huronconsultinggroup.com/resources/healthcare/reducing-waste-in-care-processes-by-documenting-direct-and-indirect-time.

operational methodologies should help better position hospitals when considering the five core principles:*

1. Striving for perfection by continually removing successive layers of waste
2. Identifying all the steps across the entire value stream
3. Making those actions that create value flow seamless and predictable
4. Only making or delivering what is required by the customer when it is required
5. Striving for perfection by continually removing successive layers of waste

If hospitals can reengineer value stream processes by focusing on the value-added activities aligned with the five core principles, hospitals will begin to see improvements in quality and safety with the following benefits:

1. Increased process efficiency (e.g., reduced scheduling times)
2. Improved productivity (e.g., ability to see more patients)
3. Reduced costs (e.g., insurance, procedures, and administrative costs)
4. Improved collaboration and communication (e.g., more time with the patient)
5. The ability to gain or sustain a competitive advantage

Determinants of Process Improvements

When analyzing a value stream, three key performance measures are needed to determine the efficiency of the process.

---

* Safer Healthcare. Process improvement and Lean in healthcare. Available at: www.saferhealthcare.com/lean/process-improvement-and-lean-in-healthascare/.

1. Capacity: How many units can be produced over a given time (maximum output)?
2. Bottleneck: Which activity in the cycle takes the longest time to complete (limits the capacity)?
3. Throughput time: How long does it take to go through the entire cycle?

These three key measures are affected by several impediments throughout the value stream process. Three of the important impediments include

1. Buffer*: Storage area between stages where the output of a stage is placed prior to being used in a downstream stage
2. Blocking[†]: Where activities in a stage must stop because there is no place to deposit the item just completed
3. Starving[‡]: Occurs when the activities in a stage must stop because there is no work

In an efficient value stream process, the amount of buffer, blocking, and starving should be minimized. An example of buffer is the amount of time it takes to transport a patient to a room for an x-ray. Blocking is when all the rooms in emergency departments are filled and there are no extra rooms for new patients. Starving is when an x-ray technician is idle and not receiving any requests.

When analyzing these three value stream impediments, common patterns of behavior begin to show where waste originates. A few of the top wasteful behaviors include[50]

- Inadequate communication methods
- Duplicate documentation requirements

---

* Pearson Education. 2007. Process Analysis and Flowcharting PPT. http://slideplayer.com/slide/5220108/.
[†] Ibid.
[‡] Ibid.

- Poor patient flow
- Inappropriate hospital admissions and lengths of stay
- Incomplete medication reconciliation

These impediments have profound effects on critical transition points and in making decisions for patient care. One hospital study noted the following outcomes because of inadequate communication methods in their patient care value streams.[51]

- Patient admission[51]: Admitting one patient takes about 51 minutes, of which an average of 33 minutes (65%) is wasted due to inefficient communications. This translates into an annual loss of about $728,000 per U.S. hospital.
- Emergency response coordination[51]: Coordinating an emergency response team takes an average of 93 minutes per patient. Of this time, an average of 40 minutes (43%) is wasted due to inefficient communications. This equates to an annual loss of more than $265,000 per U.S. hospital.
- Patient transfer[51]: Transferring a patient to another facility or home care/hospice takes an average of about 56 minutes, of which an average of 35 minutes (63%) is wasted due to inefficient communications. The total annual cost of this waste is about $754,000 per U.S. hospital.

When this same study surveyed clinicians, physicians, and the business and administrative staff, the following estimates were cited regarding wasted time in value stream activities (survey responses)[51]:

Conducting patient care = 46%

Average time wasted = 34.6 minutes

Documentation = 19%

Average time wasted = 18.8 minutes

Communicating and consulting with colleagues = 23%

Average time wasted = 24.3 minutes

Prescribing and administering medications = 8%

Average time wasted = 12.9 minutes

With the right performance metrics identified, hospitals can begin to improve value stream efficiency.

Measuring Process Improvement Outcomes

When making changes and reengineering the patient care value streams, hospitals should attempt to perform as many activities in parallel as possible, change the sequence of activities, and reduce interruptions.*

There are seven key principles recommended by Pearson Education[†]:

1. The focus is on balancing flow, not on balancing capacity.
2. Maximizing output and efficiency of every resource will not maximize the throughput of the entire system.
3. An hour lost at a bottleneck or constrained resource is an hour lost for the whole system. An hour saved at a non-constrained resource does not necessarily make the whole system more productive.
4. Inventory is needed only in front of the bottlenecks to prevent them from sitting idle, and in front of assembly and shipping points to protect customer schedules. Building inventories elsewhere should be avoided.

---

* Pearson Education (2007).
† Ibid.

5. Work should be released into the system only as frequently as the bottlenecks need it. Bottleneck flows should be equal to the market demand. Pacing everything to the slowest resource minimizes inventory and operating expenses.
6. Activation of non-bottleneck resources cannot increase throughput, or promote better performance on financial measures.
7. Every capital investment must be viewed from the perspective of its global impact on overall throughput (T), inventory (I), and operating expense (OE).

In the example of Consultation Management in Physical Therapy, several process improvement outcome-oriented metrics were recommended with a special focus on "unnecessary processing time." For example, "unnecessary steps to complete high value clinical activities" or "time required to complete a consultation request."

Clinician Satisfaction

The healthcare industry is increasingly complex with new legislation, constantly changing technology and equipment, new treatments, and a wide variety of people who care for each patient.

In this environment, many different factors have been identified as the key for improving quality and lowering costs. However, one of the most significant impacts on the healthcare industry is a result of the people who work in this industry.[52]

Among the many changes occurring in the new healthcare environment, the biggest change is the shift to value-based purchasing, which ties a system's Medicare and Medicaid reimbursements to the quality of the services it provides. For many systems, this direction will improve clinical processes and ensure a high-quality patient experience, which is an outcome dependent on the commitment, dedication, and skills of a healthcare organization's employees. In fact, with a potential

2% loss in reimbursements for hospitals that cannot meet specific patient satisfaction and quality of care outcomes, the link between employee actions, patient experiences, and financial results will be very apparent.[53]

Moreover, employee satisfaction directly affects retention. With healthcare reform creating more demand for services, the competition for talent will only get more competitive.*

In other industries, this service–profit chain (first articulated in a classic 1994 *Harvard Business Review* article[54] and recently updated) has been recognized for decades. As Towers Watson's research with clients shows,†when hospitals create an engaging and high performance-oriented work experience, they not only improve patient satisfaction, but also clinical and financial outcomes. Healthcare is still a people-intensive business, and improving patient satisfaction scores requires an investment in employee engagement.[55]

In a 2005 Gallup study of 200 hospitals,[56] researchers found that the engagement level of nurses was the primary variable correlating to mortality, even more significant than the number of nurses per patient day.

In another review of engagement and clinical outcomes, the NHS in the United Kingdom showed that for every 10% increase in engagement, there was a reduction in methicillin-resistant staphylococcus aureus by .057 cases per 10,000 bed days and one standard deviation improvement in engagement-reduced mortality by 2.4% points.[57] The same study showed a strong correlation between engagement and reducing staff turnover and absenteeism.

Therefore, healthcare employees' engagement improves patient satisfaction and clinical outcomes, while reducing hospital-acquired conditions and staff turnover[57] (Figure 7.3).

---

* 2012 Global Workforce Study. Engagement at risk: Driving strong performance in a volatile global environment.

† http://www.employmentlawdaily.com/index.php/news/towers-watson-research-shows-health-and-wellbeing-programs-miss-productivity-connection/. Accessed November 20, 2016.

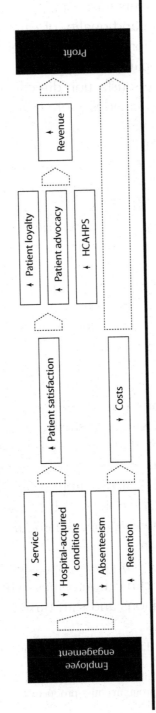

Figure 7.3 Employee engagement improves profit.[58]

Table 7.5 Reported Relationships and Outcomes from Clinician Satisfaction

Effects of Higher Employee Engagement Levels on	*Effects of Higher Employee Engagement/ Satisfaction on*	*Effects of Higher Employee Engagement/ Satisfaction on*
Employees	**Patients**	**Financial Performance**
• Improved employee productivity	• Improved care quality	• Lower employee recruitment, retention, and training costs
• Improved relationship with management	• Increased patient satisfaction	• Higher patient loyalty to the organization
• Reduced job stress	• Increased patient loyalty	• Potential lower costs related to the delivery of patient care (reduced length of stay)
• Increased employee satisfaction		
• Increased retention		

Table 7.5 presents the overall findings from previous studies about the relationships between employees, patients, and the financial performance of the organization.[57]

> Without employee engagement, you're never going to get the kind of ultimate patient experience you're hoping for.

Mike Packnett
CEO, Parkview Health

Measuring employee engagement in healthcare is vitally important, as happy employees tend to provide better care to patients.

Determinants of Employee Satisfaction and Engagement

In Towers Watson's most recent global workforce study,[59] less than half (44%) of the overall U.S. hospital workforce was highly engaged. A large proportion of employees across all workforce segments reportedly felt somewhat disconnected from their hospital system and its goals, and unsupported to some extent in doing their jobs well. The study also shows a strong relationship between employees' level of engagement and their likelihood to remain with their employer, with just 17% of the highly engaged hospital workers interested in other employment options versus 43% of the disengaged group. Improving engagement, therefore, carries another important advantage for the many hospitals already competing to find and keep a dwindling supply of people with critical skills, especially in clinical areas.

Based on the analysis of over 10 million healthcare workers in 150 countries, the top 3 drivers of engagement are[59]

■ Growth: People feel like they are advancing and learning new things
■ Recognition: People feel appreciated
■ Trust: People trust the organization has a bright future

In healthcare employee engagement, based on the survey study that included 717 senior-level healthcare professionals, the following results were found[59]:

■ More than 60% of employees are satisfied with the training they get from their organization
■ More than 70% are satisfied with the level of interaction they have with patients
■ But only 45% say senior management staff are good communicators

Measuring Employee Satisfaction

More than half of healthcare providers measure employee satisfaction as part of their effort to offer superior care.* Employee engagement surveys measure how passionate healthcare professionals are about the work they are doing. They also make it easier to identify changes that will help doctors and staff do an even better job. As an example, Gallup has a measurement called the Q12 to measure engagement, which includes the following questions[60]:

- I know what is expected of me at work.
- At work, my opinions seem to count.
- I have the materials and equipment I need to do my work right.
- The mission or purpose of my company makes me feel my job is important.
- At work, I have the opportunity to do what I do best every day.
- My associates or fellow employees are committed to doing quality work.
- In the last 7 days, I have received recognition or praise for doing good work.
- I have a best friend at work.
- My supervisor, or someone at work, seems to care about me as a person.
- In the last 6 months, someone at work has talked to me about my progress.
- There is someone at work who encourages my development.
- This last year, I have had opportunities at work to learn and grow.

---

* Healthcare Employee Engagement Surveys. Available at: www.surveymonkey. com/mp/healthcare-employee-engagement-survey/.

Healthcare Users Satisfaction with Health Information Technologies

Several survey studies have been performed in recent years to measure and monitor clinician satisfaction and reflect individual evaluation concepts such as efficiency or benefits regarding health information technologies (HIT) with a special focus in EHR systems.[61]

For example, a survey of 6536 physicians in 7 countries found that adoption of health information technology (IT) is highly variable, with the United States lagging well behind other countries. Physicians with greater IT capability were more likely to report feeling well prepared to manage patients with chronic diseases, among other benefits.[62]

One framework that has emerged for the evaluation of clinician satisfaction is the Health Information Technology Reference-based Evaluation Framework (HITREF). HITREF's use in a range of HIT evaluations by researchers new to the HITREF demonstrates that it can be used as intended. HITREF can be used as a comprehensive, research-based HIT evaluation framework to increase the capacity of informatics evaluators' use of best practice and evidence-based practice to support the credibility of their findings for fulfilling the purpose of HIT program evaluations.[63]

Several clinician satisfaction metrics were recommended earlier in the example about Consultation Management in Physical Therapy: improve clinician satisfaction regarding clinical satisfaction with the EHR support workflow, or clinical satisfaction with the EHR provision of care.

Learning and Growth

The rate of transformation currently affecting the healthcare landscape will continue to accelerate as public and private sector stakeholders introduce and implement improved strategies, processes, technologies, and organizational models. Learning and growth outcomes relate to developing and adopting a knowledge-based culture of medical best practices that continuously improves enterprise operations and performance. For stakeholders in the healthcare ecosystem, the learning and growth objectives include developing internal or understanding external strategies, planning the transformation, driving the change toward a value-oriented organization, and fueling continuous improvement.

In healthcare organizations, this translates into developing content that enhances current operations and performance, while also ensuring that the developed content is adopted and applied by stakeholders. When developing content, healthcare organizations must be mindful of the initial users so that the content can be tailored to them.

The adoption curve proposed by Everett Rodgers illustrates that innovations are accepted initially by a group of stakeholders known as "innovators." Adoption of innovations can then increase gradually over time as additional stakeholders become aware of the innovations and understand their applicability and value. The role of healthcare organizations and their respective Value Management Offices is to complete activities that prompt the release of new innovations and facilitate the adoption of those innovations (Figure 7.4).

Determinants of Learning and Growth

Robert S. Kaplan and David P. Norton, pioneers in organizational transformation and creators of the Balanced Scorecard, suggest that the role of learning and growth effort in organizations is to answer the following question:

> *"To achieve our vision, how will we sustain our ability to change and improve?"*[64]

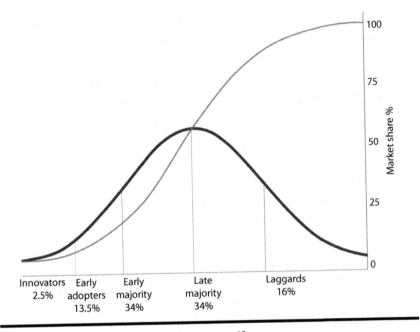

Figure 7.4   Innovation adoption curve.[65]

To aid organizations in answering this question, Kaplan and Norton developed the Managing Strategy Framework,[64] which outlines key tasks that directly connect with learning and growth objectives that healthcare organizations are tackling (Figure 7.5).

Measuring Learning and Growth

Stakeholders in the healthcare ecosystem can achieve their learning and growth objectives by understanding the activities in the Kaplan and Norton model, translating what those activities mean for their respective organizations, and measuring the effectiveness of their learning and growth efforts.

Table 7.6 provides information on how healthcare organizations can approach learning and growth objectives and how they can evaluate their success in the rollout and adoption of value-based policies, technologies, and processes.

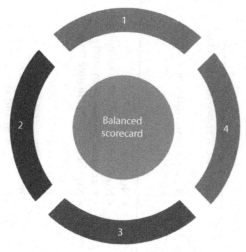

1. Translating the vision
   - Clarifying the vision
   - Gaining consensus

2. Communicating and linking
   - Communicating and educating
   - Setting goals
   - Linking rewards to performance measures

3. Business planning
   - Setting targets
   - Aligning strategic initiatives
   - Allocating resources
   - Establishing milestones

4. Feedback and learning
   - Setting targets
   - Aligning strategic initiatives
   - Allocating resources
   - Establishing milestones

Figure 7.5   Kaplan and Norton Managing Strategy Framework.

The example of the Value Realization Framework application for Consultation Management in Chapter 5 of this book was mostly focused on "feedback and learning" for the process improvement outcome perspective. Some of the indicators that were suggested are: "provider adoption of new consultation management technology" or "number of training courses planned vs. conducted (by location)."

Summary of Key Points to Remember

The learning outcomes from this chapter that are important to remember include the following points:

- Why is it important to measure all of the six perspectives of healthcare?
  The Value Realization Framework provides organizations with an approach toward defining its core foundation in a measurable way. In order to do so effectively, the HDO

Table 7.6 Learning and Growth Objectives

Step	Activities	Goal	Potential Metrics
Translating the vision	• Clarifying the vision • Gaining consensus	• Survey management determine comprehension of value-based strategy • Measure consensus through submission of operational plans	• Strategy comprehension scores—management • Number of submitted operational plans
Communicating and linking	• Communicating and educating • Setting goals • Linking rewards to performance measures	• Monitor distribution of strategy communications to staff • Ensure strategy comprehension at staff level	• Number of communications distributed • Strategy comprehension scores—staff
Business planning	• Setting targets • Aligning strategic initiatives • Allocating resources • Establishing milestones	• Ensure operational plans are aligned with value-based strategy • Operational plans identify critical milestones and resources	• Number of approved operational plans • Number of performance targets set
Feedback and learning	• Articulating the shared vision • Supplying strategic feedback • Facilitating strategy review and learning	• Share how operational achievement contribute shift toward value-management approach • Facilitate upstream communications to remove operational hurdles and drive continuous improvement	• Number of trainings • Number of milestones completed • Percent of adoption by users • Number of performance targets achieved • Number of feedback communications from management and staff • Management and staff satisfaction scores

must not solely focus its outcomes on clinical at the expense of process or patient satisfaction. Each perspective is intertwined with the other and can either positively or negatively impact a desired outcome. For example, if a new EHR feature is implemented to correct previous process defects and is providing accuracy, availability, and efficiency within specified thresholds, there should be a corollary increase in employee satisfaction, return on investment, and improvement in quality of care due to clinicians having more time to spend with their patients. The result is that for every action, there can be a reaction in other perspectives.

■ What are the six focus areas of healthcare?
The six focus areas of healthcare are also consistent with the definition of quality of healthcare by the World Health Organization:

- *Safety: Avoiding injuries to patients from the care that is intended to help them*
- *Effective: Providing services based on scientific knowledge to all who can benefit and refraining from providing services to those not likely to benefit (avoiding underuse and overuse)*
- *Patient-centered: Providing care that is respectful of and responsive to individual patient preferences, needs, and values while ensuring that patient values guide all clinical decisions*
- *Timely: Reducing waits and delays for both those who receive and those who give care*
- *Efficient: Avoiding waste, in particular, waste of equipment, supplies, ideas, and energy*
- *Equitable: Providing care that does not vary in quality because of personal characteristics, such as gender, ethnicity, geographic location, and socioeconomic status*

■ How does an organization measure clinical outcomes?
Organizations must first follow a process in defining an outcome and reach agreement on standards. The following steps are provided to help define critical success

factors, KRIs, and KPIs, as described earlier. The main three principles of measuring clinical outcomes that must be remembered include the following:

- *Outcomes should be measured by the patient's medical condition or primary care patient segment, and not by procedure or intervention.*
- *The outcome should reflect the full cycle of care for the patient's condition.*
- *Outcomes are multidimensional and should include the health results most relevant to the patient.*[66]

■ What if an organization does not measure patient and employee satisfaction?

Both providers and patients view the same episode of care through their own subjective lenses. Satisfaction with overall treatment is an essential outcome to measure. Poor patient satisfaction can reflect poor quality of care or treatment contrary to a patient's desired outcome. Poor employee satisfaction adversely affects HDOs' recruiting, retraining, and retaining of skilled providers. To not "keep the finger on the pulse" of both patient and employee satisfaction scores will likely cause problems for the HDO, for example, the potential 2% loss in CMS reimbursements for hospitals that cannot meet specific patient satisfaction and quality of care outcomes will show the direct link between employee actions, patient experiences, and financial results.[67]

References

1. Porter, M. E. 2010. Measuring health outcomes: The outcome hierarchy. *N Engl J Med*. 363:2477–2481. Appendix 2.
2. Porter. (2010)
3. Porter (2010).
4. Porter, M. E. and Lee, T. H. MD., 2013. The strategy that will fix health care. *Harvard Business Review*. Available at: https://hbr.org/2013/10/the-strategy-that-will-fix-health-care. Accessed October 12, 2016.

5. Cappelleri, J. C. and Spielberg, S. P. 2015. Advances in clinical outcome assessments. *Ther Innov Regul Sci.* 49(6):780–782.
6. Porter, M. E. 2014. Outcome measurement. Harvard Business School. Available at: www.isc.hbs.edu. Accessed October 14, 2016.
7. Miyagi, M. 2008. 10 key metrics as components to measuring financial health. The Camden Group. Available at: www.the-camdengroup.com/top10/08%20March%20(Miyagi).pdf.
8. Needleman, J. https://archive.ahrq.gov/data/safetynet/needleman.htm. Accessed November 15, 2016.
9. Miyagi (2008).
10. Porter and Lee (2013).
11. Kaplan, R. S. and Porter M. E.. 2011. The big idea: How to solve the cost crisis in health care. Available at: https://hbr.org/2011/09/how-to-solve-the-cost-crisis-in-health-care. Accessed October 12, 2016.
12. Novak, P. and Popesko, B. Application of AMB in hospital management. *Researches in Economics and Management Transformation.*
13. Udpa, S. 1996. Activity-based costing for hospitals. *Health Care Manage Rev.* 21(3):83.
14. Anderson, S. R. and Kaplan, R. S. 2004. Time-driven activity-based costing. *Harvard Business Review.* Available at: https://hbr.org/2004/11/time-driven-activity-based-costing. Accessed October 14, 2016.
15. Udpa (1996).
16. Kaplan and Porter (2011).
17. Demeere, N., Stouthuysen, K. and Roodhooft, F. 2009. Time-driven activity-based costing in an outpatient clinic environment: Development, relevance and managerial impact. *Health Policy.* 92(2–3):296–304.
18. Kaplan and Anderson (2004).
19. Porter, M. E. 2009. A strategy for health care reform: Toward a value-based system. *N Engl J Med.* 361(2):109–112.
20. Berger, S. 2008. Best practice in hospital key financial indicators: Setting and achieving goals. Healthcare insights. https://www.researchgate.net/file.PostFileLoader.html?id=55c958406225ff62bc8b45cf&assetKey=AS%3A273829203513344%401442297377219.
21. Miliard, M. Jan. 2015 HHS plans big Medicare reimbursement changes. Healthcare IT News.

22. Llewellyn, R. and Moore, K. August 2014. Best practice concepts in revenue cycle management. National Rural Health Resource Center.

23. Llewellyn and Moore (2014).

24. Prakash, B. 2010. Patient satisfaction. *J Cutan Aesthet Surg.* 3(3): 151.

25. Bjertnaes, O. A., Sjetne, I. S., and Iversen, H. H. 2011. Overall patient satisfaction with hospitals: Effects of patient-reported experiences and fulfillment of expectations. *BMJ Qual Saf.* Available at: http://qualitysafety.bmj.com.

26. Ahmad, I., Nawaz, A., Khan S., Khan, H., Rashid, M. A., and Khan, M. H. 2011. Predictors of patient satisfaction. *Gomal Journal of Medical Sciences.* 9(2).

27. Castle, N. G., Brown J., Hepner, K. A., and Hays, R. D. 2005. Review of literature on survey instruments used to collect data on hospital patients' perceptions of care. *Health Services Research.* 40(6 Pt 2).

28. Cheng S., Yang M., and Chiang T. 2003. Patient satisfaction with and recommendation of a hospital: Effects of interpersonal and technical aspects of hospital care. *Int J Qual Health Care.* 15(4): 345–355.

29. Boyer, L., Francois, P., Doutre, E., Weil, G., and Labarere, J. 2006. Perception and use of the results of patient satisfaction surveys by care providers in a French teaching hospital. *Int J Qual Health Care.* 18(5):359–364.

30. Clever, S. L., Jin, L., Levinson, W., and Meltzer, D. O. 2008. Does doctor-patient communication affect patient satisfaction with hospital care: Results of an analysis with a novel instrumental variable? *Health Science Research.* 43(5 Pt 1):1505–1519.

31. Rama, M. and Kanagaluru, S. K. 2011. A study on the satisfaction of patients with reference to hospital services. *International Journal of Business Economics and Management Research.* 1(3).

32. Schoenfelder, T., Klewer, J., and Kugler, J. 2011. Determinants of patient satisfaction: A study among 39 hospitals in an in-patient setting in Germany. *Int J Qual Health Care.* 23(5):503–509.

33. Rickert, J. 2014. Measuring patient satisfaction: A bridge between patient and physician perceptions of care. Health Affairs Blog. Available at: http://healthaffairs.org/

blog/2014/05/09/measuring-patient-satisfaction-a-bridge-between-patient-and-physician-perceptions-of-care/. Accessed November 1, 2016.

34. Daly, R. 2013. A satisfactory measure? Modern Healthcare. Available at: www.modernhealthcare.com/article/20130105/ MAGAZINE/301059942. Accessed November 5, 2016.

35. Rashid, A. and Amina, A. 2014. Patient satisfaction survey as a tool towards quality improvement. *Oman Medical Journal.* 29(1):3–7.

36. Agrawal, D. 2006. Health sector reforms: Relevance in India. *Indian J Community Med.* 31(4).

37. Jenkinson, C., Coulter, A., Bruster, S., Richards, N., and Chandola, T. 2002. Patients' experiences and satisfaction with health care: Results of a questionnaire study of specific aspects of care. *Qual Saf Health Care.* 11(4):335–339.

38. McKinley, R. K. and Roberts, C. 2001. Patient satisfaction with out of hours primary medical care. *Qual Health Care.* 10(1):23–28.

39. Rao, K. D., Peters, D. H., and Bandeen-Roche, K. 2006. Towards patient-centered health services in India: A scale to measure patient perceptions of quality. *Int J Qual Health Care.* 18(6):414–421.

40. Swayne, L. E., Duncan, W. J, and Ginter, P. M. 2008. *The Strategic Management of Health Care Organizations.* CA: Jossey-Bass.

41. Urden, L. D. 2002. Patient satisfaction measurement: Current issues and implications. *Outcomes Manag.* 6(3):125–131.

42. Quintana, J. M., Gonzalez, N., Bilbao, A., Aizpuru, F., Escobar, A., Esteban, C., San-Sebastian, J. A., et al. 2006. Predictors of patient satisfaction with hospital health care. *Health Services Research.* 6(102) [online]. Available at: www.biomedcentral. com/1472-6963/6/102.

43. Rashid and Amina (2014).

44. Dawn, A. G. and Lee, P. P. 2003. Patient satisfaction instruments used at academic medical centers: Results of a survey. *Am J Med Qual.* 18(6):265–269.

45. CMS.gov. 2014. HCAHPS: Patients' perspectives of care survey. Available at: https://www.cms.gov/Medicare/Quality-Initiatives-Patient-Assessment-Instruments/HospitalQualityInits/ HospitalHCAHPS.html.

46. CMS.gov. 2014. CAHPS clinician and group patient-centered medical home survey 2.0. Available at: www.cms.gov/Medicare/Quality-Initiatives-Patient-Assessment-instruments/HospitalQualityInits/HospitalHCAHPS.html.
47. PBS.org. 2012. Health costs: How the US compares with other countries. Available at: www.pbs.org/newshour/rundown/health-costs-how-the-us-compares-with-other-countries/.
48. McManus, H. 2012. Application of Lean to healthcare processes: A complex system perspective. Lean Advancement Educational Network. Available at: http://web.mit.edu/hmcmanus/Public/McManusTalkLeanHealthcare0312.pdf.
49. McManus (2012).
50. Henry, J. Feb 2015. 5 basic hospital inefficiencies and their quick fixes. HealthcareDive.
51. Ponemon Institute. June 2014. The Imprivata report on the economic impact of inefficient communications in healthcare. https://www.ponemon.org/.
52. Peltier, J. and Dahl, A. 2009. *The Relationship between Employee Satisfaction and Hospital Patient Experiences*. University of Wisconsin: Whitewater, Frank Mulhern, Northwestern University.
53. Sherwood, R. Employee engagement drives health care quality and financial returns. *Harvard Business Review*. Available at: https://hbr.org/2013/10/employee-engagement-drives-health-care-quality-and-financial-returns.
54. Heskett, J. L., Jones, T. O., Loveman, G. W., Sasser Jr. W. E., and Schlesinger, L. A. 2008. Putting the service-profit chain to work. *Harvard Business Review*. Available at: https://hbr.org/2008/07/putting-the-service-profit-chain-to-work.
55. Kruse, K. The ROI of employee engagement in hospitals. Available at: www.forbes.com/.
56. Blizzard, R. December 2005. Nurse engagement key to reducing medical errors. Available at: http://www.gallup.com/poll/20629/nurse-engagement-key-reducing-medical-errors.aspx.
57. West, M. and Dawson, J. 2012. Employee engagement and NHS performance. The King's Fund, 1–23.
58. Sherwood, R. 2013. Employee engagement drives health care quality and financial returns.
59. Global Workforce Study. 2012. Engagement at risk: Driving strong performance in a volatile global environment. Employee Engagement Drives Health Care Quality and Financial Returns.

Harvard Business Review's Leading Health Care Innovation Insight Center. November 8, 2013. United States by Rick Sherwood.

60. Hein, R. July 2014. Tips for measuring and improving employee engagement. Available at: www.cio.com/article/2459447/careers-staffing/tips-for-measuring-and-improving-employee-engagement.html.

61. Sockolow, P. S., Weiner, J. P., and Lehmann, H. P. 2011. A new instrument for measuring clinician satisfaction with electronic health records. *Comput Inform Nurs*. 29(10):574–585.

62. Davis, K., Doty, M. M., Shea, K., and Stremikis, K. 2009. Health information technology and physician perceptions of quality of care and satisfaction. *Health Policy*. 90(2): 239–246.

63. Sockolow, P. S, Bowles, K. H., and Rogers, M. 2015. Health information technology evaluation framework (HITREF) comprehensiveness as assessed in electronic point-of-care documentation systems evaluations. *Stud Health Technol Inform*. 216:406–409.

64. Kaplan, R. S. and Norton, D. P. 2007. Using the balanced scorecard as a strategic management system. *Harvard Business Review*. Available at: https://hbr.org/2007/07/using-the-balanced-scorecard-as-a-strategic-management-system. Accessed October 12, 2016.

65. Rogers, E. 2003. *Diffusion of Innovations (5th Edition)*. New York: Simon and Schuster.

66. Porter (2010).

67. Sherwood (2013).

Chapter 8

Common Operating Picture

Learning Objectives

After reading this chapter, the reader will be able to answer the following questions:

- Why is a Common Operating Picture (COP) important for an organization?
- What are the three dimensions of the COP?
- How can business analytics (BA) be used to better assist the hospital assign appointments when referring a patient to physical therapy to increase patient satisfaction and reduce wait times?
- Why analyze population health simulations? What would happen if other factors or variances of the variable were considered?

Getting Insight from Data

Health Delivery Organizations (HDOs) generate a vast amount of data; but the question is, how to use this data to produce valuable insight to enhance decision making. A new wave of data transformation into information such as "big data," "Internet of Things," "business intelligence," and "business analytics" has opened a new environment for many organizations to gain a competitive advantage. A *Harvard Business Review* article, "Why health care may finally be ready for big data,"[1] states that providers and payers are increasingly investing in their analytical capabilities to help them make better sense of the changing healthcare environment. In addition, according to Rock Health, growth in healthcare data from 500 petabytes in 2012 is expected to reach 25,000 petabytes in 2020.[2]

One of the biggest challenges for HDOs is the integration of healthcare analytical data across the organization. In the past, most analysis for decision making used information collected in a heterogeneous manner. Another factor to take into consideration is the lack of standardization in healthcare data, given that there are different formats of data from insurance claims, medical history, and images, to name just a few. In addition, healthcare industries are seeing an increase in the digitization of medical records and the use of wearable technologies, mobile devices, and the Internet of Things. These innovations are contributing to new intakes of data and innovations in technology. Added to the challenge is the ever-elusive "interoperability" and successful data exchange between disparate providers and different Electronic Health Record (EHR) vendors.

In December 2015, the Office of the National Coordinator listed five roadblocks to achieving interoperability, and emphasized the need to "develop and implement meaningful measures of health information exchange-sensitive health outcomes and resource use for public reporting and payment."[3]

Nevertheless, healthcare industries are just starting to get in the game of investing in new capabilities that will allow them to cross-reference information by using several variables such as medical history notes, patient family histories, surveys, and medications to gain meaningful insight to provide a better assessment of a patient's needs, improve overall patient care, transform business, and reduce costs.

The updated Federal Health IT Strategic Plan 2015–2020* is already working toward healthcare data integration and standardization as "The first two goals of this plan prioritize increasing the electronic collection and sharing of health information while protecting individual privacy. The final three goals focus on federal efforts to create an environment where interoperable information is used by healthcare providers, public health entities, researchers, and individuals to improve health, healthcare, and reduce costs."

To better meet the demands of this revolutionary healthcare era, it is important that HDOs are aligned with any technological initiatives that will assist in gathering the right data, have the right tools to capture the data, and are focused on the strategic objectives. For this reason, a COP for value management has been designed as a tool for collecting data, integrating data to analyze trends, and managing performance improvement for HDOs. This is accomplished by three complementary components—business scorecards, business intelligence (BI) analysis, and continuous feedback (Figure 8.1).

In Figure 8.1, the first component consists of the business scorecards that analyze three different categories: strategic outcomes, program operations, and interoperability and technical. These are three business dimensions that focus on analyzing each component separately. However, the real value is when the data from all three dimensions is integrated and the output, BI analysis, provides a new visual representation of critical

---

* Federal Health IT Strategic Plan 2015–2020. Available at: https://www.healthit.gov/sites/default/files/federal-healthIT-strategic-plan-2014.pdf.

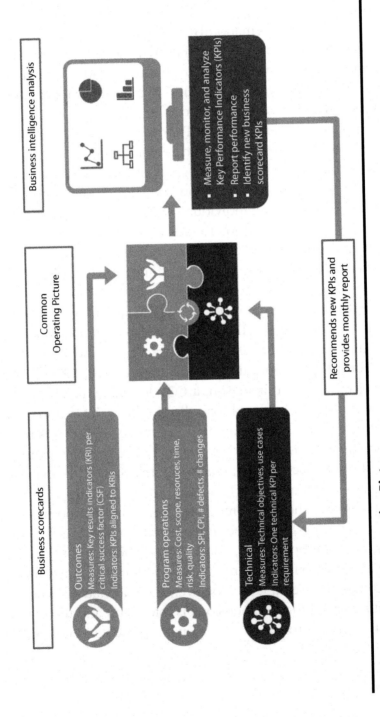

Figure 8.1 Common Operating Picture.

information. Using BI will help HDO leaders make more informed decisions and act to improve performance and deliver cost-efficient, quality care. As the performance management process matures, data and information can be filtered back into the business scorecards by providing them with new Key Performance Indicators (KPIs) and other relevant information.

In the next two sections, the reader will be introduced to the COP functionality and given an overview of BA in a healthcare environment.

How Does the Common Operating Picture (COP) Work?

Beginning with business scorecards, the use of this tool has evolved from views of organizational performance to now involve sophisticated process and results measures. The main objective of a traditional Balanced Scorecard is to provide valuable information by being able to view the organization from four perspectives (learning and growth, business process, customer, and financial), and to develop metrics, collect data, and analyze information.[4] The value management methodology has adapted the traditional goals to form six perspectives related to the healthcare environment and its three business dimensions.*

The COP takes into account three business dimensions:

- *Strategic outcomes* measures the Key Results Indicators (KRI) per Critical Success Factor (CSF) of each of the outcomes that are related to a healthcare organization's initiative.
- *Program operations interoperability* measures the cost, scope, resources, time, risk, and quality that allow one to understand how the overall projects are performing.

---

* The six perspectives for healthcare outcomes are clinical, financial, process improvement, employee satisfaction, patient satisfaction, and learning and growth.

■ *Technical* measures technical objectives and use cases that allow an understanding of how the systems are performing and the degree to which systems and devices can communicate (and exchange data); this dimension also interprets that shared data.

Each dimension carries out actions to improve its own KPIs, but each does not have the vision of other departments and does not know how it may affect performance or goals. This leads to the "transformation box" part of the COP where the data is transformed into meaningful and actionable information. This box is where several multivariants are put together to create what is known as BI (the last piece of the COP).

TechTarget* defines BI as "a technology-driven process for analyzing data and presenting actionable information to help corporate executives, business managers, and other end users make more informed business decisions. BI encompasses a variety of tools, applications, and methodologies that enable organizations to collect data from internal systems and external sources. The data is then prepared for analysis, queries, and reports. Dashboards and data visualizations make the analysis available for corporate decision support."

The following examples show how the COP can support BI managers/executives with information to make better decisions and how the COP can be used to create new KPIs for specific scorecards.

The first example shows how the COP can produce analysis maps. In this case, the COP provides several ways to characterize the projects within the program in terms of the alignment with the organization's strategic priorities; the value that the projects are providing to the organization; and the risk associated with the initiatives, their categorization, and their typologies (Figure 8.2).

---

* TechTarget. 2014. Business intelligence (BI). Available at: http://searchdatamanagement.techtarget.com/definition/business-intelligence.

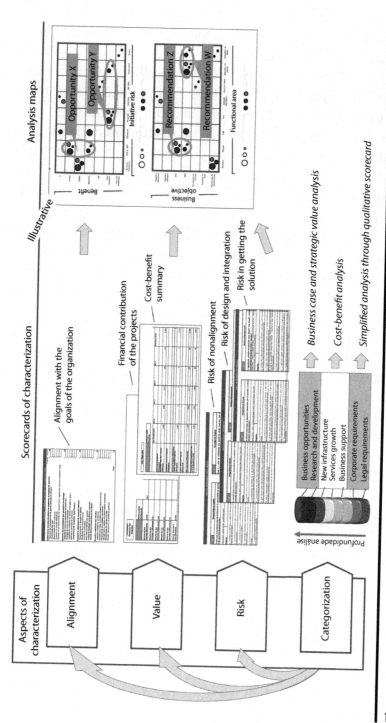

Figure 8.2 Characterization model.

To find correlations between different variables in the COP, analysis maps are used for decision support within the program and the organization.

Figure 8.3 shows a detailed outcome of four characterizations of different types of variables. Using different variables helps to explain the behavior and account for variance.

Another example uses correlation dashboards output. The left side of Figure 8.4 shows the correlation between the CSF and KRIs depicting past performance and a future trend. The right side shows the correlated performance of related technical KPIs.

The fourth example focuses on the combination of big data transactional technologies and predictive analysis. BI tools provide a comprehensive view of impacts related to business processes and information technology (IT) performance (business applications and infrastructure). Providing information on what happens to infrastructure and applications can show impacts on the organization's operations and business performance (Figure 8.5).

When applying big data transactional technologies, three levels of monitoring should be automated to collect from the systems to supply information to the COP.

- Level 1: Infrastructure
  - Objective: Analyze hardware status (for IT operations)
  - To measure: Thin clients, load balancers, network communications, physical and virtualized machines
  - Metrics: CPU usage, reserved memory, memory swapping, network latency, etc.
  - Needs: Analysis processes need to execute some operating system commands
- Level 2: Application
  - Objective: Analyze software status (for IT development)
  - To measure: Web applications, web services, application servers

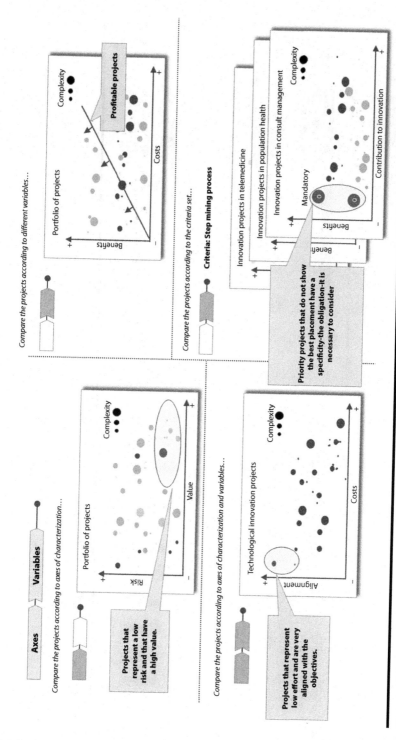

Figure 8.3 Analysis maps.

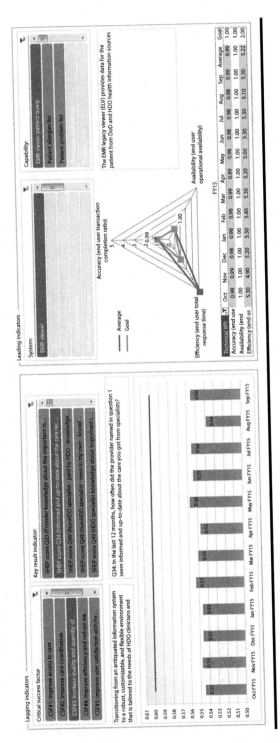

Figure 8.4 Correlation dashboards.

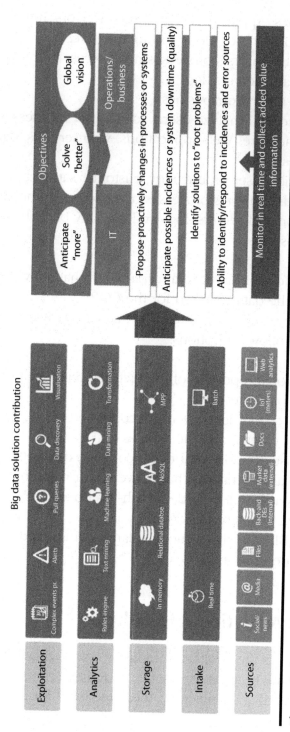

Figure 8.5 Transactional big data analytics.

- Metrics: Application errors, server errors, http sessions, response time, server throughput, etc.
- Needs: Analysis processes need access to the application and servers' logs
■ Level 3: Operation/business
- Objective: Analyze users' activity (for business areas)
- To measure: Web applications, web services, databases, etc.
- Metrics: User productivity, customer satisfaction, etc.
- Needs: Analysis processes need access to the application and servers' logs and possibly other business repositories

To conclude, BI has several capabilities that allow for cross-referencing the data required for the COP.

BI has several delivery methods that can be used. These include the following options:

■ Operational reporting of a structured template of how the data is presented.
■ Ad hoc reporting that can be controlled by the person (look, feel, etc.) and the queries.
■ Data visualizations that distill complex data sets into graphical illustrations that convey clear meaning.
■ Dashboards that provide a high-level overview of an organization and can drill down by report.
■ Other BI capabilities such as data mining, predictive analytics, desktop widgets, etc.

Business Analytics in Healthcare

So where does the healthcare industry stand with advanced BA? According to a case study by the Kelley School of Business at Indiana University, the stage is set for the application of advanced analytics given the high investments in healthcare IT implementation and a shift in focus from quantity of treatment to overall healthcare value.[5] So why is technology implementation investment so important? The answer is that having more data available allows an organization to cross-reference and analyze more information. However, with more available data for BI or BA, the data must be reliable, clean, and correctly extracted.

Understanding healthcare BA trends is important to enabling organizations make better decisions in a more scientific way. In short, applying mathematical models offers more predictive accuracy of future behaviors based on historical data.

Figure 8.6 shows how BA goes beyond BI and transforms data into information that explains what has happened or what will happen—and allows us to better understand why it has happened or estimate what will occur. In other words,

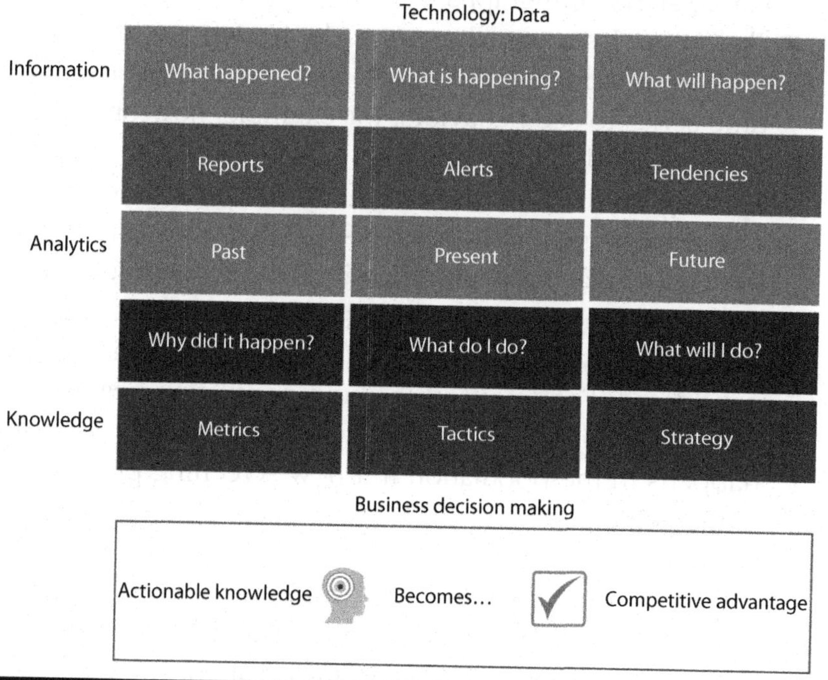

	Technology: Data		
Information	What happened?	What is happening?	What will happen?
	Reports	Alerts	Tendencies
Analytics	Past	Present	Future
	Why did it happen?	What do I do?	What will I do?
Knowledge	Metrics	Tactics	Strategy
	Business decision making		

Actionable knowledge 🧠 Becomes... ✓ Competitive advantage

Figure 8.6 Overview of business analytics.

analytics transforms data to provide knowledge and understanding of the business. This approach helps users see the root cause of the problem by being able to understand why it happened and estimate what will happen. This is an important aspect of the COP. For example, BI shows that 20 patients left their healthcare provider, whereas analytics comprehends who will leave and why according to their behaviors.

Coming back to the foundations, there are three categories of analytics that can be used: descriptive, predictive, and prescriptive.

- *Descriptive*: Involves gathering, organizing, tabulating, depicting, and then describing the characteristics of current or historical data. This category explains what happened in the past but not why or what will change. This can be seen through outputs such as dashboards, scorecards, alerts, and graphs.
- *Predictive*: Uses past data to model future outcomes. It is about anticipating the information that can be used in time series to see behaviors, for example, how organizations respond to changing regulations.
- *Prescriptive*: Uses optimization and BA testing models to advise managers on how to best do their jobs. In simple terms, it is placing intelligence in the data to suggest a course of action by considering "What if analysis" simulations. What would happen if other factors or variables are considered? For an example about population health, a simulation might help provide an understanding of what happens in the population if a new screening process is implemented.

A key point to remember is that with any of these models carried out with BA, the healthcare organization will have greater decision support with more information. An ideal ecosystem of partners providing independent views of data from different sources can enhance the quality of BA. The more information that is typically introduced in the algorithms, the better BA can provide predictive proposals.

Many algorithms can be used. Figure 8.7 shows four of the most common statistical applications: association, segmentation, classification, and simulation.

To conclude, several models can be applied with every BA category. The most commonly used models involve text mining and data mining. Each model follows its own methodology. It should be kept in mind that one of the steps within the methodology is choosing the algorithms that have been previously presented.

For instance, for our "Consultation Management in Physical Therapy" example, the data-mining model will be applied—more specifically, the CRISP-DM (Cross-Industry Standard Process for Data Mining) standard[6] (Figure 8.8).

The next element involves the use of a data scientist specialized in the use of analytics models, managing data, analyzing data, and data interpretation. Davenport states that, "as a manager, it's more important to understand what you want the data to do for you than how to manipulate it."[7] For this reason, data scientists know how to use several models such as data mining, Bayesian statistics, optimization modeling, social network analysis, and agent-based simulation.

According to a Health Catalyst survey, healthcare analytics is the highest priority for IT investment in the healthcare industry.[8] Ultimately, understanding the business and the data transformed into information to obtain insights is the main idea. IT initiatives continue to be a hot topic for IT health vendors and governments. As previously cited from the Federal Health IT Strategic Plan 2015–2020, these initiatives revolve around upgrading systems or focusing on interoperability to help facilitate health information throughout the health ecosystem. These data sources come from HDOs' healthcare delivery systems such as EHRs, laboratory

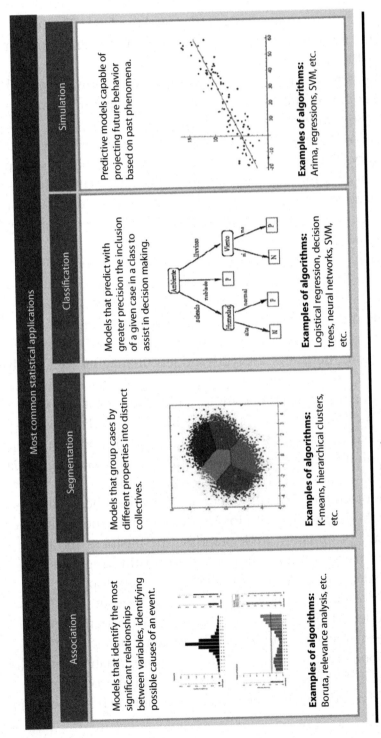

Figure 8.7   Most common statistical applications.

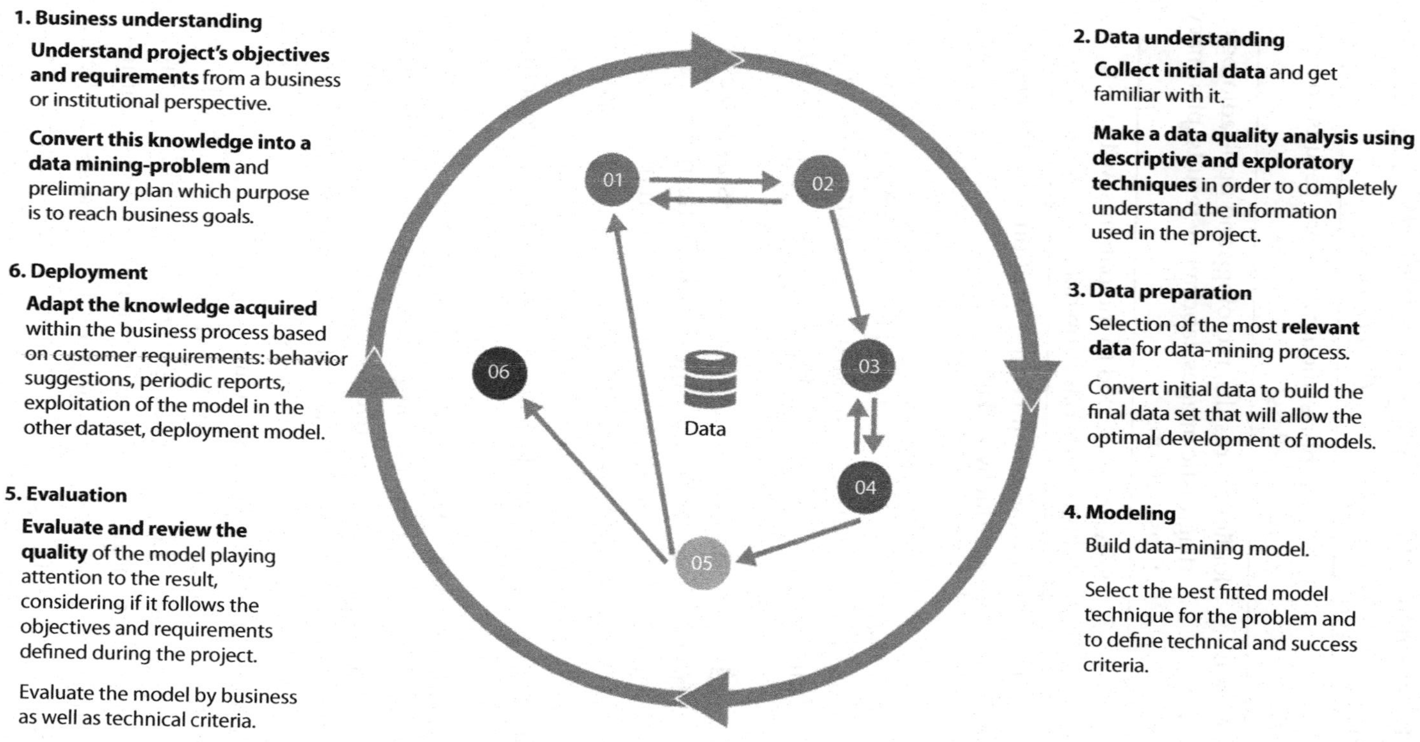

2. Data understanding

Collect initial data and get familiar with it.

Make a data quality analysis using descriptive and exploratory techniques in order to completely understand the information used in the project.

3. Data preparation

Selection of the most relevant **data** for data-mining process.

Convert initial data to build the final data set that will allow the optimal development of models.

4. Modeling

Build data-mining model.

Select the best fitted model technique for the problem and to define technical and success criteria.

1. Business understanding

Understand project's objectives and requirements from a business or institutional perspective.

Convert this knowledge into a data mining-problem and preliminary plan which purpose is to reach business goals.

6. Deployment

Adapt the knowledge acquired within the business process based on customer requirements: behavior suggestions, periodic reports, exploitation of the model in the other dataset, deployment model.

5. Evaluation

Evaluate and review the quality of the model playing attention to the result, considering if it follows the objectives and requirements defined during the project.

Evaluate the model by business as well as technical criteria.

Figure 8.8   CRISP-DM phases.

Table 8.1   Examples of Data Sources in Healthcare

Data Source	Data Generated
EHR	Clinical reports, medical history, results and medical orders
Departmental systems	Radiology results, radiology and non-radiology diagnostic images, laboratory results, pharmacy prescriptions
Billing/claims systems	Services provided to the patients, with cost, billing, and collection data
Operational systems	Human resources information, labor hours, productivity data

information management systems, diagnostic or monitoring instruments, insurance claims/billing records, pharmacy systems, human resources and supply chains, and real-time locating systems (Table 8.1).

Having this data is key to being able to cross-analyze variables; however, a challenge still exists in the non-standardization of data and in ensuring data quality. In any case, there is a growing awareness about the role of data quality in EHR-based analytics and the need to characterize the data's "fitness for use" before utilizing it for any ancillary purposes.[9]

As for healthcare analytics trends for 2016, many HDOs are using data to focus on facilitating value-based care, integrating clinical and claims data, improving patient care and outcomes through cross-referencing data analysis, using predictive analysis to improve outcomes, and leveraging new tools and skills to transform large amounts of data.

The trends suggest that the use of predictive analytics will be the focus. Most healthcare organizations could use predictive analytics in areas such as reducing patient readmissions, increasing the accuracy of patient diagnosis; preventive medicine and public health; delivering more targeted care to high-risk patients; providing employers and hospitals with predictions concerning insurance product costs; recognizing the needs of the public for medications; and providing better overall outcomes for the individuals they serve.

The following section will show how different advanced data analytics techniques can be used in healthcare to improve outcomes.

Use of Propensity Modeling to Improve Outcomes

There may be several approaches to treating a specific health condition, with each approach having an expected outcome. However, which approach will result in the desired outcome for a given patient? In healthcare, propensity modeling can be used to identify best practices to treat specific patient conditions. Propensity modeling is based on a specific approach or model, and can be used to predict patient behavior, organize preventative care and treatment plans, and determine desired outcomes. It can also be applied to predict Time Activity-Based Costing and revenue.

Propensity modeling is defined as the ability to predict a specific behavior, disposition, or outcome. In the insurance industry, propensity modeling has been used to look for the likelihood of fraud, but in healthcare, the concern is for people that have a propensity for disease or a certain health condition. Both models are similar in design, but vastly different in desired outcomes. Utilizing a value management approach and a customized analytics suite, HDOs can predict patient behavior and outcomes with a high degree of probability. Through this value approach, a provider can select specific areas of the population to assist in the prevention of specific illnesses or conditions. HDOs can also leverage data to manage various payment models, increase their revenue, and improve their brand. Propensity modeling provides three important value propositions:

1. They predict which providers' patients will choose their care, based on outcomes.
2. They enhance preventative care by providing actionable data to clinicians to deliver quality care.
3. They forecast return on investment and value outcomes from reimbursement.

The four commonly accepted propensity models are demographic segmentation, clustering, regression analysis, and artificial neural nets.[10] Each has its own benefits and associated cost for collection, storage, and analysis. However, through standardization, an organization can gain a competitive advantage in healthcare delivery. The main part of a propensity model is a linear equation that consists of three components:

1. Dependent variables: The unknown behavior that the organization wants to predict
2. Independent variables: The variables used to predict the unknown behavior
3. Parameters: The numeric values that act as weights on the independent variables

Demographic Segmentation

Demographic segmentation refers to the core demographics used by many traditional marketing organizations and divides a broad target market into subsets of customers that may have similar needs. This segmentation analysis helps companies design their marketing strategies. Examples of data used in the model include gender, marital status, age, address, number of adults in a household, number of children in a household, home owner/renter code, and language.

Cluster Analysis

Cluster analysis divides data into groups so that in some way the group is similar (called clusters). This is the main task of data mining and the model is usually comprised of multisourced data from internal and external sources. Examples of the types of data used include demographic (age, income, homeownership, marital status, number of adults, number of children, language), geographic (urban/rural population density, health geo scores, summarized credit data), psychographic (lifestyles, consumption, activities, hobbies, politics, brand and product usage), media usage (listen/read/watch/web), and health (health propensities, health attitudes, CDC data, pharmaceutical propensities, health metrics [CMS]).

Regression Analysis

Regression analysis is a statistical modeling technique that involves modeling and analyzing several variables to predict an outcome. The model focuses on the relationship between a dependent variable and one or more independent variables. As an example, all non-smoking, left-handed, white male architects who have a diet rich in organic foods, and who live in a cul-de-sac in an urban neighborhood, have a lower risk of heart disease. The challenge that comes with regression analysis is understanding if one or two of the variables in the sample (e.g., left-handedness or living in a cul-de-sac) really affects heart disease. In other words, if one or two of these independent variables were removed, would the outcome change?

Artificial Neural Nets

Artificial Neural Nets (ANNs) are a family of models that depend on many inputs, and are used for pattern recognition to estimate or predict outcomes. Most ANNs contain some sort of "learning rule," which adjusts the weights of the connections based on the input patterns it is presented with. ANNs learn from observed data to predict a future event based on statistical links among known data. ANNs are commonly used for healthcare propensity modeling to construct patient behavior models that can predict who will require a specific service or procedure. If an ANN propensity model is properly configured, it can also assist HDOs in predicting patient outcomes and costs with a high degree of accuracy.

Combining the strengths of each, the four propensity models can provide HDOs with the capability to deliver high performing value-based care, gain market share, and increase return on investment. The use of propensity modeling tools can yield three distinct benefits:

1. Prioritization of billing based on patient's and insurer's propensity scores
2. Determination of propensity to treat
3. Determination of propensity to improve patient health

Propensity Score

The propensity score is the conditional probability of each patient receiving a specific treatment based on pre-treatment treatment variables. The propensity score can be used to predict desired health outcomes, that is, the propensity to improve patient health. Strategically, organizations can leverage the information to identify areas of improvement, create a recruiting model to identify propensity to deliver value, retrain key employees, and retain high performing individuals with proven records of delivering value-based outcomes.

There are several national care standard databases and "authoritative" data sources available. Understanding the benefits of each can be time-consuming and problematic. With the vast amount of data available and the various standards, understanding which database to use can be complex. It is best to first define the problem and answer the question prior to selection, "What does success look like?" In other words, choose the right tool for the job at the start.

Using Analytics with Referrals for Patients Who Need Physical Therapy

In this section, the BA techniques will be applied to the Consultation Management for Physical Therapy use case.

Before presenting the BA case, it is necessary to decide which COP output variable is to be used. Figure 8.9 illustrates an example of a visual multivariate graphical output of BI that takes into account three outcomes (process improvement, patient satisfaction, and employee satisfaction), interoperability and technical, and program operations.

For the BA case, let's focus on the variable "wait time" for employee satisfaction, given that it has decreased. There is a strong and inverse relationship between patient satisfaction and wait times in primary care and specialty care physician offices.[11] Therefore, a hypothetical BA use case has been defined in order to demonstrate how advanced analytics can understand "why it has happened" in this scenario. The question to answer in this case is "How can BA be used to better assist the hospital to assign appointments when referring a patient to physical therapy in order to increase patient satisfaction and improve wait times."

In order to set up any BA use case, it is important to have an overview of all the applicable aspects necessary to build the BA scenario, visualize the output that we want to achieve, and choose a high-level methodology, which will need to be implemented later. Figure 8.10 depicts a sample use case template that includes a brief description, benefits, impact on an organization, skills and tools required to carry out this case, KPIs, datasets, and data processing requirements. In addition,

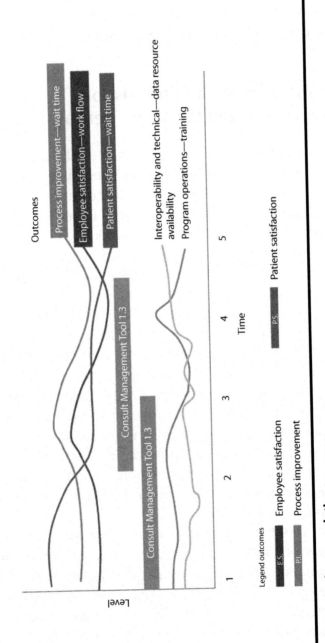

Figure 8.9 Business analytics use case.

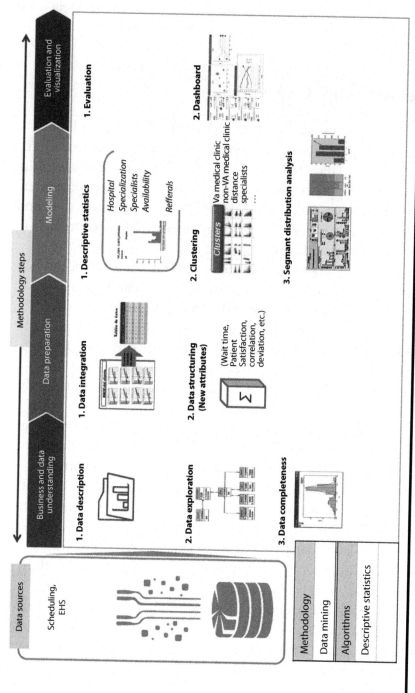

Figure 8.10 Methodology overview.

a visual representation has been included to understand the output as well as a high-level methodology of the models used to carry out this case.

Methodology Overview

As mentioned previously, different methodologies and their corresponding activities depend on the model that is used. In this case, as data will be collected from systems, a data-mining approach is applied. The following methodology incorporates all of the phases of CRISP-DM but has been adjusted to keep it high level, and other activities may need to be incorporated if this business case is implemented.

In the first phase, the business and data understanding is geared to understand business drivers/scorecards, consider business issues and gaps (constraints), perform a process assessment (to assure that data is collected correctly), and identify data availability (verify source). For this case, from the business aspect, the issue is that the FA clinic that corresponds to the patient is not available due to the unavailability of the specialist and because the physical therapy unit is not receiving images. Therefore, the patient must be referred to a non-FA care provider. The patient goes to the clinic, there are problems with the scheduling, and the whole check-in process is inefficient. This entire experience leads to low patient satisfaction, an increase in costs, and longer wait times. When carrying out the data collection, it will be important to analyze several variables such as staffing capacity, physical therapist skills, and number of appointments at a location, which the system may or may not provide.

The second phase, data preparation, is the actual readying of the data that is going to be used. The activities that need to be accomplished include data cleansing, descriptive analysis, and data structuring.

The third phase, modeling, is where one will select the best technique, whether it be linear regression, multivariate regression, self-organized maps, logistic regression, text mining, neural intelligence, or cluster analysis. For this case, descriptive statistics, cluster analysis, and efficient segment distribution analysis have been chosen. These models will help with the grouping of cases with similar/distinct properties in a homogeneous/heterogeneous group, and all will identify the most significant relationship between variables.

The last phase is the evaluation of the main variable (wait time) and the other variables to ensure that the data is consistent (Figure 8.10).

Output

The last phase of the methodology, output, is where there are multiple ways to view the outcome of the models used.

The clinician can then use this visual dashboard to make informed decisions based on several aspects, such as how wait time relates to number of patients and time, the historical availability of staff, and historical referrals. Figure 8.11 is an illustrative example of this visual dashboard.

Summary of Key Points to Remember

The learning outcomes from this chapter that are important to remember include the following points:

■ Why is a COP important for an organization?
  The value of a COP is realized when the data from all three dimensions (clinical, program, and technical) is integrated and BI is performed to enable HDO leaders to make informed decisions related to delivering cost-efficient, quality care outcomes for patients.

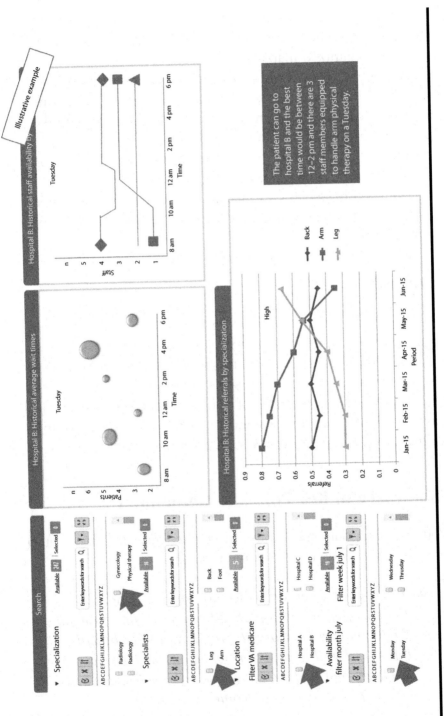

Figure 8.11 Output for physical therapy.

■ What are the three dimensions of the COP?
The three dimensions are clinical, program, and technical. Each dimension is essential and can carry out actions to improve its own KPIs. However, if not integrated into a COP, they do not have the visibility of other departments and how they may be affecting their performance or goals.

■ How can BA better assist hospitals to assign appointments when referring a patient to physical therapy in order to increase patient satisfaction and improve wait times?
Analytics transforms data to provide knowledge/understanding of the organization to help users see the root cause of the problem by being able to understand why it happened and calculate what will happen. This sort of propensity modeling is also essential in predicting patient outcomes and in determining appropriate treatment for the specific individual.

■ Why analyze population health simulations? What would happen if other factors or variances of the variable were considered?
If analyzing population health, one may want to understand (by using a simulation) what happens in the population if a new screening process is implemented.

References

1. Nilay, D. S. and Jyotishman, P. 2014. Why health care may finally be ready for big data. *Harvard Business Review.* Available at: https://hbr.org/2014/12/why-health-care-may-finally-be-ready-for-big-data.
2. Ghandi, M. and Wang, T. 2017. The future of personalized healthcare: Predictive analytics. RockHealth. Available at: https://rockhealth.com/reports/predictive-analytics/.
3. Davis, J. ONC cites security incentive woes among 5 biggest interoperability roadblocks. HealthITNews. Available at: www.healthcareitnews.com/news/onc-cites-security-incentive-woes-among-5-biggest-interoperability-roadblocks.

4. Kaplan, R. S. and Norton, D. P. 1996. *The Balanced Scorecard: Translating Strategy into Action.* Boston: Harvard Business School Press.
5. Ward, M. J., Marsolo, K. A., and Froehle, C. M. 2014. Applications of business analytics in healthcare. *Bus Horiz.* 57(5):571–582.
6. Wirth, R. and Hipp, J. 2000. CRISP-DM: Towards a standard process model for data mining. http://citeseerx.ist.psu.edu/viewdoc/download?doi=10.1.1.198.5133&rep=rep1&type=pdf.
7. Davenport, T. H. Business analytics defined. *Harvard Business Review.* Available at: https://hbr.org/video/2386816175001/business-analytics-defined.
8. Ghosh, R. 2015. What to expect in 2015. Four predictions for the healthcare analytics industry in the year ahead. Available at: www.analytics-magazine.org/january-february-2015/1190-health-care-analytics-what-to-expect-in-2015.
9. Weiskopf, N. G. and Weng, C. 2013. Methods and dimensions of electronic health record data quality assessment: Enabling reuse for clinical research. *J Am Med Inform Assoc.* 20(1):144–151.
10. Baser, O. 2006. Too much ado about propensity score models? Comparison of types of propensity score matching. *Value in Health.* 9(6):677–385.
11. Michael, M., Schaffer, S. D., Egan, P. L., Little, B. B., and Pritchard, P. S. 2013. Improving wait times and patient satisfaction in primary care. *J Healthc Qual.* 35(2), 50–60.

Chapter 9

Program Core Metrics

Learning Objectives

After reading this chapter, the reader will be able to answer the following questions:

- Why are Program Value Measurement Key Performance Indicators for the Common Operating Picture (COP) important?
- What is the role of a Project Management Office (PMO) versus a Value Management Office (VMO)?
- How can the Schedule Performance Index impact cost variance?
- What if the quality of a product does not meet user acceptance criteria?

Program Value Measurement

This book does not seek to create new project management processes or standards. Instead, the criticality of reporting program metrics for the purposes of determining value is highlighted. Whether it is a new information technology (IT)-related project or other medical program, each has an impact on value. For example, in the event that an IT Electronic Health Record (EHR) feature is released late or does not pass the acceptance criteria, this has an adverse impact on the value delivered to the patient, costs, user satisfaction, and the eventual adoption of the product. Understanding program impact deliverables is important in measuring value and creating a holistic COP for the Health Delivery Organization (HDO).

Six core program-related metrics have the most impact on value-based outcomes. It is recommended that each program should measure time, cost, resources, scope, quality, and risks and report the indicators shown in Table 9.1 for each on a weekly dashboard.

Schedule Reporting Metrics

The schedule performance metrics selected for performance indicators are the Schedule Variance (SV) Trend, Schedule Performance Index (SPI), SPI Trend, Critical Path Length Index (CPLI), and Baseline Execution Index (BEI).

The SV Trend compares the metric for a specific reporting period (usually monthly) to the same metric in prior reporting periods. An SV Trend is favorable if the SV improves in value over the course of multiple reporting periods (i.e., 3 months).

Table 9.1 Program Core Metrics Examples

Measure	Key Performance Indicator
Time	Schedule Performance Index (SPI)
Cost	Cost Performance Index (CPI)
Resources	Number of actual vs. planned staff
Scope	Number of scope change requests
Quality	Number of defects per user acceptance criteria
Risks	Number of risks vs. risks resolved

The SV may still be negative (unfavorable) but the trend is improving. Conversely, the SV Trend is unfavorable when the SV worsens over time. Again, the SV could be positive (favorable) but the trend is degrading. The following paragraphs will provide examples of both trends at a work package or control account level.

The SPI is an efficiency factor representing the relationship between the performance achieved and the initial planned schedule. The SPI for projects without an Over Target Baseline (OTB) is calculated as follows:

$$SPI = \frac{BCWP}{BCWS}$$

An index of 1.00 or greater indicates that work is being accomplished at a rate on or ahead of what was planned. An index of less than 1.00 suggests that work is being accomplished at a rate below the planned schedule. An index of less than 0.95 is used as an early warning indication of schedule slippage and should be investigated. The adjusted SPI for projects with an OTB is calculated as:

$$SPI = \frac{BCWP - BCWP @ TIME\ OF\ OTB}{BCWS - BCWS @ TIME\ OF\ OTB}$$

The SPI Trend is a comparison of the metric for this reporting period (usually monthly) to the same metric in prior reporting periods. An SPI Trend is favorable if the SPI increases in value over the course of multiple reporting periods. Conversely, the SPI Trend is unfavorable if it decreases in value.

The CPLI is a measure of the efficiency required to complete a milestone on time. It measures critical path "realism" relative to the baseline finish date, when constrained. A CPLI of 1.00 means that the project must accomplish one day's worth of work for every day that passes. A CPLI of less than 1.00 means that the project schedule is inefficient regarding meeting the baseline date of the milestone (i.e., it is going to finish late). A CPLI of greater than 1.00 means that the project is running efficiently regarding meeting the baseline date of the milestone (i.e., it is going to finish early). The CPLI is an indicator of efficiency relating to tasks on a milestone's critical path (not to other tasks within the schedule). The CPLI is a measure of the relative achievability of the critical path. A CPLI of less than 0.95 should signal the need for further investigation.

The CPLI requires determining the project schedule's Critical Path Length (CPL) and the Total Float (TF). The CPL is the length in workdays from now until the next project milestone that is being measured. TF is the number of days that a project can be delayed before delaying the project completion date. The TF can be negative, which reflects that the project is behind schedule. The analyst should coordinate with the project manager to ensure that the employee/contractor performs the calculation and provides the results to the analyst. The mathematical calculation of TF is generally accepted to be the difference between the "late finish" date and the "early finish" date (late finish minus early finish equals TF). The formula for CPLI is as follows:

$$\text{Critical Path Length Index}\,(\text{CPLI})\frac{\text{CPL}+\text{TF}}{\text{CPL}}$$

The critical path is identified in the project's scheduling tool (e.g., MS Project). The CPL is calculated by inserting a new task into the schedule, with an actual start date of the schedule status date. The CPL is determined by inserting a number value into the duration of this new task until the finish date equals the finish date of the completion milestone identified by the critical path analysis. This is a trial-and-error process to get the correct duration for the CPL. The TF for the completion milestone is recorded for conducting the CPLI calculation.

In addition to recording the CPLI results, it is important to document any rationale for the completion milestone chosen and the analysis method used to calculate the critical path. It is also important to note if the final milestone or task in the schedule has a baseline finish date beyond the project period of performance.

The BEI metric is a schedule-based metric that calculates the efficiency of tasks accomplished when measured against baseline tasks. In other words, it is a measure of task throughput. The BEI provides insight into the realism of project costs, resources, and schedule estimates. It compares the cumulative number of tasks completed to the cumulative number of tasks with a baseline finish date on or before the current reporting period. BEI does not provide insight into tasks completed early or late (before or after the baseline finish date) if the task was completed prior to the current time. If the employee/ contractor completes more tasks than planned, then the BEI will be higher than 1.00, reflecting a higher task throughput than planned. Tasks missing baseline finish dates are included in the denominator. A BEI of less than 0.95 should signal the need for additional investigation. The BEI is calculated as follows:

$$BEI = \frac{\text{Total \# of Tasks Complete}}{\text{Total \# of Tasks Completed Before Now} + \text{Total \# of Tasks Missing Baseline Finish}}$$

The BEI is always compared against the Hit Task Percentage. The Hit Task Percentage is a metric that measures the number of tasks completed early or on time to the number of tasks with a baseline finish date within a given fiscal month. This metric can never exceed a value of 1.00 since the metric assesses the status of tasks with a base finish date within a single fiscal month.

Cost Reporting Metrics

The cost performance metrics selected for performance indicators are the Cost Variance (CV) Trend, Cost Performance Index (CPI), CPI Trend, and the ratio "percent complete" to "percent spent."

Cost Variance Trend

Like the SV Trend, the CV Trend is a comparison of the metric for a specific reporting period (usually monthly) to the same metric in prior reporting periods. A CV Trend is favorable if a positive CV increases (or negative CV decreases) in value over the course of multiple reporting periods. Conversely, the CV Trend is unfavorable if a positive CV decreases (or negative CV increases) in value.

Cost Performance Index

The CPI is an efficiency factor representing the relationship between the performance accomplished (BCWP) and the actual cost expended (ACWP). The CPI for projects without an OTB is calculated as follows:

$$CPI = \frac{BCWP}{ACWP}$$

An index of 1.00 or greater indicates that work is being accomplished at a cost equal to or below what was planned. An index of less than 1.00 suggests that work is accomplished at a cost greater than planned. A cumulative index of less than 0.95 is used as an early warning indicator of cost increases and should be investigated.

The adjusted CPI for projects with an OTB is calculated as follows:

$$CPI(adjusted) = \frac{BCWP - BCWP @ TIME OF OTB}{ACWP - ACWP @ TIME OF OTB}$$

The CPI Trend is a comparison of the metric for a specific reporting period (usually monthly) to the same metric in prior reporting periods. A CPI Trend is favorable if the CPI increases in value over the course of multiple reporting periods. Conversely, the CPI Trend is unfavorable if it decreases.

Percent Complete and Percent Spent

The Percent Complete and Percent Spent metrics each provides valuable information, but as a ratio they gauge the amount of budget spent in relation to the amount of work completed. The first part of this metric, the numerator, is Percent Complete (%comp). The formula to calculate %comp is as follows:

$$Percent\ Complete(\%) = \%comp = \frac{BCWP}{BAC} \times 100$$

The value range of %comp is from 0% to 100%. It provides a measure of how far along the project is toward project completion. The second part of the metric, the denominator, is Percent Spent (%spent). The formula to calculate %spent is as follows:

$$Percent\ Complete(\%) = \%spent = \frac{ACWP}{BAC} \times 100$$

The value range of %spent starts at 0% and, since it tracks actual cost, it theoretically has no limit. It provides a measure of how far along the project is toward completion. If %spent is over 100%, this indicates that a cost overrun condition has been realized. The combination of these two metrics results in the following formula:

$$\frac{\%comp}{\%spent} = \frac{BCWP/BAC}{ACWP/BAC} = \frac{BCWP}{ACWP} = \text{Cost Performance Index}\,(CPI)$$

When measured independently, %comp and %spent provide additional insight into project performance. As shown above, the ratio of these two metrics results in the CPI. Note, when trends of SPI or CPI are seen to be dropping over time, it indicates a negative trend that needs investigation.

Resources Key Performance Indicator

A lack of resources or quality of resources can adversely affect schedule, cost, etc. Therefore, resources is a core metric and should be reported monthly.

# of available resources vs. total number required

Scope Key Performance Indicator

Scope change or "creep" can adversely affect program and project schedule, cost, and resources, so it requires careful monitoring and the reporting of all scope changes. The total number of scope changes per project should be tracked monthly.

Total # of scope changes per project

Quality Key Performance Indicator

This is the total number of defects against the user acceptance criteria. This shall be categorized by project or by system.

Total # of defects per user acceptance criteria

Risks Key Performance Indicator

A lack of a standardized Risk Management Process can create challenges for the tracking and management of pertinent risks and issues that impact programs. The use of disparate tools/processes and resistance to change negatively impact program and project performance and increase the likelihood of intended outcomes not being delivered. A risk registry is an essential mitigation tool used by programs to record, monitor, and report risk.

Every identified risk within a program should have a mitigation plan to eliminate it, or to minimize the impact if the risk cannot be eliminated. The mitigation plan includes

- The steps to be taken to minimize adverse consequences
- The impact on the project or program
- The resources that may be used
- The organizations that would be involved

Each risk will be further categorized as low (L), medium (M), or high (H) based on severity and its impact on the project. The risk is reviewed by the Risk Review Board (RRB), an Action Owner (AO) is assigned, and the mitigation plan is developed by the AO. The mitigation plan progress is tracked in the weekly RRB project meetings and reviewed monthly at the program RRB. If the RRB determines that the risk cannot be resolved at the project or program level, due to a lack of resources or authority, it is submitted to executive level for attention. For the purposes of reporting, the core metric for the Balanced Scorecard is the total number of risks identified versus risks closed.

$$\text{Total \# Risks/Risks Closed}$$

Summary of Key Points to Remember

The learning outcomes from this chapter that are important to remember include the following points:

■ Why are Program Value Measurement Key Performance Indicators for the COP important?
Time, cost, resources, scope, quality, and risks are the core metrics needed for the COP. These metrics provide insight into whether or not the project is on time, highlight staffing needs, and present risks to the organization's leadership for awareness and action. In the absence of these program metrics, it is virtually impossible to accurately predict future outcomes across the six perspectives.
■ What is the role of a PMO versus a VMO?
A PMO is a governing office for executing a successful project management approach at an organization. A PMO ensures project delivery is aligned with business requirements and delivered within cost, scope, quality, and time criteria.
The VMO serves as a center of excellence for determining evidence-based outcome measurements. The VMO facilitates the creation of value-based care models and supports IT governance by evaluating business case investments and projected benefits to link people, processes, and technology. The VMO uses measurable inputs from three dimensions— clinical, programmatic, and technical—to

define and measure value-based outcomes. This provides vertical and horizontal alignment with an organization's strategy.

■ How can the SPI impact cost variance?

Put simply, if you miss a deadline or deliver a poor-quality product, it could drive up costs in fixing the issue or hiring more people to get the job done.

■ What if the quality of a product does not meet user acceptance criteria?

In the event that a product does not meet the user acceptance criteria, the PMO in consultation with the business owner will determine the next course of action. Two predominant options exist: (1) do nothing and allow the product to be released; or (2) fix the issue. In either case, there are multiple risks, which include impact to patient safety, poor user satisfaction, low adoption of the product, and loss of market share. The negative impacts of delivering a poor product justify quality as a core metric for any Balanced Scorecard.

Chapter 10

Technical Metrics

Learning Objectives

After reading this chapter, the reader will be able to answer the following questions:

- What is the importance of Systems Performance?
- What does IT support performance measure?
- How do ISO 9126 standards influence healthcare delivery organizations (HDOs)?
- What if fault tolerances for an electronic health record (EHR)/electronic medical record (EMR) are not established prior to implementation?

Technical Value Measurement

Currently, HDOs' information technology (IT) systems make it a challenge to properly measure outcomes due to poor interoperability, the improper use of industry standards, and poor investment strategies. Common obstacles in building an enabling IT Platform include[1]

- Health IT lagging far behind other industries.
- Traditional IT siloed in departments ("best of breed" approach)
- Data definitions
- Unstructured data elements
- Systems that are designed for the revenue cycle, not for outcome and cost measurement
- Health IT vendors that have not understood the need for outcome and cost measurement
- Large capital investment

Koppel[2] has recently described the main challenges faced by healthcare organizations in measuring the value derived from investments in health information technology (HIT) initiatives and the difficulties with articulating the benefits without a credible framework. This book describes the Value Realization Framework that can be applied to that purpose, articulating the correlation between the outcomes and the Key Performance Indictors (KPIs) (ease of use, time taken by tasks, and value of the primary and secondary tasks) that are improved through the HIT program or initiative. A Value Management Office's monitoring capability can help in continuously reporting on performance and alert management when deviations are observed again to protect the value.

Koppel proposed ten recommendations to demonstrate improvements in outcomes from HIT. These recommendations, briefly summarized in the following list, are completely aligned with the framework, methodology, and tools proposed in this book:

1. *Establish clear metrics for HIT's core functions*
2. *Conduct tests both in controlled laboratory settings and in actual field conditions*
3. *Recognize the need for multi-method testing procedures*
4. *Require data standards*

5. *Establish consistent usability tests for every major screen and function*
6. *Evaluate graphic presentations of data*
7. *Use the tests to help vendors improve their products and to help healthcare providers select the best products for their needs*
8. *Make these evaluation processes transparent*
9. *Publish the findings*
10. *Do not allow hidden contractual agreements*

In 1992, Joseph Newhouse, a Harvard economist, estimated that up to 70% of medical spending growth over the last half-century might be due to acquiring new medical technology.[3] Given the high cost of acquiring new technology, it is imperative that HDOs make an informed decision. The proposal is that in order to measure the technical performance of healthcare organization technologies, each program or initiative should combine the application of the technology process index, in addition to standards-based performance metrics such as the group provided by the International Organization for Standardization (ISO) for software quality.

Technology Process Index

The Technology Process Index consists of Systems Performance, IT Support Performance, Service Level Effectiveness, New Project Index, and IT Total Cost Index. Each of the aggregate measures within the IT support services business domain assumes that the activities covered are managed through service level agreements (SLAs) with internal customers. The services measured by IT responsiveness are distinct from the other support services categories. Services measured by IT responsiveness involve the accuracy, availability, efficiency (time behavior), and agility of IT products.

Value Impact: Using the value definition of IT support services—"IT responsiveness"—the activities measured by this aggregate represent the organization's general ability to exploit IT and deal with the changing requirements of its IT resources. The value of IT support services—IT responsiveness—varies by organization and industry. In general, the higher the volume of transactional activity and the more complex the services are, the more value from support services that can be extracted.

Systems Performance

Systems Performance shows the percentage of time that applications, systems, and infrastructure are operating within their performance objectives. This metric indicates the amount of time during expected hours of operation that services are available and usable by the organization. Time outages, poor response time, degraded throughput, or other performance-related service level breaches are counted as unacceptable performance.

Systems Performance

$$= \left(\text{Time system is available to the organization} \right)$$

$$/ \left(\text{Time system is expected to be available to the organization} \right)$$

IT Performance

IT Support Performance measures the ability of IT support functions to provide organization users with support for problem resolution, questions, and unplanned change requests. The metric accounts for the availability of support (time-to-respond) and the performance of support (time-to-resolve).

IT Support Performance shows the percentage of requests completed within the SLA. Unacceptable performance would include any time a support request is not completed satisfactorily—for example, the user could not initiate the request, or the user's support falls outside of tolerable performance criteria.

IT Support Performance

= (Number of IT support requests within SLA)

/(Total Number IT support requests) Data is for standard hours

of operation

Service Level Effectiveness

Service Level Effectiveness measures the effectiveness of the expected service levels in place with all users of IT. To maintain positive working relationships with users, IT service providers must play a proactive role in ensuring that service levels are delivered effectively. Quarterly surveys to determine Service Level Effectiveness are recommended. The survey questions should be grouped into three categories:

- Does the level of expected service meet the organization's needs?
- Does the level of expected IT support meet the organization's needs?
- Does the level of partnership between IT and business units meet the organization's needs?

Service Level Effectiveness = (Surveyed users with >

= 90% satisfaction)/(Total number of surveyed users)

266 ■ *Value Management in Healthcare*

New Project Index

The New Project Index measures the ability of the IT function to deliver new projects into the organization within budget, time, and value objectives.

New Project Index

$$= \left(\begin{array}{l} \text{Total IT projects within budget, time,} \\ \text{and value objectives} \end{array} \right)$$

$$/ \left(\text{Total IT projects} \right)$$

IT Total Cost Index

The IT Total Cost Index measures the overall total cost of ownership (TCO) for technology owned, operated, or supported by the organization.

$$\text{IT Total Cost Index} = \left(\text{Sum of IT} - \text{related TCO} \right)$$

$$/ \left(\begin{array}{l} \text{Total revenue} \\ \text{of organization} \end{array} \right)$$

A brief summary of TCO costs is as follows:

■ Direct costs: Hardware and software; management; support; application development and integration; and communications fees
■ Indirect costs (i.e., unbudgeted): End user, cost of end users to support themselves and each other instead of using formal IT support channels; downtime, lost productivity due to system unavailability

ISO Standards for Software Quality

The comprehensive specification and evaluation of software products is a key factor in ensuring adequate quality and must be validated by widely accepted metrics. The ISO provides standards for the evaluation of software quality. International Standards provide any organization with world-class specifications for products, services, and systems to ensure quality, safety, and efficiency. Any healthcare organization can use ISO standards to support public policy, and by integrating an ISO standard into national regulation, the organization can benefit from the opinion of experts without having to call on their services directly.

ISO 9126* identified six quality characteristics—functionality, reliability, usability, efficiency, maintainability, and portability—along with their associated subcategories. The Value Realization Framework uses these as the starting point for categorizing and generating the technical KPIs.

Table 10.1 shows the definition for each of these categories and sub-categories.

To support the performance of any HIT system, at least the following performance categories must be evaluated:

- Accuracy
- Availability
- Time behavior
- Capacity
- Interoperability
- Security
- Fault tolerance
- Usability

* ISO/IEC 9126. Software engineering. Product quality. Part 1 and 2. Quality model. First edition 2001-06-15.

Table 10.1   Technical KPIs ISO Categories and Sub-Categories

Category	Subcategory	Description
Functionality	1. Suitability	Characterizes functional fit
	2. Accuracy	Refers to data accuracy, consistency, and precision
	3. Interoperability	Ability to integrate with other relevant systems
	4. Security	Application and infrastructure security
	5. Compliance	Refers to system compliance with regulatory checklist
Reliability	1. Maturity	Evaluates software stability (i.e., version maturity)
	2. Fault Tolerance	Ability of system to continue operating properly in the event of the failure of some of its components
	3. Availability	Proportion of time system is in a functioning condition
	4. Recoverability	Ability to restore system to full operation
Usability	1. Understandability	Refers to user interface effectiveness
	2. Learnability	Use of training approaches and documentation according to user roles
	3. Operability	The system's ease of use and any special usability requirements
	4. Attractiveness	The capability of the software product to be attractive to the user

(*Continued*)

Table 10.1 (Continued)   Technical KPIs ISO Categories and Sub-Categories

Category	Subcategory	Description
	5. Findability	The system's ease of use for finding the required information and functionalities
Efficiency	1. Time behavior (performance)	Conformance to specified time tolerances and transaction volume
	2. Capacity (IT resource utilization)	Resources required by the system during its deployment and operations (i.e., technological and human resources required)
Maintainability	1. Analyzability	Concerns software mechanisms used to identify the root cause of system failure
	2. Changeability	Describes the capability of the system to manage configurable business rules easily
	3. Stability	System's ability to avoid unexpected effects from modifications
	4. Testability	Evaluates features and tools required to support system testing
Portability	1. Adaptability	Ability of the system to change autonomously to respond to new specifications or operating environments

(*Continued*)

Table 10.1 (Continued) Technical KPIs ISO Categories and Sub-Categories

Category	Subcategory	Description
	2. Installability	Characterizes the effectiveness of system installation mechanisms/ resources
	3. Co-existence	Ability of two or more systems to perform their required functions while sharing the same hardware or software environment
	4. Replaceability	Characterizes the plug-and-play aspect of software components
	5. Serviceability	The ability of the system to be deployed in cloud environments
	6. Reusability	The ability to leverage existing information, data, code, services, etc.

In the following sections, some examples of KPIs for these categories are provided.

Accuracy

HDO systems must deliver information that is accurate by ensuring that documentation and the retrieval of the data is correct and complete from all data sources. Accuracy ensures that health information is associated with the correct patient (identity); establishes policies and guidelines in compliance with government, regulatory, and industry standards; and presents the most current information (latency).

Accurate data and proper documentation reduce medical errors, improve patient safety, reduce costs, improve caregiver efficiencies, and facilitate health information exchange (HIE) and quality measurement initiatives.

For example, some of the accuracy metrics that are currently used by the U.S. government include

- *Successful user transaction completion ratio*: Information that is retrieved by a system from a specified set of data sources/potential information that should be retrieved from the same source
- *Data accuracy (completeness—consistency—currency—precision)*: Data stored in the system that is in accordance with the right level of precision that is required/total data stored in the system

Availability

HDO systems operating at high performance are necessary to ensure that the expected values from using the systems are directly or indirectly realized or not lost (e.g., intended vs. direct impact on productivity of clinicians in delivering care to patients that requires the use of HIT systems, or the indirect impact on clinicians' satisfaction with IT systems), where highly available is understood as operating within defined thresholds (benchmarks) for established Enterprise Reference Metrics regarding the availability of IT systems.

Availability provides systems with achievable performance levels (primarily uptime rates) commensurate with corresponding expected or industry thresholds. They also allow the monitoring of defined quality of service (QoS) levels to support the use of SLAs that can be specified by a product development effort and incorporated into system procurement and the associated contract award.

For example, some of the government availability metrics in use include

- *User operational availability*: The amount of time that the system is available to the end user divided by the total possible operational time (e.g., 99.76%—downtime not to exceed 22 h/year or 110 min/month)
- *Technical operational success rate*: The amount of time that the system should be available divided by the total possible operational time as defined by the project team

Time Behavior

HDO systems shall be built as highly efficient for use as measured by defined QoS levels for the timeliness of responses to requests made to the systems, which can be monitored and enforced.

High efficiency HDO systems are necessary to ensure that the expected values from using the IT systems are directly or indirectly realized (or not lost where time-based efficiency is understood to be timely responses to requests) for operations over infrastructure during peak and nonpeak periods.

Some examples of the capacity/scalability metrics that are currently used by the U.S. government include

- *End-user total response time*: The amount of time to return a response to a request made by an end user (e.g., 750–2000 ms)
- *Transaction response time*: The amount of time to return a response to a request made by any calling component (e.g., 250–1000 ms)
- *Network response time*: The latency of requests sent and responses received over connecting networks (e.g., 250 ms per successful transaction)

■ *Presentation response time*: The latency of information submitted and returned to the presentation tier and visualized on the client device (e.g., 100–400 ms)

Capacity/Scalability

HDO systems shall be built as highly efficient for use as measured by defined QoS levels for the (current) capacity and (future) scalability of the systems, which can be monitored and enforced.

High capacity (and scalability) HDO systems are necessary to ensure that the expected values from using them are directly or indirectly realized (or not lost) where capacity is understood to be when IT systems are operating within current and projected capacities over infrastructure during peak and nonpeak periods.

For example, some of the capacity/scalability metrics that are currently used by the U.S. government include

■ *Transaction throughput rate*: Expected transaction throughput volumes divided by maximum transaction volume of the system rate (e.g., 8.5–5.0 million TPM)
■ *Data transmission rate*: Expected transmission of data loads divided by maximum rate commensurate with the implementing platform (e.g., 25 MBPS)
■ *Data input/output operations rate*: Processing of data input/output operations divided by total processing speed of the implementing platform (e.g., 200 I/O per second)
■ *Utilization rate*: Operation within the current volumes divided by operation with scaling up to projected volumes commensurate with the implementing platform (e.g., 90% of capacity)
■ *Concurrency rate*: Expected concurrent processing of data by end users and other connections divided by total number of connections commensurate with the implementing platform

Interoperability

HDO systems shall be made highly interoperable for use as measured by defined QoS levels for high informational interoperability by the U.S. government. Informational interoperability is understood to be

- *Syntactic (or technical)*: Where data exchanged between systems in different domains conforms to established and mutually recognized standards for general format and structure
- *Semantic*: Where data exchanged between systems in different domains is mapped so that the meaning of data is translatable or mutually understood
- *Process-Based*: Where data exchanged between systems in different domains supports the seamless interaction between related and contiguous processes, the success of which is testable based on the occurrence of corresponding errors at each of these levels

Some examples of the interoperability metrics that are currently used by the U.S. government include

- *Syntactic interaction success rate*: Messages conforming to the established and mutually agreeable data exchange standards divided by total messages exchanged (e.g., HL7 and a rate of 99.9%)
- *Semantic terminology mapping success rate*: Messages conforming to the established and mutually agreeable data exchange standards that are mapped to domain-specific terminology divided by total messages exchanged
- *Process interaction success rate*: Data exchanges successfully threaded across domains via established and mutually understood interfaces for ensuring continuity of processing across multiple domains divided by total data exchanges (e.g., 99.9%)

If a HDO participates in a health exchange, two outcome-oriented metrics for measuring interoperability cost savings/avoidance include

1. Reduction in duplicate testing
2. Reduction in imaging

Security

Healthcare organizations need to provide authentication and authorization of users, detect attempted intrusions by unauthorized persons, prevent infection from malicious attacks, and ensure that communication is private. Security is essential for the protection of patient identity, the diagnosis of conditions, and the performance of procedures and tests. Consent and custody is important with controls to prevent, deter, and detect security breaches (and react and recover when they happen).

Some examples of the security metrics currently used by the U.S. government include

■ *Incidents reporting and fixing*: Number of incidents reported on time divided by the total number of reported incidents, and the number of incidents fixed on time divided by the total number of reported incidents (for each incidence category)
■ *Venerability management*: Number of vulnerabilities identified and mitigated within the target time frame during the time period divided by the number of high vulnerabilities identified within the time period
■ *Access control/single sign-on satisfaction*: Number of satisfied employees with the three benefits of the four-point satisfaction scale divided by the total number of employees taking the satisfaction survey
■ *Identification and authentication*: Number of breaches without two-factor authentication minus the number of

breaches with two-factor authentication divided by the number of breaches without two-factor authentication

■ *Security awareness and training*: Number of personnel taking the appropriate test and getting scores over the threshold divided by the number of personnel taking the test, and the number of personnel taking the test divided by the total number of personnel in the organization

■ *Access control*: Number of people rejected who had valid credentials divided by the total number of people who had valid credentials, and the number of people accepted who had invalid credentials divided by the total number of people who had invalid credentials

■ *Risk assessment*: Number of vulnerabilities remediated according to the plan of action and milestones (POA&M) schedule divided by the total number of POA&M-documented vulnerabilities identified through vulnerability scans

Fault Tolerance

HDOs need to develop software that is dependable and trustworthy. Fault tolerance is the capability of the software product to maintain its level of performance under the stated conditions for a specified period of time.

Fault tolerance reduces the loss of data (and service) due to system failure; prevents diminishing credibility and patient trust from diminishing and avoids the resultant churn of patients; reduces the penalties for violated government and industry regulations (HIPAA, HITECH, and JCAHO); reduces the costs of recovering and repairing lost data due to having unreliable systems; and reduces the legal costs of meeting internal and external compliance requirements.

Some examples of fault tolerance metrics currently used by the U.S. government include the following measurements:

- *Mean time to failure (MTTF)*: The time it takes from one failure to the next (in minutes and hours) must correspond with the SLAs that are established
- *Mean time to repair (MTTR)*: The time it takes to repair and restore the operational system (in minutes or hours)
- *Data recovery (DR)*: The total data recovered after an incident divided by the total data in the system that was there before the incident (must be close to 100%)

Usability

Any healthcare organization should develop systems that promote clinician usability, adoption, and acceptance to provide a user experience that exceeds expectations.

Usability solutions enhance the effectiveness and efficiency of software based on industry-defined standards, as well the satisfaction level of users. When measuring effectiveness, there are two aspects that are normally analyzed: did the user accomplish the designated task resulting in the desired outcome, and did the user complete the designated task in the desired amount of time. When measuring efficiency, the focus is on the path the user takes to accomplish the task. The solution checks that the user took all the correct steps and only used the required steps to complete the task. When measuring user satisfaction, the solution wants to get the user's impression of the system.

Highly usable systems increase clinician productivity and efficiency, decrease user errors, increase safety, and improve cognitive support. These enhancements lead to improved patient and provider outcomes. Usability also increases organizational efficiencies and decreases maintenance costs, training and support costs, and development time and costs.

For example, some of the usability metrics that are currently used by the U.S. government include the following measurements:

- *Efficiency Index*: The number of people who score greater than 80% in the test divided by the total number of people taking the test (a high score indicates an efficient system)
- *Effectiveness Index*: A measure of the number of people who can locate the task compared to the total number of people taking the test
- *Satisfaction Index*: The number of users who indicate a positive response to satisfaction in the personal interview divided by the total number of people in the interview
- *Learnability Index*: The number of people passing the evaluation after learning the basic and advanced functions divided by the total number of people taking the evaluation

Summary of Key Points to Remember

The learning outcomes from this chapter that are important to remember include the following points:

- What is the importance of Systems Performance? *Systems Performance shows the percentage of time that applications, systems, and infrastructure supported by the IT organization and its service providers are operating within their performance objectives. This metric indicates the amount of time during expected hours of operation that services are available and usable by the organization. Time outages, poor response times, degraded throughput, or other performance-related service level breaches are counted as unacceptable performance.*

■ What does IT support performance measure?
IT support performance shows the percentage of requests completed within the SLA. Unacceptable performance would include any time that a support request is not completed satisfactorily—for example, the user could not initiate the request, or the user's support falls outside of defined performance criteria.

■ How do ISO 9126 standards influence HDOs?
The ISO provides standards for the evaluation of software quality. International standards provide any organization with world-class specifications for products, services, and systems to ensure quality, safety, and efficiency. Any healthcare organization can use ISO standards to support public policy, and by integrating an ISO standard into national regulation, the organization can benefit from the opinion of experts without having to call on their services directly. ISO 9126*identified six quality characteristics—functionality, reliability, usability, efficiency, maintainability, and portability—along with their associated subcategories. The Value Realization Framework uses these characteristics as the starting point for categorizing and generating the technical KPIs.

■ What if fault tolerances for an EHR/EMR are not established prior to implementation?
Fault tolerance is the capability of the software product to maintain its level of performance under stated conditions for a specified period of time. If a new or existing EHR/EMR does not have fault tolerance specifications within an industry standard, it can negatively impact HDOs' investment strategies and ultimately quality of care. Fault tolerance reduces the loss of service and data due to system failure; prevents diminishing credibility and patient trust

---

* Ibid.

and avoids the resultant churn; and reduces legal costs, government penalties, and industry violations (HIPAA, HITECH, and JCAHO).

References

1. Dr. Thomas Feeley. April 2016. Presentation at Harvard Business School.
2. Koppel, R. 2016. Great promises of healthcare information technology deliver less. In *Healthcare Information Management Systems* (pp. 101–125). Springer International Publishing.
3. Peden, E. A. 1998. Freeland MS. insurance effects on US medical spending (1960–1993). *Health Econ.* 7(8): 671–687.

Chapter 11

Other Index Metrics

Learning Objectives

After reading this chapter, the reader will be able to answer the following questions:

- Why consider using other metrics?
- What is a Product Portfolio Index?
- How can a Research and Development (R&D) Success Index benefit my organization?
- What other index metrics can be used?

Other Metrics

Six other useful index metrics include the Product Portfolio Index, New Products Index, Feature Function Index, Time-to-Market Index, and R&D Success Index. Each of these index metrics provides greater insight into portfolios and the value of products delivered.

Value Impact: Product development effectiveness may have the single biggest effect on financial performance and savings from all aggregate measures.

Product Portfolio Index

The Product Portfolio Index identifies and validates current and projected patient needs in existing and targeted demographics. This metric shows the product portfolio by size and margin contribution. The underlying assumption is that high-margin products serve patient needs better than low-margin products, and that high growth rates indicate that patient needs are being met. The index combines these factors to create a metric that shows an organization's ability to serve patient needs compared with its industry peer groups.

$$\text{Product Portfolio Index} = \text{Sum}\{\text{Revenue/Cost Savings of products}$$

$$\text{where } [(g > G/2) \text{ AND}(m > M/2)]\}/\text{Sum}\{\text{Revenue/Cost savings of}$$

$$\text{all products}\}$$

where
- G = product with highest growth rate
- G = growth rate of each individual product
- M = product with highest gross margin
- M = gross margin of each individual product

New Products Index

The New Products Index shows the organization's emphasis on adapting its products and services to the changing demands of patients.

$$\text{New Products Index}$$

$$= (\text{Revenue of products and services released in last 12 months})$$

$$/ (\text{Total company revenue})$$

Feature Function Index

The Feature Function Index shows the level and extent of the changes found in new products and services offered by the organization.

Feature Function Index

$$= (\text{New component items for products released last year})$$

$$/(\text{Total component items for those products})$$

where
- New component items have been added specifically for products released on the market during the past 12 months.
- For services, component items are substituted by skill sets.

Time-to-Market Index

The Time-to-Market Index shows the ability of the product development function to release new products and services on a timely basis.

Time − to − Market Index

$$= \text{Average}(\text{time from approval to launch for each product})$$

Research and Development Success Index

The R&D Success Index shows the ability of the product development function to bring products to the market.

R&D Success Index

$$= (\text{New products launched in last 12 months})$$

$$/(\text{Development projects due to be complete in 12 months})$$

Summary of Key Points to Remember

The learning outcomes from this chapter that are important to remember include the following points:

- Why consider using other metrics?
  Depending on organizational needs and preferences, these tools may be helpful, in particular for organizations managing large portfolios. In theory, the more metrics used, the more details of a project that can be attained. However, it has been found that it is best to keep things "simple" for value management and focus on a specific outcome.
- What is a Product Portfolio Index?
  The Product Portfolio Index identifies and validates current and projected patient needs in existing and targeted demographics. The underlying assumption is that high-margin products serve patient needs better than low-margin products, and that high growth rates indicate that patient needs are being met.
- How can the R&D Success Index benefit my organization?
  The R&D Success Index demonstrates the ability of an organization's product development function to bring new products to the market. This metric is useful for an innovative organization developing several products internally.
- What if other index metrics are required?
  The choice of metrics is dependent on organizational need and leadership. There is a wide variety of project management and project management office literature available on metrics related to managing projects. The focus of this book has been to research existing indexes and, where applicable, to incorporate them into the value management methodology. A useful book for traditional IT project management is Project Management for Healthcare Information Technology *by Masuda and Coplan.**

---

* Coplan, S. and Masuda, D. 2011. *Project Management for Healthcare Information Technology*. New York: McGraw Hill.

Chapter 12

Change Management

Learning Objectives

After reading this chapter, the reader will be able to answer the following questions:

- What are the most important recommendations for adopting the Value Management Office (VMO) in the organization?
- Why is it so important to manage the change?

Transformation Process Overview

A sustained transformation to a value-based organization not only requires the VMO and Value Realization Framework, but also a change in organizational culture, stronger staff skills, better performance management, and clear leadership. This section presents an eight-step process based on Kotter's book, *Leading Change*[1] (Figure 12.1). Considered by many to be the seminal work in the field of change management, Kotter's research revealed that only 30% of change programs succeed.[2]

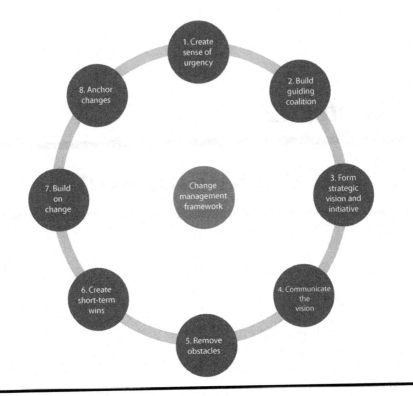

Figure 12.1   Transformation process overview.

Step 1: Create Urgency

The world is recognizing that cost containment is the highest priority for the healthcare system. However, healthcare providers face a dilemma in attempting to ensure that patients receive the highest quality care while containing healthcare costs. To some degree, they are moving toward identifying the value of the care provided to patients. However, measuring value and training healthcare professionals to look at value has been challenging thus far, which has delayed the transformation.

Maintaining the status quo is no longer viable. The research conducted by the New England Health Institute found that 30%, or nearly $700 million[3] (now close to $1 trillion dollars), of all healthcare spending is wasteful, meaning it could be eliminated without reducing the quality of care. Waste factors include unexplained variation in clinical care, patient medication adherence, misuse of drugs and treatments, emergency department overuse, underuse of appropriate medications, and overuse of antibiotics.

By establishing a VMO and learning the Value Realization Framework, physicians can ensure quality of care while keeping cost in mind—maximizing the value of the care provided. The technology and operational investment decisions could be based on the value provided to the patients, the attainment of key performance indicators (KPIs), and the satisfaction of the care providers in reducing risk and waste.

Several leading organizations have realized the importance of a value-based agenda and created urgency within their respective organizations to implement a value management approach. Some suggestions are to

1. Educate and train individuals on the value concept
2. Engage with thought leaders
3. Collaborate with others interested in or implementing value management
4. Pilot portions of the agenda incrementally
5. Establish a VMO with leadership support[*]

Case study: Based on Harvard Business School's 2013 article "Boston Children's Hospital: Measuring Patient Costs (Abridged)" by Kaplan, Witkowski, and Hohman[4]

Our review shows that the current system of healthcare payment is not always value-based, and healthcare providers throughout the state are compensated at widely different rates for providing similar services of a similar quality and complexity. To control cost growth, we must shift how we purchase healthcare to align payments with value, measured by those

---

[*] "Early successes made subsequent implementation easier." Dereesa Reid, CEO HOAG Orthopedic Institute. April 2015.

factors the healthcare market should reward, such as better quality.*

Boston Children's Hospital (BCH) has long been considered a worldwide leader in providing high-quality care for children. In 2011, BCH provided care for over 500,000 patient visits and its surgeons performed more than 26,000 procedures. As the only freestanding pediatric hospital in Boston, BCH had historically reported higher costs and prices than other hospitals in the Massachusetts area. Tufts' Floating Hospital for Children had been recognized for charging prices 50% lower than BCH's while producing comparable health outcomes. Floating Hospital had seen its volume and revenue from pediatric care grow significantly over the last few years. Payors began excluding BCH from certain offerings while increasing cost sharing in their network plans that still included BCH. This left a very limited market for BCH. BCH had been experimenting with new reimbursement approaches and in 2012 started an Alternative Quality Contract (AQC), shifting from fee-for-service to fixed payments.[5]

A Strengths, Weaknesses, Opportunities and Threats (SWOT) analysis of BCH created the urgency to improve. The urgency led to a revamped strategic plan and objectives. A key objective was to improve the hospital's data collection and reporting of health outcomes. This led to a value management approach that has helped propel BCH further as a leader in delivering predictable health outcomes based on a patient's condition (Table 12.1).

Step 2: Build a Guiding Coalition

Identifying key stakeholders and true leaders in clinical and information technology and obtaining their acceptance of and

---

* Office of the Attorney General Martha Coakley, Commonwealth of Massachusetts. 2010.

Table 12.1   Boston Children's Hospital SWOT Analysis

Strengths	Weaknesses	Opportunities	Threats
#1 ranked pediatric hospital in United States	Limited data and outcomes	Contracts that earn more with higher quality	Competitors—much lower prices for same services and outcomes
Only dedicated pediatric hospital in New England	No understanding of costs by medical control SVCS	New treatment possibilities from research	Under scrutiny from public (Medicaid) payer and Attorney General of Massachusetts
Top research hospital	Complex and confusing billing	Demonstrate lower total costs over episode of care	New "value based" payment models for performance
Delivers highly complex care	Complex organizational structure	Develop regional integrated network or excluded from some areas	Placed in higher patient cost tiers by insurance companies
Treats low-income population (free or reduced price)		Expand nationally and internationally based on brand	

commitment to the framework is the next step. This team can help institute the specific attitudes and practices necessary to launch the change initiative.

Leaders must understand the trade-offs in healthcare and be confident in communicating them to other team members. Important trade-offs are the variation in the cost per intervention and the patient's ability to afford healthcare, the long-term and short-term impact of the intervention, the balance between utility (refers to the desirability of a health outcome) and usability (refers to the patient's willingness and ability to adhere to the intervention), the risk of intervention, and the likelihood of errors or adverse events and their associated consequences.

Finally, the team should understand that the larger community is not trained in medical economics and teaching them the value of performance may not be an easy task. Identifying resources with training in multiple areas and enrolling them in the program is also equally important.

Imagine that you are the value management project leader for implementing the value-based approach within a department. What would you actually say to the various people you must interact with in order to be successful? The following are four roles that you will likely encounter— Chief Executive Officer (CEO), Chief Financial Officer (CFO), Chief Information Officer (CIO), and Chief Medical Officer (CMO)—and their possible statements when approached about implementing the value agenda.

CEO/Executive Representative

1. How does a value management approach yield outcomes that align with our strategic objectives? *A value management approach addresses healthcare challenges (rising costs, new policies, low patient satisfaction) that healthcare ecosystem providers face today. Leading institutions (Harvard, Cleveland Clinic) and subject matter experts (Dr. M. E. Porter) give this approach credibility. Also, improving healthcare outcomes in the most efficient manner is an objective that all healthcare providers should strive for.*

2. Do we have the resources (e.g., financial, people or organizational support) to implement a value management
approach? *Implementing a value management approach
is more about shifting how an organization defines and
measures success. Most organizations have performance
management personnel and systems. These existing
resources could be leveraged when implementing a VMO.
Lastly, external experts familiar with implementing VMOs
are available to assist with the implementation and organizational change management.*

3. What are the risks and how can we mitigate them?
*There's risk in choosing the right success criteria. This
can be mitigated by identifying and engaging all the
right stakeholders from the very beginning. There's also
risk around showing early results that validate the new
approach. This can be mitigated by identifying what success looks like in the short term and long term. Lastly, there
is a risk that key stakeholders will have concerns about the
shift to value management. This risk can be mitigated by
sharing leading research, inviting subject matter experts,
communicating successful implementation examples, and
sharing the insights from this book with key stakeholders.*

CFO/Financial Representative

1. Things are very hectic right now because it is budget
season and the Board has mandated we cut costs by 10%.
What have you got? *Time-Driven Activity-Based Costing
(TDABC) applies here because it strategically allows the
CFO to see exactly where each cost is being processed.
Within a care delivery cycle, they will be able to see for
each process step the money spent on each (1) specialty;
(2) technology; and (3) equipment involved. Therefore, the
CFO may see where they can better utilize each of these
three categories to make these cost cuts.*

2. I learned about Activity-Based Costing in my accounting class over 20 years ago. We've already made a substantial investment in our existing costing system and quality and safety initiatives. It has served us well in managing costs. Why reinvent the wheel and do something new? *Activity-Based Costing is not as modern as TDABC because it, simply put, does not include the time function of the equation. Once you are able to write out your costing equation including this piece, it will be much easier to update as well as maintain, at a fraction of the cost. This is because you will not need to start anew each time. Rather, it can easily be changed based on any simple fluctuation (which in today's healthcare system happens frequently), for example, personnel and/or equipment changes.*

3. We are already swamped and dealing with multiple issues, such as the government introducing new payment models that increase our risk and could lower our revenues. No one else uses TDABC so why should we? *TDABC has been proven to work as shown by leading major health systems that have already incorporated the value management approach. These include, but are not limited to, MD Anderson, Cleveland Clinic, and Schon Klinik. Therefore, it would not be reinventing the wheel but rather using an efficient methodology that has been proven to not only work, but be successful as well. You would continue to follow in these prime organizations' steps while also being another major health system to incorporate the use of value management and, with that, TDABC.*

CIO/Technology Officer

1. Does value management lead to clinical improvements, such as better health, faster recovery, less pain, improved quality of life for patients, etc.? *Value management promotes quality by defining critical metrics to ensure that*

clinical improvements and value for the patients have been achieved.

2. Does value management help deliver the "right" care at the "right" time, as determined by medical staff for specific patient conditions? *Value Management shows if a process is operating in a timely manner by communicating the current status and goals through the COP.*

3. Does value management help staff members be better equipped to provide the highest levels of care? *Value management helps executives and staff members become more knowledgeable of performance measures and provides insights to make data-supported decisions to deliver the highest value to patients.*

4. Does value management provide improved customer service and/or stronger relationships and better outreach with patients? *Value Management aligns information technology (IT) investments with enterprise objectives, ensuring that the best quality service can be provided to the patient.*

CMO/Medical Officer

1. Our medical team leaders and business-side leaders sometimes have clashed views. How would value management help bring their respective views together? *Value management is a resource that would allow the physicians and business leaders to see each other's combined efforts to make the healthcare organization be the best it can be.*

2. I know how to do my work as a physician, as well as my learned administrative skills through additional training. How would value management continue my growth in both areas? *One of the greatest benefits of the incorporation of a value management methodology is that each position is encouraged to wear 'more than one hat' within their role. This means that the COO should know skills of the CEO, and vice versa, etc. An upcoming trend for*

CMOs is, in addition to physician practice, to know about finance, strategic management, and quality improvement. This means incorporating all the skills of the CFO, CEO, and quality manager (QM) within this one position. Value management would promote this knowledge of each role's skills, and the increased learning will stimulate the advancement of providing value to the patient.

Essential within any successful VMO is a successful analytics team. Business Analytics is one of the best internal sources for any provider in keeping the Healthcare Delivery Organization (HDO) alive and growing. However, a 2016 *Harvard Business Review* article by Chris McShea, Dan Oakley, and Chris Mazzei pointed out that most providers have found the incorporation of such a team difficult.[6] Management should focus on keeping these items in check on implementation of a new analytics team. These items include the following (which reflect the principles of a guiding coalition):

1. Actively manage C-suite dynamics. With this, management must proactively care for traditional leaders who may feel that they now have a lack of influence in making decisions. This would mean following the principle of remaining confident and ready to embrace the new trade-off for change.
2. Choose the right analytics leader. They should have these three qualities:
   a. An ability to collaborate
   b. An understanding of how the enterprise currently functions and a vision for how it may drastically change with the influence of analytics
   c. A hunger to create an environment of discovery
3. This new leader would also have the duty to make sure the team has the resources to develop as better analysts.
4. Challenge existing mental models. A company should encourage members of their team to challenge their mental models and think differently.

5. Create an environment of rapid innovation. Experimentation must be rewarded. (HBS found that only around 17% of employers have enacted a compensation system tied to a discovery method of payment for analysts.)

Step 3: Form Strategic Vision and Initiatives

The mission of the VMO is to establish processes to enable the HDOs to evaluate strategic, operational, and financial benefits from business process changes and initiatives. Moreover, the vision is to apply value management as a way of doing business to ensure the efficient deployment of capital; improved clinical outcomes; and the achievement of strategic, operational, and financial objectives.

One initiative that could help in accomplishing the vision is to build a center of excellence for the efficient deployment of capital. A center of excellence would ensure that investments are made in areas with short-term returns and that evidence-based medicine capability is enhanced. Use of the same will improve outcomes while reducing costs, optimize the operations of the healthcare organizations by streamlining the supply chain, and reduce operating costs. Collaborating with complimentary healthcare providers will also have a positive effect on improving quality and access to care and will improve the satisfaction of care providers and patients.

Case Study: Referenced from a 2013 *Harvard Business Review* article by Cosgrove as well as a 2011 Cleveland Clinic "Model of Care" video

The Cleveland Clinic is a prime example of an organization leading the charge for a value-based care delivery system. It has instilled this practice since first opening its doors in 1921, founded on the principles of cooperative medical practice, research, and education. It was one of the first hospitals to incorporate performance reviews with its doctors, showing early on a commitment to measuring performance with data.

This measurement of quality of care distinguished this hospital from all others.[7]

As Michael Porter and Tom Lee write, the Cleveland Clinic is one of only two to achieve all six components of a high-value care delivery system. The six components are: (1) integrated practice units (IPU); (2) cost and outcomes measurement; (3) bundled payments; (4) integrated care delivery across facilities; (5) expanded services across geography; and (6) an IT platform to enable those processes. As Porter further reflects about the Cleveland Clinic's ways, he states, "What makes Cleveland Clinic different stretches back to their founding 92 years ago as a physician-led group practice that runs a hospital—not a hospital that employs doctors."[8]

The Cleveland Clinic today holds true to its original founding values. To achieve the first component of making a high-value care delivery system stems from IPUs. The Cleveland Clinic was reorganized around 16 institutes in 2007, where the CEO practiced cardiovascular surgery in an IPU-like structure. The first true institute was neurological. It has now moved to 106 IPUs after hiring its head of strategy, but is still achieving continued growth.

In fulfillment of the cost and outcomes measurement, the Cleveland Clinic has made this a commitment within every institute. It believes outcomes are the ultimate measure of quality, and with this, each institute is provided with outcome books to annually benchmark its status.

Along with outcome measurement, the Cleveland Clinic has been just as focused on cost measurement. To perform this, it has posted supply costs in operating rooms (ORs) and other locations while also having started a few TDABC projects. These projects have mainly covered bundles direct to employer for hip and knee replacement, valve repair, coronary artery bypass grafting, and vertebroplasty.

To achieve a satisfactory IT department, the clinic has included an integrated EMR (Epic) and data warehouse with a cloud-based analytics platform.

To attain integrated care delivery across facilities, the Cleveland Clinic has prepared a regional integration structure. With this, it not only has the foundations of regionalized services in hospitals and clinics based in Ohio, but it wants to ensure that there is the right care provided at the right place. This is ensured with common processes and health kiosks with advanced practice nurses (APNs). Cleveland Clinic also believes that with an integrated practice framework it can expand geographically. This will encompass all heart and vascular affiliates, national kidney transplant affiliates, and national telemedicine second opinion services in a Florida hospital as well as Las Vegas. Lastly, it will provide neurology services within an Abu Dhabi hospital and clinic, as well as Canadian executive physicals.

Step 4: Communicate the Vision

The success of a change initiative depends on clearly communicating the vision across all activities. The following five-step approach has been very effective and could be applied to the VMO:

- Identify the challenges of the organization in the current state and present them in a manner that is easy for everyone to understand
- Demonstrate the difficulty experienced by the organization in monetary and service terms with a clear explanation as to why the status quo is not viable
- Outline the opportunity of moving toward a value-based organization and help the organization visualize the future state to obtain buy-in and support
- Articulate and communicate the benefits quantitatively (dollars) and qualitatively (satisfaction) for the organization and for everyone in the system
- Produce evidence of leading healthcare organizations that have embraced value management and the growth they are experiencing to solicit support

Complementing these steps by documenting the as-is process, simulating it to identify bottlenecks and inefficiencies, and documenting the to-be process is helpful in communicating gaps, overlaps, and automation. Talk often about the change vision; over-communicate during periods of rapid change. Place a high value on two-way communication as feedback can be used to improve messaging and obtain buy-in from the entire group.

> MD Anderson is a prime example, being one of the first organizations to be at the forefront of incorporating value management into its processes. The following excepert is taken from the "About Us" section created in 2016 by MD Anderson.
>
> In 1941, MD Anderson's first hospital was created while in the midst of World War II. Creating a new cancer and research hospital during this time was a very hard task. Doctors were in short supply, building matcrials were not easy to obtain, there were very high government restrictions, etc.
>
> The Texas Legislation ultimately created MD Anderson as part of the University of Texas System. It is one of only three cancer centers designated by the National Cancer Act of 1971. The core values of MD Anderson show that it revolves around a high-value care delivery system: "(1) Caring: By our words and actions, we create a caring environment for everyone; (2) Integrity: We work together to merit the trust of our colleagues and those we serve; and (3) Discovery: We embrace creativity and seek new knowledge."[9]
>
> MD Anderson keeps its vision alive by communicating to others (alongside Dr. Thomas Feeley) as Senior Fellows at Harvard. It has also demonstrated the practice of IPUs since the 1990s. It first delivered value in genitourinary cancers in 1994 to make care more

convenient for patients. Head and neck cancers soon followed this. This transition was completed by 1996.

The Cancer Center created a dedicated institute solely focused on value. This contained a small group of full time staff (total of 7 including the faculty head). The faculty and administrative associates were appointed to the institute, with additional project work done by graduate students.

Outcome measurement was also a focus for MD Anderson. It first developed an outcome beyond survival for head and neck cancer. IT functionality makes it difficult to measure speaking and swallowing; therefore, MD Anderson was one of the first to break through and ask its patients what they thought was important. It is now also reorganizing its IT approach due to data extraction difficulties as well.

TDABC programs began with MD Anderson in 2010. This started with head and neck cancer, mapping over 160 processes. This is currently moving toward software solutions for regular reporting. Also to be noted with head and neck cancers is the use of a bundled reimbursement payment method.

Lastly, MD Anderson is hoping to achieve geographic expansion as well. Nationally, this has been a success. Internationally, however, there remain mixed results, which is why work is still in progress with this ongoing reorganization.

Step 5: Remove Obstacles

Obstacles to change can come from people, processes, and organizational structures. These obstacles must be addressed to avoid the negative forces from moving forward. Specifically, these challenges arise from a lack of management commitment; the misallocation of resources; unproven performers;

poorly documented processes; the use of unproven tools; and tolerance for deficits in cost, schedule, and performance.

Establishing a structure for change and implementing the following changes—improving the skills and understanding of people in value management and healthcare economics to reduce their resistance for change; recognizing and rewarding people for moving toward value-based decision making; streamlining the process to capture their performance in the form of availability, efficiency, and accuracy; and developing automated checklists—will empower people in executing the vision and help them in accelerating the processes. Note that in all these situations, taking action early is important and will save both time and money.

As noted by Dr. Feeley and Dr. Anderson at Harvard, the major obstacles are

- Traditional academic departments
- Specialty focus in medical education, certification, legislative advocacy, and quality measure development
- Team medicine not being totally embraced
- Tradition of the eminent physician
- Fragmentation of services leading to low volume by condition and families of conditions
- People working in different places

Case Study: Referenced from a 2014 Harvard Business School Review by Kaplan, Witkowski, and Hohman[10]

Schon Klinik, the fifth largest hospital group in Germany, consists of 15 hospitals that primarily focus on neurological and orthopedic conditions. Schon actively monitors over 3300 performance indicators across 130 physical and mental health conditions. The oversupply of beds, rising costs, stagnant reimbursement rates, hospital inefficiencies, and projected closures led to Schon's leadership's willingness to try a TDABC pilot project. However, from the onset, physician resistance to change was a leadership concern. Schon's leadership previously led multiple initiatives to standard-ize equipment and materials in hospitals with little success. Leadership had also tried to impose on doctors the mandatory use of a single type of implant for total knee replacement. The lack of involvement in the selection process for the implant and inadequate training led to poor adoption of the practice and negatively impacted quality. Had a change management process been followed, these initiatives may have been more widely accepted and adopted by doctors.

In the early 2000s, Schon leadership attempted to develop standardized care pathways for selected medical conditions. However, physicians blocked the initiative based on the argu-ment that patients were different and required customized treatment plans to meet individual needs. Failure to execute a change management plan and actively engage the physicians prior to implementation contributed to this initiative's demise.

Step 6: Create Short-Term Wins

Early successes are important. They motivate committed people to move forward while deterring critics and negative thinkers that might hinder progress.

For example, coordinating the VMO with a proven ini-tiative, such as Consultation Management—which focuses on reducing duplication, errors, and adverse events, while improving access and the experience of patients—will be an important facilitator for the success of the organization.

To demonstrate success, develop a baseline using the met-rics from the current operations on the factors indicated previ-ously. In the earlier example, these could be in the form of the percentage of data shared in a consultation, average time spent by the physicians with patients, number of duplicate tests and images in the system, time it takes for patients to get an appoint-ment, etc. After implementation, measure the same performance measures and report the difference. Note that the VMO must collect, categorize, and communicate all wins, early and often, to track progress and energize collaboration to drive change.

In April 2016, at Harvard Business School's Value Measurement course, Dr. Feeley noted that to get started with the value management approach an organization must

- Have committed leadership
- Build teams around conditions as transition (i.e., virtual IPUs)
- Build around organ systems and move to conditions
- Start with practices already using the IPU philosophy
- Initially, work with the willing: Who believes in the concept?
- Scale as others come on board
- Reward innovation with resources/facilities

Step 7: Build on Change

Quick wins are good, but they do not guarantee sustained success. It is advisable that after every win, analyze what went right and what needs improving. Incorporate the feedback for continuous improvement of the process and the success of other projects or initiatives. Keep ideas fresh by bringing in new change agents and leaders from the change coalition. Many organizational change efforts fade before the organization ever reaches the desired goals.

A change vision can take a long time to achieve and generating and celebrating wins along the way is vital to achieving the goal. These successes prevent the organization from reverting to old ways and counter resistance to change.

Step 8: Anchor the Change in Corporate Culture

Finally, to make any value management measure permanent, it should be made a central part of the healthcare organization.

The HDO's corporate culture often determines what is possible. The values behind the organization's vision must be present in day-to-day work. It is also important that a HDO's leaders continue to support the change. It is important to make continuous efforts to ensure that the change is present in every aspect of the organization. This will help give the change to value-driven initiatives an obvious place in the organization's culture.

Some actions that can be used for continuous improvement are: talking about progress often, highlighting change process success stories, discussing change ideals and values when hiring and training new staff, publicly recognizing key members of the original change coalition, and making sure the rest of the staff—new and old—remember their contributions. Creating plans to replace key change leaders if they should leave the organization will help ensure that continuity is maintained.

Case Study: From 2014 article "Martini Klinik: Prostate Cancer Care" by Porter, Deeberg-Wittram, and Marks

Established in 2005, Hamburg's Martini Klinik focuses on prostate cancer care and is the largest prostate cancer treatment program in the world with 5000 outpatient cases and more than 2200 surgical cases annually. The organization is a good example of sustaining value management and incorporating it into its daily culture. This process has helped the organization in recruiting, retraining, and retaining clinicians, and setting standards for others to follow. Martini Klinik follows a regimented schedule, and to the casual observer it may seem that it has too many meetings.

The purpose of establishing a care improvement process is not to create more meetings, but rather to learn and grow as an organization in order to achieve desired outcomes. A transparent discussion of what went right and what went wrong can help to improve an organization. As an example, Martini Klinik has embraced a standardized care improvement process, which has contributed to the organization's

widely recognized success in delivering value-based outcomes. Martini Klinik focuses on continuing education for
its faculty and residents, organizes itself around the patient
condition, routinely discusses difficult cases, and transparently
reports outcomes. In fact, every 2 years the Martini Klinik
invites referring doctors from all over Germany to the Martini
Seminar to discuss medical outcomes and recent scientific data
based on lessons learned.[11] Bottom line, Martini Klinik has
anchored continual learning and improvement into its organizational culture (Table 12.2).

Working Groups

Establishing Working Groups is an essential piece of a successful Value Management Team. The establishment of these
groups requires the use of a specific process. Our recommendation is to use the following process method:

Value is determined by measuring key outcomes. The VMO
Governing Board (GB) determines which outcomes to measure
(in the form of both KPIs and KRIs). The GB is comprised of:
(1) experts; and (2) Working Groups (WGs).

Value Management Working Groups (VMWGs) define the
metrics to "assess the value of significant releases of IT capability to the HDO community." These releases can be new IT
capabilities, existing capabilities, or minor releases with distinct new features expected to be of high value. The VMO and
VMWG go together. As the VMO begins new efforts, VMWGs
will then be created to determine metrics.

Three classes of metrics will be defined:

- *Programmatic metrics:* Measuring the execution of the IT
  program developing the capabilities
- *Clinical metrics:* Measuring the health and other
  outcomes

Table 12.2 Meeting Schedule Example (Adapted from Martini Klinik, 2016)

Meeting	Topic	Participants	When
Morning huddle	Review last day's surgical cases, current patients on ward, and scheduled surgeries of the day	All physicians	7:00 a.m. daily
Resident lecture	A resident presents a topic around X condition from recent literature on the subject	All physicians	9:00 a.m. every Tuesday
X condition board (e.g., tumor board)	Discussion of treatment for all patients	Example participants: faculty, surgeon, oncologist, uropathologist, radiologist, etc. *Participant list can vary based on hospital needs	9:00 a.m. every Wednesday
Pathology conference	Discussion of all patients with unexpected pathological findings (positive surgical margins and metastasis)	Example participants: faculty, surgeon, oncologist, uropathologist, radiologist etc. *Participant list can vary based on hospital needs	9:00 a.m. every Thursday

(Continued)

Table 12.2 (Continued)   Meeting Schedule Example (Adapted from Martini Klinik, 2016)

Meeting	Topic	Participants	When
Advanced X condition for outpatient clinics. (e.g., prostate cancer outpatient clinic)	Interdisciplinary discussion of patients with advanced X condition (e.g., advanced prostate cancer)	Example participants: Faculty leading the clinical trial center and oncologist	9:00 a.m. every Friday
Literature review	Discussion of any recent relevant articles	All physicians	3:00 p.m. every Friday
Interdisciplinary X condition board (e.g., uro-oncological tumor board)	Discussion of difficult cases from outpatient physicians and hospital	Example Participants: Faculty, surgeon, oncologist, uropathologist, radiologist, etc. *Participant list can vary based on hospital needs	Last Friday of the month
Morbidity and mortality conference	Discussion of all cases with complications	Example Participants: Faculty, surgeons, oncologist, radiologist, nurses, quality management, pathologist. *Participant list can vary based on hospital needs	Monthly

(Continued)

Table 12.2 (Continued)   Meeting Schedule Example (Adapted from Martini Klinik, 2016)

Meeting	Topic	Participants	When
Quality review	Compare outcomes of surgeons	All faculty	Semi-annually
Seminar	Present health outcomes and research findings	All faculty and guests	Annually

- *Technical metrics:* Measuring the performance and operations of the IT capabilities

A VMWG operates by

1. Defining metrics pertinent to new initiatives or capabilities and the business outcomes they are anticipated to affect.
2. Monitoring metrics and recommending actions based on measurements and trends over time. These actions will be reported to the Governing Board.

The VMWGs follow the pattern of a life cycle. The number of VMWGs created and operating at one time will be of a "minimal, manageable quantity, balanced against the need to measure key value metrics that may not yet be defined." The process of phases that occur (three in total) is as follows:

Phase I. The first phase of VMWG operation is the most active, requiring meetings on a regular basis. Metrics are developed for collection and use in future phases.

1. Formation: A VMWG is created by the GB and chartered to measure the anticipated IT capabilities. A work breakdown structure (WBS) is developed to define deliverables and deadlines.

2. Staffing: The VMWG chair, with support from the perspective team leads, selects members of the VMWG as described earlier.
3. Initial meeting(s): The newly formed and staffed VMWG meets to normalize their goals and adjust staffing as needed.
4. Establish metrics and thresholds: The VMWG meets to define metrics and target values, using reference metrics, VMO and program expertise, and business/provider input. These metrics are then approved by the GB.
5. Approve metrics and thresholds: The VMWG delivers a document containing the metrics, thresholds, and guidance on the collection and interpretation of the metrics. The GB approves the metrics and thresholds, and directs the transition of responsibility for implementation and analysis of the metrics to appropriate VMO organizations.

Phase II. Once the metrics are approved, the VMWG may be called to meet on an ad hoc basis, providing revisions and consulting with the implementation team on the collection of metrics.

1. Design and implement dashboard: The implementation team within the VMO develops and maintains the VMO dashboard and works with the VMWG to understand and implement metrics collection.
2. Acquisition and contracts: For metrics that cannot be collected using existing means, new tools or modifications may be needed. The program/acquisition representatives to the GB enable the implementation of the collection of these metrics.

Phase III. After metrics are collected, they will be analyzed by the VMO analysis team who will consult with VMWG team members on an ad hoc basis.

1. Monitor dashboards: The VMWG will meet on a regular basis to review collected measurements, compare them against thresholds, and look for trends.
2. Analyze and report: On a periodic basis, the VMWG will analyze measurements and trends, report them to the GB, and make any recommendations for corrective action.
3. Take corrective action: The GB will review the VMWG reports and recommendations, and will use the resources of the GB members to take any corrective actions needed. Collection of additional metrics or data may be necessary.
4. Assess: The VMWG and GB will assess the corrective actions, and potentially recommend further corrective actions.
5. Disband: At the discretion of the GB, when the objectives of the VMWG have been achieved and/or have been transitioned to maintenance by other organizations, the GB may disband the VMWG.

Activities of a VMWG will be comprised of: (1) developing metrics to measure the value and success of IT investments (Phase I); (2) monitoring the collected metrics (Phase II, as needed); and (3) analyzing the collected metrics (Phase III, as needed).

The deliverables of a VMWG will include
∎ Metrics
  – Critical Success Factors (CSFs), KPIs, KRIs, values (these may include risk adjustment factors)
  – Prioritization
    • Emphasize higher priority metrics in dashboard
    • Option not to collect lower priority or higher cost metrics
∎ Context for metrics
  – Determine if proposed metrics duplicate existing metrics
  – Specify the lifespan for collection of the new metrics

- If all metrics are collected forever, and new metrics are added on each release, proliferate a collection of many metrics
  - When appropriate, recommend existing metrics for retirement
    - Note: Some metrics (e.g., uptime) should persist indefinitely
- ■ The roles of stakeholders who will view, monitor, and act on these metrics once they are available in a dashboard
  - Decisions/actions to be enabled by the dashboard
  - Associated queries

The main take-away from a VMWG is what it can provide, that is, to define the metrics to "assess the value of significant releases of IT capability to the HDO community."

Summary of Key Points to Remember

The learning outcomes from this chapter that are important to remember include the following points:

- ■ What are the most important recommendations for adopting the VMO in the organization?
  Several steps are advised following recommendations from John Kotter in his book Leading Change *but applied to the value management concept in healthcare:*
  - *Step 1: Create urgency*
  - *Step 2: Build a guiding coalition*
  - *Step 3: Form strategic vision and initiatives*
  - *Step 4: Communicate the vision*
  - *Step 5: Remove obstacles*
  - *Step 6: Create short-term wins*
  - *Step 7: Build on change*
  - *Step 8: Anchor the change in corporate culture*

■ Why is it so important to manage the change?

Change management is the approach to driving adoption and usage so new initiatives and projects in value management deliver expected results and outcomes to the organization.

For many change leaders, there is no doubt that change management must be used on projects that impact how people do their jobs. Value management involves an important transformation in the way healthcare organizations manage their business, so change management is paramount. Managing the human side of change is key to meeting program objectives.

References

1. Kotter, J. P. 1996. *Leading Change.* Harvard: Harvard Business Press.
2. Aiken, C. and Keller, S. 2009. The irrational side of change management. *McKinsey Quarterly.* 2(10):100–109.
3. Carrus, B., Corbett, S., and Khandelwal, D. 2010. A hospital-wide strategy for fixing emergency-department overcrowding. McKinsey & Company. Available at: www.mckinsey.com/industries/healthcare-systems-and-services/our-insights/a-hospital-wide-strategy-for-fixing-emergency-department-overcrowding. Accessed December 5, 2016.
4. Kaplan, R. S., Witkowski, M. L., and Hohman, J. A. 2013. Boston Children's Hospital: Measuring patient costs (abridged). Harvard Business School.
5. Kaplan et al. (2013).
6. McShea, C., Oakley, D., and Mazzei, C. 2016. How CEOs can keep their analytics programs from being a waste of time. *Harvard Business Review.* Available at: https://hbr.org/2016/07/how-ceos-can-keep-their-analytics-programs-from-being-a-waste-of-time. Accessed November 10, 2016.
7. Cleveland Clinic. 2011. Model of care: National. YouTube. 30 June 2011.

8. Cosgrove, T. 2013. Value-based health care is inevitable and that's good. *Harvard Business Review*. Available at: https://hbr.org/2013/09/value-based-health-care-is-inevitable-and-thats-good. Accessed November 11, 2016.

9. Anderson, M.D. 2016. About us: Facts and history. Available at: www.mdanderson.org/about-md-anderson/facts-history.html. Accessed December 15, 2016.

10. Kaplan, R. S., Witkowski, M. L., and Hohman, J. A. 2014. Schon Klinik: Measuring cost and value. Harvard Business School.

11. Porter, M. E., Deeberg-Wittram, J., and Marks, C. 2014. Martini Klinik: Prostate cancer care. Harvard Business School.

Reflections

Thanks to the power of social collaboration, my son Sebastian achieved a desired health outcome. If it wasn't for a complete stranger, we would never have known what provider to choose. If sick, injured, diagnosed with cancer, or suffering from a chronic disease, it is the health *outcome* that matters most to any parent, child, or person. As people, we deserve to know a predictable outcome prior to receiving a given treatment, while also being accountable for our own behavior that may affect the outcome. Sebastian has made a full recovery and, at only 3 years old, displays empathy and kindness at a level remarkable for his age. We have watched him interact with the newest addition to our family, Indra, in a manner that makes me wonder if there was another outcome outside the physical one. He suffered through 2 years uncomfortably, in and out of doctors' offices to the point that he still fears them, but emotionally he has calmed into an "old soul," someone who repays kindness to his baby sister and others ... without asking for anything else in return. Despite his early age, there is no doubt that my son has learned the value of selflessness. Shouldn't we all take note?

In 2007, Dr. Regina Herzlinger said it best, "Soaring health care costs that cripple our global competitiveness, uneven quality of care, 46-plus millions uninsured, and Medicare and Medicaid programs whose deficit threatens our children's economic welfare—who can best solve these mind-numbing problems? The government? A technocratic elite? Status quo insurers and hospitals? Or you and me?"[1]

As citizens, we have a social responsibility to think "outside the box" and find an innovative solution that creates the change we collectively seek—transparent health care. Sitting on the sidelines is not an option.

Despite the widespread adoption and use of health information and mobile technologies, no consumer-driven healthcare platform exists that utilizes a value-based approach. As healthcare reform and the economy continue to present challenges, innovative advancements in healthcare information technology and mobile applications will be key drivers in reducing costs and improving patient care. Central to reducing costs and improving patient care is a value-based approach to empowering consumers through transparency.

> Transparency would at least help uninsured patients and all consumers of care know what they were going to be charged and the quality of the services they would receive.
>
> **Dr. Regina Herzlinger[1]**
> *Who Killed Health Care?*

Inspired by my son, it occurred to me that we need a platform to see firsthand the outcomes of those that administer care. Each of us should be able to choose a provider that best meets our individualistic family needs. Thanks to a few other active citizens, we've recently developed an innovative application, My Doctor Knows, that leverages the power of data to provide transparent reporting of health outcomes and improve access to care. In fact, it received the Predictive Analytics Innovation Award for best use of data for public good. The platform utilizes a value-based approach toward recruiting new patients, retaining current patients, and providing patient-reported outcomes that can educate and retrain clinicians to deliver patient-centric value. The outcome measurements are standardized and approved by clinicians to create a "value score." In addition, a cost ranking and net promoter score are provided so that patients can make an informed decision. My Doctor Knows provides value to patients, providers, and payers by

- Scheduling the right appointment with the right provider at the right time
- Choosing a provider based on real health outcomes (i.e., "value")
- Reducing wait times
- Reducing "no-shows"
- Reducing readmissions and improving quality of care by collecting patient-reported outcomes
- Providing an analytics dashboard for providers and exportable outcomes for reimbursement
- Assisting insurers in building networks based on provider outcomes

The mission for My Doctor Knows is to improve provider efficiency and effectiveness, resulting in demonstrably better patient outcomes. It creates an environment in which patients can make truly informed choices about their healthcare in ways that democratize access to the best available healthcare options. The application is tied into a dynamic database that makes it possible for healthcare providers and consumers to work collaboratively. This is accomplished in a way that reduces bureaucratic work for the former and increases choice and quality of care for the latter. Ultimately, this concludes in an improvement of outcomes for *both* in a way that is: (1) empirically demonstrable; and (2) reportable to regulators. Whether you're a patient, a provider, or a payer, we all benefit from embracing the Value Equation.

Over a decade ago, the Institute of Medicine identified timely access to healthcare as an essential way to improve health care quality in the United States. Appointment wait times continue to be an essential measure of access as the healthcare system continues to struggle with long wait times. Negative consequences of delayed access to care include poor health outcomes, especially among older and more vulnerable patient populations, and lower patient satisfaction. My Doctor Knows is the *only* value-based solution for improving patient access and providing the transparency needed to reduce negative consequences and deliver desired health outcomes.

As the launch of My Doctor Knows fast approaches, I'd ask each of you, whether you are a patient, provider, or payer, to embrace value as the equation and support the application by reporting your outcomes. After all, shouldn't every parent regardless of race or ethnicity be able to choose the best doctor for their child based on condition-specific outcomes?

As we look to the future, I owe considerable thanks to my friend Francisco for deciphering my "chicken-scratch" diagram and Value Explorer is now on the horizon for healthcare organizations (providers), payers, and patients. I'm constantly amazed that Francisco has the uncanny ability to translate my ad hoc drawings and vision into a product that will benefit us all. Thank you my friend.

The ehCOS Value Explorer provides the following capabilities to users:

- The selection of a desired Critical Success Factor within each initiative accomplished by the healthcare organization, utilizing the Value Realization Framework
- The selection of up to 15 Key Results Indicators (KRIs) categorized into the six different outcomes perspectives (clinical, financial, employee satisfaction, patient satisfaction, process improvement, and learning and growth). The clinical outcomes are also structured into three tiers as proposed by Dr. Porter[2]

- The ability to combine and correlate outcome-oriented metrics (KRIs), program metrics and Key Performance Indicators (KPIs) (user perspective and technical)
- The visualization of indicators (both KRIs and KPIs) in the "selection" frame
- Multiple views to visualize and analyze selected indicators (Radar, Timeline)
- The comparison of several alternatives or treatment options using the Radar view to assess how each indicator is performing compared to their targets
- The ability to hide or show all the labels for all the selected indicators using the Radar view
- The ability to automatically and manually identify correlations among the outcomes or understand how the program or technical indicators are impacting the outcomes using the Timeline view
- The expansion of graphs to allow users to explore correlations in more detail.
- Indicators on a scale of 0–100 with values that are proportionally calculated regarding the achievement of targets and the comparison of selected alternatives
- The evaluation of alternative courses of action through filtering by Healthcare Delivery Organization, integrated care unit, and condition
- A final calculated value for selected alternatives according to the Value Equation
- Graphs and tables that can be printed, saved, or exported

An initiatives management function shall also be provided. The Value Management methodology described in this book enables the validation of KRIs and KPIs for each Critical Success Factor. ehCOS Value Explorer includes the following features and capabilities to facilitate A3 problem-solving thinking:

- Creates A3 reports with figures and pictures, and edits them as needed.
- Implements fishbone, 5 whys, and Pareto diagrams as described in the Value Management Methodology.
- Details and assesses identified indicators through A3 analysis using checklist options.
- Analyzes indicators with advanced analytics.

In short, we are finally racing ahead of technology as opposed to behind it in a matter most dear to us all—our health and quality of life. If that's not something to look forward to, I don't know what is.

As George Orwell pointed out, "People sleep peacefully in their beds at night only because rough men stand ready to do violence on their behalf."[3] In this case, the "rough men" are the innovators in our society, regardless of race, sex, or ethnicity, who standby ready to create solutions and best practices to deliver predictable health outcomes on our behalf. To each of you active citizens who read this book and find something of value, I say thank you and good luck in your endeavors.

References

1. Herzlinger, R. E. 2007. *Who Killed Health Care? America's $2 Trillion Medical Problem—and the Consumer-Driven Cure*. New York: McGraw-Hill (p. 3).
2. Porter, M. E. and Lee, T. H., MD. 2013. The strategy that will fix health care. *Harvard Business Review*. Available at: https://hbr.org/2013/10/the-strategy-that-will-fix-health-care. Accessed October 12, 2016.
3. Orwell, G. (n.d.) (Attributed) Quotes. Available at: www.quotes.net/quote/40074. Accessed May 3, 2017.

Summary of Key Points

The key points to remember from this book include the following:

There are three primary stakeholders affected by Value Management: the "3 Ps." The measurable value story should be applied to each of the 3Ps:

1. Patients shall choose the providers for their care based on outcome value scores.
2. Providers shall be data-informed to make targeted improvements and learn.
3. Payers shall measure return on investment and direct patients to high-value providers.

Value is defined as: Outcomes (Benefits) / Costs (Inputs). For healthcare, the outcome is measured as the patient's overall health as a result of care over time, whereas costs are the summation of all costs measured over time for the patient's condition and not the cost of individual services. For clinical outcomes, Porter's Outcomes Hierarchy is recommended as a construct: Tier 1 Health status achieved or retained, Tier 2 Process of recovery, and Tier 3 Sustainability of health (post-recovery).[1]

The Value Management Office (VMO) serves as a center of excellence for determining evidence-based outcome measurements. This can facilitate the creation of value-based care models and support information technology (IT) governance by evaluating business case investments and projected benefits to link people, processes, and technology. A VMO is different from a Project Management Office (PMO) because it combines elements from project, clinical quality, financial, and value-based management.

A VMO collaborates with clinical quality and financial offices (not just from a process point of view) and provides five key deliverables:

1. Defined clinical outcome metrics
2. Defined program outcome metrics
3. Defined IT investment outcome metrics
4. Time-Driven Activity-Based Costing for each clinical outcome
5. The construction of new payment models (e.g., bundled payments)

The Value Realization Framework provides the methodology for aligning mission, vision, and values with concrete Critical Success Factors (organizational goals), measurable Key Results Indicators (outcomes), and objective/measurable Key Performance Indicators (actions). The framework consists of six outcomes perspectives: clinical, financial, process improvement, patient satisfaction, clinician satisfaction, and learning and growth. Each of these six perspectives is part of the Value Scorecard.

The execution of the Value Realization Framework enables the creation of a Common Operating Picture when the data from all three dimensions (clinical, program, and technical) is integrated and business intelligence is performed to enable Healthcare Delivery Organization leaders make informed decisions related to delivering cost-efficient, quality care outcomes for patients.

Reference

1. Porter, M. E. and Lee, T. H., MD. 2013. The strategy that will fix health care. *Harvard Business Review*. Available at: https:// hbr.org/2013/10/the-strategy-that-will-fix-health-care. Accessed October 12, 2016.

Appendix I:
Acronym List

ACWP	actual cost of work performed
AHRQ	agency for healthcare research and quality
AO	action owner
BA	business analytics
BCWP	budgeted cost for work performed
BEI	baseline execution index
BI	business intelligence
CAH	critical access hospital
CEO	chief executive officer
CMS	centers for Medicare and Medicaid services
COP	common operating picture
CPLI	critical path length index
CPRS	computerized patient record system
CQM	clinical quality measures
CRISP-DM	cross-industry standard process for data mining
CSF	critical success factor
DCF	discounted cash flow
DMAIC	define, measure, analyze, improve, control
EHR	electronic health record
EMR	electronic medical record
ER	emergency room
FPD	federal project director

HCAHPS	hospital consumer assessment of healthcare providers and systems
HDO	healthcare delivery organization
HEDIS	healthcare effectiveness data and information set
HHS	Health and Human Services (U.S. Department of)
HIPAA	Health Insurance Portability and Accountability Act
HIT	health information technology
HITECH	health information technology for economic and clinical health
HITREF	health information technology reference-based evaluation framework
HSS	hospital for special survey
I/O	input/output
ICHOM	International Consortium for Health Outcomes Measurement
iDSI	International Decision Support Initiative
IQWiG	Institute of Quality and Efficiency in Healthcare (Germany)
IRR	internal rate of return
ISO	International Organization for Standardization
IT	information technology
JCAHO	Joint Commission on Accreditation of Healthcare Organizations
KPI	key performance indicator
KRI	key results indicator
LIMS	laboratory information management system
MH	mental health
NHI	National Health Institute
NHS	National Health Service
NICE	Institute for Health and Care Excellence
NPV	net present value
NQF	National Quality Forum
OECD	Organizations for Economic Co-operation and Development
PCMH	patient-centered medical home
PCP	primary care provider

PDSA	plan-do-study-act
PI	performance indicator
PMO	project management office
PP	payback period
QI	quality improvement
QoS	quality of service
R&D	research and development
ROI	return on investment
RRB	risk review board
SHEP	survey of the health experiences of patients
SLA	service level agreement
SMART	specific, measurable, attainable, relevant, time-bound
SPI	schedule performance index
SUS	system usability score
SV	schedule variance
TCO	total cost of ownership
TF	total float
VA	Department of Veterans Affairs
VfM	value for money
VHA	Veterans Health Administration
VMO	value management office
VRM	value realization framework

Appendix II: SMART Criteria

The Value Management Office ensures the robustness of enterprise and technical measures by checking the SMART criteria before the metrics and including them in the set. The SMART criteria comprise the following:

- *Specific*: Addresses the need for a specific goal rather than a more general one. This means that the goal is clear and unambiguous. To make goals specific, the Value Management Office must tell a team exactly what is expected, why it is important, who is involved, where it is going to happen, and which attributes are important. A specific goal will usually answer the five "W" questions: What: What do I want to accomplish? Why: Specific reasons, purposes, or benefits of accomplishing the goal. Who: Who is involved? Where: Identify location. Which: Identify requirements and constraints.
- *Measurable*: Addresses the need for concrete criteria for measuring progress toward the attainment of the goal. If a goal is not measurable, it is not possible to know whether a team is making progress toward its successful completion. Measuring progress is supposed to help a team stay on track, reach their target dates, and experience the feeling of achievement that spurs them on to maintain the

continued effort required to reach the goal. A measurable goal will usually answer questions such as: How much? How many? How will I know when it is accomplished? Indicators should be quantifiable and have a position of reference.

- *Attainable*: Addresses the importance of goals that are realistic and attainable. While an attainable goal may stretch a team to achieve it, it should not be too far out of reach. When important goals are identified, the team develops the attitudes, abilities, skills, and financial capacity to reach them. The theory states that an attainable goal may cause goal-setters to identify previously overlooked opportunities to bring themselves closer to the achievement of their goals. An achievable goal will usually answer the question "How?" How can the goal be accomplished? How realistic is the goal?

- *Relevant*: Addresses the importance of choosing goals that matter. A manager's goal to "Make 50 peanut butter and jelly sandwiches by 2 p.m." may be specific, measurable, attainable, and time-bound, but it lacks relevance. Many times, you will need support to accomplish a goal: resources, a champion voice, and someone to knock down obstacles. Goals that are relevant to your boss, your team, and your organization will receive that needed support. Relevant goals (when met) drive the team, department, and organization forward. A goal that supports or is in alignment with other goals would be considered a relevant goal. A relevant goal can answer yes to these questions: does this seem worthwhile? Is this the right time? Does this match our other efforts/needs? Are you the right person? Is this applicable in the current socioeconomic environment?

- *Time-bound*: Addresses the importance of grounding goals within a time frame, giving them a target date. A commitment to a deadline helps a team focus their efforts on the completion of the goal on or before the due date.

This part of the SMART goal criteria is intended to pre-vent goals from being overtaken by the day-to-day cri-ses that arise in an organization. A time-bound goal is intended to establish a sense of urgency. A time-bound goal will usually answer the question "When?" What can I do 6 months from now? What can I do 6 weeks from now? What can I do today?

Appendix III

Value Management Outcome-Oriented Metrics Meeting			
Date: month/day/year		**Dial-In:** xxx-xxx-xxxx	
Time:		**Participant Code:** xxxxxx#	
Facilitator:		**Owner:**	
Link:			
Attendee		**Attendee**	
Outcome-Oriented Metrics Meeting Purpose			
The purpose is…			

Value Management Outcome-Oriented Metrics Meeting	
Topics	**Discussion Lead**
Opening remarks	
Outcome-oriented metrics	(shared)
Status update	
Possible topics are specific conditions to review	

MEETING MINUTES

Agenda Item: *Welcome/Opening Remarks*

Discussion:

-

-

Agenda Item: *Status Update*

Discussion:

-

-

Agenda Item: *Topic*

Discussion:

-

-

Agenda Item: *Topic*

Discussion:

-

-

Value Management Outcome-Oriented Metrics Meeting			
Agenda Item: *Topic*			
Discussion:			
•			
•			
Agenda Item: *Topic*			
Discussion:			
•			
•			
Agenda Item: *Topic*			
Discussion:			
•			
•			
Agenda Item: *Topic*			
Discussion:			
•			
•			
Agenda Item: *Topic*			
Discussion:			
•			
•			
ACTION ITEMS			
Item No.	Action Item	Assigned To	Due Date
1			
2			
3			
4			

Index

Printed in the United States
by Baker & Taylor Publisher Services